W9-CLL-825

MASTERS OF HEAVY METAL

MASTERS OF HEAVY METAL

EDITED BY JAS OBRECHT

Quill/A Guitar Player Book
New York 1984

Special thanks to Mike Varney and John Strednansky for their metal expertise.

Copyright © 1984 by GPI Publications

The text of this book has been edited from material originally published in *Guitar Player* magazine from 1968 to 1983.

All rights reserved. No part of this book may be reproduced or utilized in any form or by any means, electronic or mechanical, including photocopying, recording or by any information storage and retrieval system, without permission in writing from the Publisher.
Inquiries should be addressed to
Quill, an imprint of William Morrow and Company, Inc., 105 Madison Avenue, New York, N.Y. 10016.

Library of Congress Catalog Card Number: 83-60067

ISBN: 0-688-02937-X

Printed in the United States of America

First Quill Edition

1 2 3 4 5 6 7 8 9 10

Art Director
Dominic Milano

Graphics Assistant
Mark Medalie

Darkroom
Cheryl Matthews
Paul Haggard

Typesetting
Leslie K. Bartz
Ellayn M. Evans
Frank Fletcher
Pat Gates

Proofreading
Jake Hunter
Alis Rasmussen

Director, GPI Books
Alan Rinzler

Editor, Guitar Player Magazine
Tom Wheeler

Publisher, GPI Publications
Jim Crockett

Cover photo by Neil Zlozower

CONTENTS

MASTERS OF HEAVY METAL

The Rise Of Heavy Metal

By Jas Obrecht

Heavy metal was born in the mid '60s. Its roots extend back to the British blues and R&B booms, which emphasized players' technical virtuosity and were perfect testing grounds for extended soloing. Early metal players drew from the chord-based patterns of blues-rock and the free-form, experimental approach of psychedelic music to develop a concise, riff-based form of playing. Today the term has come to mean intense, high-energy, guitar-dominated rock taken to its extremes.

From the beginning, metal bands have played upon larger-than-life rock star traditions, using massive sounds and flashy showmanship to produce rock and roll at its grandest scale. For metal guitarists, tone, vibrato, and speed are essential. Their screaming solos emphasize fluidity, sustain, and distorted tones. In the early stages of the art, so much importance was placed on soloing that guitarists commonly set aside ten or fifteen minutes a set for their extravaganzas.

The pioneer of heavy metal was Jimi Hendrix, who in 1967 recorded the first major metal hit, "Purple Haze." During the next three years he set an unparalleled standard for hard rock guitar. Despite his excursions into psychedelic music, blues, and other styles, Jimi returned to what we know today as heavy metal often during his career, blending soul and finesse with an incredible mastery of sound. His talents were first recognized by English audiences, and he had achieved superstar status abroad before most Americans had heard of him. *Metal Rendez-Vous* editor John Strednansky points out that since Hendrix' time, British and American heavy metal guitarists have developed different approaches: "The British rely on a lot of riffs. The songs are structured around crashing guitar sounds, and the vocals are of secondary importance. The stronger the riff, the more important the song. In America, it's the other way around. The vocals carry the song, and the riffs are there to enhance them. American heavy metal sounds more polished because of this emphasis on the melody and voice."

The seeds of English heavy metal were planted with Cream, formed in 1966, and the mid-'60s Yardbirds. In general, Cream had a bluesier, more psychedelic approach than heavy metal, although cuts such as "Sunshine Of Your Love" and "Crossroads" certainly hinted at trends to come. Similarly based in the blues, the Yardbirds usually used clean, trebly tones. English heavy metal really came to fruition with Led Zeppelin, which arose in 1968 from the remnants of the Yardbirds (the group's original name was New Yardbirds). Lead guitarist Jimmy Page utilized fatter, more distorted tones and pushed beyond his blues influence to break new ground. Their first three albums—*Led Zeppelin*, *Led Zeppelin II,* and *Led Zeppelin III*—are considered heavy metal classics.

Following in Zep's wake in the late '60s was Deep Purple. Ritchie Blackmore proved inspirational to countless guitarists before going on to organize Blackmore's Rainbow in 1975, while other members of Deep Purple joined Whitesnake. In the early '70s Black Sabbath, Status Quo, Uriah Heep, Budgie, and Skid Row took up the metal gauntlet in Great Britain.

In America, the earliest metal bands tended to blend psychedelic elements with riff-oriented playing. Blue Cheer produced a landmark metal album in 1968 with *Vincebus Eruptum*. The MC5 similarly displayed heavy metal traits on their records. Although he was stylistically inconsistent, Leslie West thundered forth in 1969 to become one of America's first bona fide metal guitar heroes. As his hits "Blood Of The Sun" and "Mississippi Queen" clamored up the charts, he turned in a stunning performance with Mountain at Woodstock. After several albums with Mountain and West, Bruce & Laing, Leslie continued his career as a solo artist. Years later, Michael Schenker and Randy Rhoads would credit West as being a major influence.

The first prominent American heavy metal act of the '70s was Blue Oyster Cult. (In fact, Strednansky points out, B.O.C. producer Sandy Pearlman was reportedly the first person to use novelist William Burroughs' phrase "heavy metal" to describe a musical style.) Among the competent, lesser-known American metal bands at the time were Dust, Sir Lord Baltimore, Tucky Buzzard, and Bang. Grand Funk occasionally leaned towards metal, although most of their music was good-time, driving rock.

Ted Nugent, who began his career with the psychedelic Amboy Dukes of the '60s, turned to heavy metal in the '70s. The first Montrose album—*Montrose*, which paired Sammy Hagar and Ronnie Montrose—was hailed as a milestone in 1973. In the mid '70s American metal softened a bit, with Aerosmith and Kiss leading a list of headbanging acts that included Starz, the Godz, Rex, and Legs Diamond. One of the first well-exposed female rockers to create blistering metal solos was Lita Ford, who debuted in 1976 with the Runaways and went on to form her own band in the '80s.

Continental Europe's most enduring metal contribution came with the Scorpions. Their 1974 *Fly To The Rainbow*, featuring guitarists Ulrich Roth and Rudolf Schenker, is regarded as a classic metal album. In its earliest incarnation, the Scorpions lineup included Rudolf's younger brother Michael, a virtuosic soloist who went on to become mainland Europe's most influential metal guitarist. He was only 15 when he played on the Scorpions' *Lonesome Crow* in 1971. Two years later he replaced Mick Bolton in U.F.O. and helped propel the English band to the top of the metal heap before going solo with the Michael Schenker Group in the late '70s. Meanwhile, Judas Priest emerged in 1974 with the blazing twin-guitar lineup of K.K. Downing and Glenn Tipton. Gary Moore, formerly of Skid Row, played bluesy metal with Thin Lizzy.

By the mid '70s, metal was on its way to becoming a global phenomenon. Australia's AC/DC, powered by the ballsy guitar wizardry of Angus Young, gathered an enormous following and went on to become one of rock's most popular bands. Following in their countrymen's footsteps, Angel City (formerly Angels) released several albums in America. Krokus broke in Switzerland, while Japan found its first certified metal hero in the brilliant Kyoji Yamamoto of Bow Wow, a group with over a dozen albums dating back to 1976. Scotland's Nazareth took to demolishing familiar pop songs with thunderous riffs. Omega provided the voice of heavy metal in Hungary. Although they later became more progressive, the Canadian trio Rush made a strong heavy metal statement on their Zeppelinesque 1974 debut album, *Rush*. Fellow Canadians Frank Marino & Mahogany Rush, Triumph, and Goddo carried on the tradition.

Guitarists had a dramatic glance at the future with the 1978 release of *Van Halen*, on which Dutch-born, California-raised Eddie Van Halen broke more new ground than any American metallist since Hendrix. His impact was immediate, his influence enormous. Eddie's tone, unusual fingering methods, and kamikaze approach to the vibrato bar have become highly imitated elements of the metal vocabulary.

Although Van Halen, AC/DC, U.F.O., Judas Priest, and the Scorpions consistently packed concert halls and stormed the charts, heavy metal in general slumped during the late '70s. This trend was partly attributable to the rise of punk and new wave, as well as the shift in media attention to disco. The movement was rejuvenated in 1980 with the emergence of what's been termed the New Wave Of British Heavy Metal. Taking a lesson from punk, young metallists trimmed the average length of a song down to about three minutes. Where a decade before metal albums would often contain seven or eight tracks, players now jammed ten or more cuts on a disk. Numerous bands that had been building up in the English underground were signed. Iron Maiden, Def Leppard, Tygers Of Pan Tang, Motorhead, Girlschool, and Saxon achieved international success, while other acts such as Diamond Head, Trespass, Fist, Angelwitch, Witchfynde, and Tytan gathered strong English support. Gillan brought recognition to a talented guitarist named Bernie Torme, who has since formed Electric Gypsies.

Former Black Sabbath singer Ozzy Osbourne used American musicians to form one of the leading metal acts of the early '80s. On the first two Blizzard Of Ozz releases, Randy Rhoads brought new excellence to metal guitar. A stunning soloist, Rhoads had nearly achieved superstardom when, in March 1982, he was killed in a plane crash. He was briefly replaced in the group by Bernie Torme before Brad Gillis took over.

In the last few years, metal bands have sprung up all over the free world. Warning, Ocean, and Trust are the leaders in France, while Mercyful Fate has gathered a fanatical following in Denmark. The E.F. Band and Rising Force hail from Sweden, Picture and Vandenberg from Holland, Smack from Yugoslavia. Belgium has Killers. Iceland's resident metal band is Start. Italy's Strike imitate Judas Priest. Loudness has provided Japan's latest guitar hero in Akira Takasaki. Even South Africa has an ensemble for headbangers. Britain's Reading Festival, which in the late '70s became increasingly devoted to heavy metal, has helped familiarize English-speaking audiences with Spain's Baron Rojo and Japan's Bow Wow.

Today America is in the midst of a metal renaissance similar to what occurred in England a few years ago, with hundreds of new bands playing clubs from coast to coast. The strongest acts to emerge on major labels are Riot and Y&T (formerly Yesterday And Today). Some bands—led by Portland's Crysys, Kansas' Manilla Road, and New York's Virgin Steele and Talas — have independently produced and released their own albums. Others have surfaced on small-label metal compilations. Producer Mike Varney, founder of Shrapnel Records, has released tracks from dozens of unknown, innovative American heavy metal bands on his acclaimed *U.S. Metal* album series.

Metal mania continues to flourish worldwide. Bands pack stadiums; albums go platinum. Hordes of young players are drawn to the style. And with masters such as Jimi Hendrix, Jimmy Page, Michael Schenker, Eddie Van Halen, and Randy Rhoads to emulate, the guitarists keep getting better.

* * * *

Founded in 1967, *Guitar Player* was one of the first magazines to cover heavy metal. Jimi Hendrix appeared in the December 1968 issue; Jimmy Page was interviewed the following summer. During the early '70s the magazine explored the views and techniques of Leslie West, Ritchie Blackmore, Tony Iommi, and Led Zeppelin's John Paul Jones. The contributions of Hendrix, Page, and Blackmore were comprehensively updated for their subsequent mid-decade cover stories.

Eddie Van Halen gave his first nationally published interview to *Guitar Player* during the opening days of his debut American tour in 1978. Two years later he unveiled secrets of his style and sound in one of the most sought-after issues in the magazine's history. Meanwhile, Ted Nugent, Michael Schenker, Gary Moore, and guitarists in the Scorpions, Judas Priest, and Def Leppard were given free rein in the magazine to express themselves. The publication's 1982 tribute to the late Randy Rhoads was composed by his family, friends, and fellow musicians. The *Guitar Player* stories reprinted in this volume were chosen for their ability to convey the spirit and power of heavy metal.

THE PIONEER: JIMI HENDRIX

GENE KESTER

Hendrix in 1968

GENE KESTER

For many, Jimi Hendrix' "Purple Haze" signaled the birth of heavy metal. The pioneer American psychedelic superstar, Jimi was interviewed by *Guitar Player* for this December 1968 cover story.

* * * *

When Jimi Hendrix plays, the house comes down. It doesn't fall in small pieces, but in chunks. The whole place topples on the audience, but it doesn't touch them because he's got them flying up there with him somewhere. That's the way it was at Winterland in San Francisco when we interviewed Jimi Hendrix. That's the way he makes it.

"All my songs happen on the spur of the moment," he says, and you know he's leveling with you. So you ask him if he has to compensate for this spontaneity by using gimmicks: "On some records you hear all this clash and bang and fanciness, but all we're doing is laying down the guitar tracks and then we echo here and there, but we're not adding false electronic things. We use the same thing anyone else would, but we use it with imagination and common sense. Like in 'House Burning Down' [*Electric Ladyland*], we made the guitar sound like it was on fire. It's constantly changing dimensions, and up on top that lead guitar is cutting through everything."

He tells you his most important thing is to honestly communicate with the audience. His stage presence is usually expected to be sort of obscene, with lots of gesturing, but this is not true most of the time. Jimi's presence is always cool, and he lets his emotions come through strong. At times he has turned his back on the audience—if that's the way he really felt: "When I don't say 'thank you,' or I turn my back to the audience, it's not against them. I'm just doing that to get a certain thing out. I might be up-tight about the guitar being out of tune or something. Things have to go through me and I have to show my feelings as soon as they're there."

One problem Jimi has is that his instruments won't hold up. He explains: "Like these two guitars I have now, they've been around for a while and just don't stay in tune. They might slip out of tune a bit right in the middle of the song, and I'll have to start fighting to get it back in tune. We tune up between every song because it's not a Flash Gordon show—everything all neat and rehearsed. It's not one of those kind of things. It's important for us to get our music across the best way we can. It means we have to do it natural, like tuning up before songs."

Jimi adds that it sometimes is tough working with the other members of the Experience, drummer Mitch Mitchell and bassist Noel Redding: "Sometimes they might want to tell me something, and I might not be able to understand. It gets frustrating. Any time you make a song, you want your own personal thing in it as well as the group. We don't compromise with each other very much, you know. Like one guy thinks one thing and he's going to stick with that one thing, so he does it the way he wants it."

Jimi admits the trio doesn't do much practicing: "Most of our practice is thinking about it. They might hear the same tune I have, so they throw it around in their minds and picture the fingerboard. So when we go to the studios and I give them a rough idea, maybe Mitch and I will lay a track down completely by ourselves and then add the rest. As far as jamming out here on a show . . . we try to listen to each other.

"I just keep my music in my head. It doesn't even come out to the other guys until we go to the studio. Sometimes if I have a new song or if the guys want to take a vacation or something like that, maybe I'll go to the studio by myself and have an acid tape made with a rough idea about the drums, guitar, bass, and vocal. Then other times, I'll just come in banging away on the guitar and be singing and say this is a new song. We try to put our own self into it no matter what song we play."

What does Jimi look for in other musicians? "When I see a group, I look for feeling, but not the jump-around kind of feeling. Then I look for togetherness, a communication between the musicians. Originality comes about fourth or fifth."

The night we talked with Jimi Hendrix was the second anniversary of the trio. Jimi himself was born in Seattle, Washington, 21 years ago. He left school early to join the Army Airborne. "I've played with millions of groups, played behind cats who are making it now." Jimi feels that those who influenced him while he was trying to make it were Muddy Waters, Elmore James, Eddie Cochran, and B.B. King, among others. But Jimi's style is not a mixture of the past. It is something which comes out of himself: "I write songs to release frustration. I like to play lead sometimes so I can express myself. But the way I play lead is a raw type of way. It comes to you naturally."

The way Jimi Hendrix plays may be natural for Jimi Hendrix, but it's the opposite of most other guitarists. A left-hander, he usually plays a right-handed Stratocaster that's flopped upside down and restrung the normal way with Fender light-gauge strings. He also has two Gibsons: "Some of the tracks on our new LP have a Gibson on them. I also use Sunn amps. It doesn't make any difference what size the amps are, as long as I know I have it. I'm not necessarily trying to be loud. I'm just trying to get this impact. I don't like to use mikes. To get the right sound, it's a combination of both amp and fretting."

Jimi feels it's important not to have a closed mind to new things that are happening: "You can't just get stuck up on guitar. You have to use a little bit of imagination and break away. There's millions of other kinds of instruments. There's horns, guitars, everything. Music is getting better and better, but the idea now is not to get as complicated as you can, but to get as much of yourself into it as you can.

"Music has to go places. We'll squeeze as much as we really feel out of a three-piece group, but things happen naturally. We've got about four tracks that we haven't released yet. One has a very simple rhythm with a funky horn pattern in it, and a tiny bit of echo to make the horn sharper. It happens naturally, like when you hear something you might want to use strings with. But we haven't been able to get these things together because we've been on tour."

Jimi's advice to guys who are still out there trying to

make it? "It's pretty hard to give advice, but if these guys have really gotten into it and everyone — mothers and friends — have said 'Wow,' then they should try to get in touch with a major musician or have a representative of a record company come to one of their gigs. But tell them it's best not to sign anything too soon. Tell them to get some lawyers. Managers may not know it all, and a lawyer knows what's right."

"You have to stick with it," he adds. "Sometimes you are going to be so frustrated you want to give up the guitar. . . you'll hate the guitar. But all of this is just a part of learning, because if you stick with it, you're going to be rewarded."

Jimi Hendrix
Nov. 27, 1942—Sept. 18, 1970

GENE KESTER

Don Menn faced the challenge of his career as a *Guitar Player* assistant editor when he was asked to organize the September 1975 Jimi Hendrix special issue. Spending several weeks on the project, Don interviewed over 50 people, including Jimi's dad, crew, and fellow musicians John McLaughlin, Johnny Winter, John Hammond, and Mike Bloomfield. The original magazine included a soundsheet recording of "Beginnings." The material was subsequently reissued in magazine form (without the record) in 1976, and portions of the biography appear as the liner notes in Reprise Records' *The Essential Jimi Hendrix*. Through the years, the Jimi Hendrix issue has remained the most popular in the magazine's history.

His hands are what made him look so tall. They could have been stitched onto someone a foot taller. But James Marshall Hendrix, who only stood 5′ 11″, made good use of what he had and what he heard.

What he heard to begin with were the sounds of the '40s and '50s blaring out of radios, phonographs, and the televisions in his hometown of Seattle, Washington. He was acquainted as well with the sounds of other eras preserved in his father's extensive record collection, which contained primarily blues and R&B artists. The sounds from those around him must have stayed in his ears, too — his father slapping the spoons on his thighs and palms, his mother (Lucille, who died when he was ten) running her fingers occasionally up and down a piano, and his aunt playing keyboard with authority at the Dunlap Baptist Church (where Jimi's funeral was later to be held).

Jimi's dad, James Allen Hendrix, a landscape gardener, traded in his sax for an acoustic guitar to replace the broom his 12-year-old boy strummed. Jimi began to train himself. He'd watch other guitarists and see them playing things which he'd pick up and try himself, usually left-handed, but sometimes right-handed. Though he never learned to read music, he was always jamming, and logged much practice time gigging in a half-dozen rock-oriented groups in Seattle. They played the local clubs or traveled 120 miles north to Vancouver to work dances for 50¢ an hour and all the Cokes and hamburgers they could consume. Mr. Hendrix still has a mental image of his elder son (Jimi's brother, Leon, was five years younger) flopped on the sofa playing along with records, radio, and television, and that's where Jimi probably got that Peter Gunn theme he plays on the *War Heroes* album.

Jimi's parents were originally from Vancouver, and he spent much time there in elementary school and visiting his grandmother when gigging around British Columbia in the days after he'd entered Garfield High School back in Seattle. But, however highly he was later to be thought of, in Seattle a lot of people didn't consider Jimi that extraordinary a guitar player. Not then anyway.

In 1959, when he was 17, Jimi convinced his father to sign the military enlistment papers (he wasn't 18 yet, and needed parental approval), and off he went with the 101st Airborne Division. This 26-month excursion into paratrooping ended on his 26th jump, which wracked his back and foot and brought him an early discharge. But he'd kept up with his music. Earlier in boot camp, he had written his father begging him to send a guitar because Jimi thought he was going crazy. With the instrument he jammed with anyone, including Billy Cox, who would later play bass with Jimi in the Band Of Gypsys.

Between 1963 and 1964, Jimi toured the South, "the chitlin circuit" as he called it, with a wide variety of acts. He landed in New York in 1964. His prominence as a sideman grew, and by the time he joined King Curtis in 1965, he had worked with Ike & Tina Turner, Little Richard, Joey Dee, Jackie Wilson, James Brown, Wilson Pickett, B.B. King, the Isley Brothers, and Curtis Knight and the Squires.

Chuck Rainey, who played bass with King Curtis while Jimi and Cornell Dupree shared lead guitar roles, recalls that Hendrix was an exceptional musician who was just happy to be included. "If he was hired as the third guitar player," Rainey says, "he was happy; he never had a bad thing to say about anything." He also remembers that Jimi had perfect pitch, was ambidexterous, and had enough finesse with jazz numbers to lead him to conclude that Jimi had some knowledge of the Billy Butler and Charlie Christian eras. For anyone who doubted it, Jimi could and did play jazz solos as opposed to strictly rock and rhythm and blues.

Jimi formed his own New York group in 1965. He called it the Blue Flames and himself Jimmy James. By mid 1966, they were gigging in pop music's backyard — Greenwich Village. Accepting a position as lead guitarist for John Hammond Jr., this Jimmy James character

TOM COPI

began to make a name for himself among an even more elite crowd that included Bob Dylan, the Beatles, and the Animals.

This led to a fortuitous visit from Bryan "Chas" Chandler, formerly the bass player with the Animals, who decided that his and this wild guitar player's futures should be zipped together. After arranging for passports, Chas presented Jimmy James with a ticket, some money, and a promise of meeting Eric Clapton—whom the young guitarist was just hearing about and gaining some interest in. After the arrival in England, Mr. Hendrix received a call from his son saying that he was going to be made into a star. He had also redeemed his original surname, but changed the spelling of his first. Now he was Jimi Hendrix.

In London, Chas snatched up Mitch Mitchell (a drummer) and Noel Redding (a lead guitarist who was handed a bass), and the Jimi Hendrix Experience was born. An immediate success in Europe at smaller and then larger clubs, the group signed a contract with Track Records, who released "Hey Joe" and "Purple Haze," which became instant hits. Though then considered to be the hottest act in Europe, the Experience was an underground rumor on Jimi's side of the ocean.

However, the group did not remain obscure long in the United States. On the recommendation of Paul McCartney, the planners of the Monterey Pop Festival (June 16-18, 1967) booked the Experience. At the last show on Sunday, Jimi Hendrix flabbergasted those attending, and America got its first glimpse of what he could do with an electric guitar and lighter fluid. But guitar players were stunned less by his theatrics than by Jimi's unusual approach to music and his fluent control over and use of distortion, which had previously been a game of chance or a factor to be eliminated from (not added to) one's sound system.

The second glimpse for America was from the wrong eye. The Experience was put on tour with the Monkees in early 1967, and the idea was not a bright one. The Monkees' young fans were not prepared for Jimi's wild sensuality and roaring music. After less than a half-dozen performances, management fabricated a story that the Daughters of the American Revolution had had the Experience banned, so the group pulled out of the tour.

Hendrix returned to England where his popularity had remained high. Positive response from his records in America, coupled with word of his performances in Europe, helped erase the memory of the Monkees fiasco. Jimi played to standing-room-only crowds in tours of the United States in 1968 and 1969.

Hendrix became a guitarists' guitarist, jamming constantly with the top musicians in the pop field in famous after-hours meetings that included luminaries such as Johnny Winter, John McLaughlin, Stephen Stills, and artists from other realms, such as reed virtuoso Roland Kirk. The members of the Experience began to drift apart in late 1968. Jimi was showing signs of desiring to work with other musicians, most notably the Band Of Gypsys, which included Buddy Miles on drums and Billy Cox on bass. Their performance at the Fillmore East in New York was recorded and portions were remixed in their only album — *Band Of Gypsys* — though the group never did tour together.

Talk of reforming the Experience and going on tour in the spring of 1970 came to nothing. Jimi apparently went through a period of intense reevaluation of his music and artistic goals. In the spring and summer he toured with Mitch Mitchell and Billy Cox, and in August of 1970 he played at England's Isle Of Wight Festival after staying awake all night with Eric Barrett for the opening of his own recording studio, Electric Lady Studios in New York. There he gave a bad performance which has been regarded often as indicative of depression or a general decline in his abilities as opposed to being a to-be-expected slip-up resulting from sleep deprivation, jet lag, and the 2:00 A.M. slot.

On September 18, 1970, James Marshall Hendrix was pronounced dead on arrival at St. Mary Abbots Hospital in London, England. Professor Donald Teare, the pathologist, explained the cause of death had been "inhalation of vomit due to barbiturate intoxication." Though there were not enough drugs in Jimi's body to have caused his death, speculation arose as to whether or not he had attempted suicide. This has been discounted by nearly every person who knew Jimi, many who recall that he was in fact rather enjoying life and the prospect of entering a new, highly creative phase of his career. It should be noted that the sleeping pills which he took were not his own, and were in fact a German brand which are normally broken into quarters before ingesting. Jimi probably had no idea of the dose he was taking to catch a little sleep in the early morning hours of that day. Moreover, in the ambulance Jimi had been placed in a sitting position with his head back; if he had not been sick enough to die — and he wasn't — the impossibility of clearing his throat and breathing at this angle was enough to kill him, and it did. From all appearances, his death was a tragic and avoidable mistake.

Gerry Stickells, his road manager, had Jimi's body flown home for the funeral, attended by such notables as Johnny Winter and Miles Davis, as well as many of the musicians with whom he had performed. His burial took place on October 1, 1970 at Greenwood Cemetery in Seattle.

What would Jimi have done had he lived? All is speculation, but he expressed many dreams to those around him; some may have been pipe dreams, some may or may not have been brought to reality. Eric Barrett says he sensed "that a whole new trip was coming down." Jimi would call him, and they'd sit up all night discussing ideas. Hendrix had wanted to buy a big top, hire his own security guards, and set up three- and four-day concerts on the outskirts of towns. Guards would have been there to keep order and things running smoothly as opposed to turning a concert into a drug bust.

Jimi died the week before he was to have completed preliminary meetings with master jazz arranger Gil Evans to do some recordings. (*The Gil Evans Orchestra Plays The Music Of Jimi Hendrix*, RCA, CPL1-0667, contains selections that Evans presented in his all-Hendrix concert at Carnegie Hall as a part of the New York Jazz Repertory Company's 1974 programs.)

Jimi himself spoke of a desire to take a year or so off to study music more systematically to learn to write and read. In one interview he expressed an interest in mixed media, in exploring the healing power of sound and color used in coordination. He told Roy Hollingworth in an interview published the day before his death that, "In older civilizations they didn't have diseases as we know them. It would be incredible if you could produce music so perfect that it would filter through you like rays and ultimately cure." As to his musical horizons, he told the same interviewer, "I dig Strauss and Wagner. Those cats were good, and I think they are going to form the background of my music. Above it will be blues — I still got plenty of blues — and then there will be Western Sky music and sweet opium music, and these will be mixed together to form one." Jimi also wanted to complete the work he'd begun on the *Cry Of Love* album, as well as put together a big band with brass instruments and competent musicians for whom he could conduct and write.

Alan Douglas mentions innumerable plans of Jimi's to expand into film-making and book writing. Douglas also suggests that Hendrix was considering doing a fantasy biography about "Black Gold" (a character that was basically Jimi) done in ten tunes linked together into a total story much like *Tommy*, the Who's rock opera. Douglas and Hendrix conceived of developing this theme in an animated film (perhaps this is what Jimi alludes to as "cartoon material" in the following interview), on a record, and in an illustrated book. Unfortunately, the cassette on which Jimi had sketched out the original rough was among the items stolen from his apartment immediately following his death.

Regardless of the wealth of ideas that seems to have tumbled through his fertile mind, Jimi Hendrix, though untimely silenced, left a legacy of musical creativity that was richly satisfying in every way. His death was a tragedy, but his life was not.

— Don Menn

A Rare Interview

On February 4, 1970, a day so cold and snowy that all the cabs in New York were occupied, John Burks (then managing editor of *Rolling Stone*), shivering in his California clothes, trudged and skidded through frozen slush to a chic midtown apartment to conduct what proved to be one of Jimi Hendrix' last major interviews. In attendance were Jimi, Noel Redding, Mitch Mitchell, various management personnel, and Baron Wolman, the well-known photographer-journalist. The meeting had been initiated by Hendrix' management primarily to trumpet the reunification of the original Jimi Hendrix Experience, which turned out to be a short-lived regrouping that ran concurrently with the Band of Gypsys.

Burks and Wolman remember sensing an anxiety on the part of the interviewees. "Though the setup was like you do for a fan magazine writer," John recalls, "they knew they could not manipulate the interview for their own publicity purposes because they were dealing with *Rolling Stone*. Moreover, that particular time jag contained memories of a disturbingly dull concert in January at a peace rally at Madison Square Garden at which an uninspired Jimi had simply stopped playing. Nevertheless, it is difficult to make a case for a depressed Hendrix, for if Madison Square had been a bummer, he also had the memory of a concert with the Band of Gypsys that Bill Graham described as the finest he'd ever heard at Fillmore East. Whatever the initial mood, cognac, a warm fire in the fireplace, and a relaxed pace of questioning loosened things up."

Obviously, it did not occur to John that the Hendrix portions of this interview with the Experience would be used five years later in a memorial edition of *Guitar Player*. In fact, the tape itself — a hissy jumble of voices interrupting voices, captured by a wobbly recorder — was so discouraging in quality that Burks snatched from it what phrases he could for a quick article and stashed it away in a box where it rested untranscribed, unpublished, but fortunately not erased for the last half-decade. When he learned of this special issue, John dug the cassette out, and we present here the discernible portions. Whenever possible, topical events, recordings, and individuals have been identified in brackets. Some elude clarification. Though it does not always dwell on areas normally covered by *Guitar Player*, this interview nevertheless provides a last intriguing glimpse of a guitar genius.

— Don Menn

Are you still living with a lot of musicians at your house?

No, I just try to have some time by myself so I can really write some things. I want to do more writing.

What kind of writing?

I don't know. Mostly just cartoon material. Make up this one cat who's funny, who goes through all these strange scenes. I can't talk about it now. You could put it to music, I guess. Just like you can put blues into music.

Are you talking about long extended pieces or just songs?

Well, I want to get into what you'd probably call "pieces," yeah — pieces, behind each other to make movements, or whatever you call it. I've been writing some of those. But like I was into writing cartoons mostly.

If the cartoon is in your head, do you have the music too?

Yeah, in the head, right. You listen to it, and you get such funny flashbacks. The music will be going along with the story, just like "Foxey Lady." Something like that. The music and the words go together.

When you put together a song, does it just come to you, or is it a process where you sit down with your guitar or at a piano, starting from ten in the morning?

The music I might hear I can't get on the guitar. It's a thing of just laying around daydreaming or something. You're hearing all this music, and you just can't get it on the guitar. As a matter of fact, if you pick up your guitar and just try to play, it spoils the whole thing. I can't play the guitar that well to get all this music together, so I just lay around. I wish I could have learned how to write for instruments. I'm going to get into that next, I guess.

So for something like "Foxey Lady," you first hear the music and then arrive at the words for the song?

It all depends. On "Foxey Lady," we just started playing actually, and set up a microphone, and I had these words [*laughs*]. With "Voodoo Child (Slight Return)," somebody was filming when we started doing that. We did that about three times because they wanted to film us in the studio, to make us [*imitates a pompous voice*] "Make it look like you're recording, boys" — one of them scenes, you know, so "Okay, let's play this in *E*; now a-one and-a-two and-a-three," and then we went into "Voodoo Child."

When I hear Mitch churning away and you really blowing on top and the bass getting really free, the whole approach almost sounds like avant-garde jazz.

Well, that's because that's where it's coming from — the drumming.

Do you dig any avant-garde jazz players?

Yeah, when we went to Sweden and heard some of those cats we'd never heard before. These cats were actually in little country clubs and little caves blowing some sounds that, you know, you barely imagine. Guys from Sweden, Copenhagen, Amsterdam, or Stockholm. Every once in a while they start going like a wave. They get into each other every once in a while within their personalities, and the party last night, or the hangover [*laughs*], and the evil starts pulling them away again. You can hear it start to go away. Then it starts getting together again. It's like a wave, I guess, coming in and out.

For your own musical kicks, where's the best place to play?

I like after-hour jams at a small place like a club. Then you get another feeling. You get off in another way with all those people there. You get another feeling, and you mix it in with something else that you get. It's not the spotlights, just the people.

How are those two experiences different, this thing you get from the audiences?

I get more of a dreamy thing from the audience — it's more of a thing that you go up into. You get into such a pitch sometimes that you forget about the audience, but you forget about all the paranoia, that thing where you're saying, "Oh, gosh, I'm onstage — what am I going to do now?" Then you go into this other thing, and it turns out to be almost like a play in certain ways.

You don't kick in many amps any more or light guitars on fire.

Maybe I was just noticing the guitar for a change. Maybe.

Was that a conscious decision?

Oh, I don't know. It's like it's the end of a beginning. I figure that Madison Square Garden was like the end of a big long fairy tale, which is great. It's the best thing I could possibly have come up with. The band was out of sight as far as I'm concerned.

But what happened to you?

It was just something where the head changes, just going through changes. I really couldn't tell, to tell the truth. I was very tired. You know, sometimes there's a lot of things that add up in your head about this and that. And they hit you at a very peculiar time, which happened to be at that peace rally, and here I am fighting the biggest war I've ever fought in my life — inside, you know? And like that wasn't the place to do it, so I just unmasked appearances.

How much part do you play in the production of your albums? For example, did you produce Are You Experienced?

No, it was Chas Chandler and Eddie Kramer who mostly worked on that stuff. Eddie was the engineer, and Chas as producer mainly kept things together.

The last record [Electric Ladyland] *listed you as producer. Did you do the whole thing?*

No, well, like Eddie Kramer and myself. All I did was just be there and make sure the right songs were there, and the *sound* was there. We wanted a particular sound. It got lost in the cutting room, because we went on tour right before we finished. I heard it, and I think the sound of it is very cloudy.

You did "All Along The Watchtower" on the last one. Is there anything else that you'd like to record by Bob Dylan?

Oh yeah. I like that one that goes, "Please help me in my weakness" ["Drifter's Escape"]. That was groovy. I'd like to do that. I like his *Blonde On Blonde* and *Highway 61 Revisited.* His country stuff is nice too, at certain times. It's quieter, you know.

Your recording of "Watchtower" really turned me on to that song when Dylan didn't.

Well, that's reflections like the mirror [*laughs*]. Remember that "Roomful Of Mirrors"? That's a song, a recording that we're trying to do, but I don't think we'll ever finish that. I hope not. It's about trying to get out of this roomful of mirrors.

Why can't you finish it?

[*Imitates prissy voice*] Well, you see, I'm going through this health kick, you see. I'm heavy on wheat germ, but, you know what I mean [*laughs*] — I don't know why [*takes a pencil and writes something*].

You're not what I'd call a country guitar player.

Thank you.

You consider that a compliment?

It would be if I was a country guitar player. That would be another step.

Are you listening to bands doing country, like the Flying Burrito Brothers?

Who's the guitar player for the Burrito Brothers? That guy plays. I dig him. He's really marvelous with a guitar. That's what makes me listen to that, is the music.

It's sweet. It's got that thing to it.

[*In a deep drawl*] "Hello walls" [*laughs*]. You hear that one, "Hello Walls"? "Hillbilly Heaven."

Remember Bob Wills And The Texas Playboys?

[*Laughs*] I dig them. The Grand Ole Opry used to come on, and I used to watch that. They used to have some pretty heavy cats, heavy guitar players.

Which musicians do you go out of your way to hear?

Nina Simone and Mountain. I dig them.

What about a group like the McCoys?

[*Sings intro to "Hang On Sloopy," which featured Rick Derringer on guitar.*] Yeah, that guitar player's great.

Do you dig parodies like the Masked Marauders or the English radio program, The Goon Show?

I never heard it [Masked Marauders]. I heard about it. The Fugs, they're good. I've heard they don't have it [*The Goon Show*] over here. They're masterpieces. Those are classics. They're the funniest things I've ever heard, besides Pinkie Lee. Remember Pinkie Lee? They were like a classic of a whole lot of Pinkie Lees put together, and just flip them out together.

You a Pinkie Lee fan?

Used to be. I used to wear white socks.

Were you really rehearsing with Band Of Gypsys 12 to 18 hours a day?

Yeah, we used to go and jam actually. We'd say "rehearsing" just to make it sound, you know, official. We were just getting off; that's all. Not really 18 hours — say about 12 or 14, maybe [*laughs*]. The longest we [the Experience] ever played together is going onstage. We played about two and a half hours, almost three hours one time. We made sounds. People make sounds when they clap. So we make sounds back. I like electric sounds, feedback and so forth, static.

Are you going to do a single as well as an LP?

We might have one from the other thing coming out soon. I don't know about the Experience, though. All these record companies, they want singles. But you don't just sit there and say, "Let's make a track, let's make a single or something." We're not going to do that. We don't do that.

Creedence Clearwater Revival does that until they have enough for a record, like in the old days.

TOM COPI

Well, that's the old days. I consider us more musicians. More in the minds of musicians, you know?

But singles can make some bread, can't they?

Well, that's why they do them. But they take it after. You'll have a whole planned-out LP, and all of a sudden, they'll make, for instance, "Crosstown Traffic" a single, and that's coming out of nowhere, out of a whole other set. See, that LP was in certain ways of thinking; the sides were played on in order for certain reasons. And then it's almost like a sin for them to take out something in the middle of all that and make that a single, and represent us at that particular time because they think they can make more money. They always take out the wrong ones.

How often will you space these concerts with the Experience so that you won't feel hemmed in?

As often as we three agree to it. I'd like for it to be permanent.

Have you given any thought to touring with the Experience as the basic unit, but bringing along other people? Or would that be too confusing?

No, it shouldn't be. Maybe I'm the evil one, right [*laughs*]. But there isn't any reason for it to be like that. I even want the name to be Experience anyway, and still be this mish-mash moosh-mash between Madame Flipflop And Her Harmonite Social Workers.

It's a nice name.

It's a nice game. No, like about putting other groups on the tour, like our friends — I don't know about that right now. Not at a stage like this, because we're in the process of getting our own thing together as far as a three piece group. But eventually, we have time on the side to play with friends. That's why I'll probably be jamming with Buddy [Miles] and Billy [Cox]; probably be recording, too, on the side, and they'll be doing the same.

Do you ever think in terms of going out with a dozen people?

I like Stevie Winwood; he's one of those dozen people. But things don't have to be official all the time. Things don't have to be formal for jams and stuff. But I haven't had a chance to get in contact with him.

Ever think about getting other guitar players into your trip?

Oh, yeah. Well, I heard Duane Eddy came into town this morning [*laughs*]. He was groovy.

Have you jammed with Larry Coryell, Sonny Sharrock, and people like that?

Larry and I had like swift jams down at The Scene. Every once in a while we would finally get a chance to get together. But I haven't had a chance to really play with him, not lately anyway. I sort of miss that.

Do you listen to them?

I like Larry Coryell, yeah.

Better than others?

Oh, not better. Who's this other guy? I think I've heard some of his things.

He's all over the guitar. Sometimes it sounds like it's not too orderly.

Sounds like someone we know, huh [*laughs*]?

Have you played with people like [*tenor saxman*] *Roland Kirk?*

Oh yeah, I had a jam with him at Ronnie Scott's in London, and I really got off. It was great. It was really great. I was so scared! It's really funny. I mean *Roland* [*laughs*]. That cat gets all those sounds. I might just hit one note, and it might be interfering, but like we got along great, I thought. He told me I should have turned it up or something.

He seems like a cat you might record particularly well with. I hear these bands like Blood, Sweat, & Tears and their horns, and CTA [*Chicago Transit Authority*], *though I haven't heard them in person.*

Oh yeah, CTA. In person, listen, that's when you should hear them. That's the only time. They just started recording, but in person. The next chance you get, you should check them out.

Do you listen to the Band?

It's there. They got their own thing together that takes you to a certain place. Takes you where they want to go [*laughs*], you know. Where they want to. They play their things onstage exactly how they play it on record.

Have movie people tried to lure you into films by saying you'd be a hell of a gunslinger or an astronaut?

Astronaut [*laughs*]! Fly in space! We have one called "Captain Coconut." No, well, you know. I'm trying to get the guitar together really.

Do you find American audiences more violent than those of other countries?

In New York, it's more of a violent climate. It's very violent, actually. They don't know it, really. But Texas is really fine. I don't know why. Maybe it's the weather, and the feeling of it. I dig the South a little more than playing in the North. It's more of a pressure playing in the Midwest, like Cleveland or Chicago. It's like being in a pressure cooker, waiting for the top to blow off. The people there are groovy, but it's just the atmosphere or something, you know? But the South is great. New Orleans is great. Arizona is great. Arizona's fantastic. Utah.

How did they treat you in Utah?

[*Laughs*] Well, once we're off stage, it's another world, but like the people are great. But when we play at the gigs, they were really listening; they were really tuned in some kind of way or another. I think it was the air.

Your tastes seem broader than the typical rock and roll fan or listener.

This is all I can play when I'm playing. I'd like to get something together, like with Handel, and Bach, and Muddy Waters, flamenco type of thing [*laughs*]. If I can get that *sound*. If I could get *that* sound, I'd be happy.

— John Burks

Jimi's Guitars, Amps, & Devices

CHUCK BOYD

"You name it, he used it," states Eric Barrett, Jimi's equipment manager from 1967 to 1970. This fact is what makes a complete accounting of all of Hendrix' guitars, amps, distortion devices, and accessories so formidable a task. Fortunately, however, five years after Jimi's death many of those who played with him, purchased for him, and equipped him — his father, his road managers, his fellow musicians — still recall information that he cannot tell us himself.

Somewhere between his eleventh and thirteenth birthday, Jimi received his first guitar — an inexpensive acoustic — from his father, who bought it after seeing his son holding the neck of a broom and strumming the bristles. This first guitar was replaced by an inexpensive electric when the youngster reached 12 and by an Epiphone when he was about 15.

Jimi and the Fender Stratocaster eventually became the perfect match. He bought the right-handed model because he preferred to have the controls on top, restrung it, and turned the nut to accommodate having the high *E* closest to his toes. The necks of his Stratocaster during '67 and '68 were usually made of rosewood (there were exceptions), which tended to be thinner than the maple necks on the '69 and '70 models. Jimi made his own adjustments at the bridge and around the pickups. He owned innumerable Stratocasters (he often carried 13 or more at a time) — black, white, sunburst, whatever was in that day. Only half a dozen can be accounted for today, these being instruments in the possession of Buddy Miles and Mr. Hendrix.

Jimi also favored Gibson Les Pauls, and he owned at least three Flying V's throughout his career (only one remains, a black V with gold pickups, now treasured by Eric Barrett).

One other Fender model — the Telecaster — was always on hand, though Jimi rarely used it, and then usually only in the studio. On one occasion he may have played a Stratocaster with a Telecaster neck.

Once Jimi became wealthy enough to buy whatever he needed, his accumulation of instruments began. Henry Goldrich of Manny's recalls selling him everything from a Gibson ES-330 to a Firebird to a Mosrite double-cutaway electric dobro (which he dropped and broke the same night he purchased it). Other guitars were: a Guild 12-string acoustic; a Gibson stereo; an acoustic Black Widow (Mr. Hendrix salvaged it); two Hagstrom 8-string basses (Jimi played them on "Spanish Castle Magic" on *Axis: Bold As Love*); three Rickenbackers—a bass, a 6-, and a 12-string guitar; a Gibson Dove acoustic; a Martin, new when bought; and an old Hofner electric. Eric Barrett adds that Jimi generally had more than one of everything except the Rickenbackers.

Modifications to his instruments were scarce or minimal. He had purely decorative designs hand-painted on some of his Stratocasters (as with the one he burned at the Monterey Pop Festival of 1967) and on his Black Flying V. Barrett does not recall Jimi doing this himself, though his road manager of four years, Gerry Stickells (who was also his equipment manager, preceding Barrett) thinks that Jimi *did* do the painting.

Frets were rarely reworked because Hendrix' guitars didn't last long enough to become worn. In the early days before the Experience carried extra equipment, Stickells says Jimi used to take the small panel off the back of his Stratocasters because that made it easier to change strings. If he broke one during a performance, Stickells would make the change while Jimi kept playing.

Jimi spent hours bending his tremolo bars (by hand) to get them near enough to the body so that he could tap the strings individually as well as raise and lower their pitches. In a sense, he also "modified" his guitars by smashing them, since often the axe he used at the next performance would be an assemblage of the unsplintered parts gathered up in a box and stuck together by Barrett.

There are two other alterations to Jimi's guitars that may or may not have happened. Jess Hansen of the Jimi Hendrix Archives stood onstage at Jimi's last concert in Seattle. He clearly remembers seeing another toggle switch on the back of the black Strat, located approximately where the neck joins the body. Jimi manipulated this switch throughout the evening, though its effect, purpose, or permanence is not known. Bill Lawrence, one of the world's foremost experts on guitars and their electronics, says he suggested a design to Jimi for rewiring his Stratocasters. Dan Armstrong, another fine craftsman who learned much of what he knows from Lawrence, may have actually done the work. (Lawrence was not certain whether it happened, and Armstrong did not respond to repeated queries.) Whatever, it may have been a one-time modification, since Goldrich, Barrett, and Stickells — those most immediately responsible for Jimi's equipment — know nothing of such a rewiring of the stock instruments with which they kept Jimi supplied.

Jimi experimented with various amplification systems, but to use Barrett's words, "It was 99% Marshall." In his rhythm and blues days, Jimi had a Fender Twin Reverb (which he very occasionally used in the studio after he became a worldwide phenomenon). Jimi also sniffed out Orange amps at the December '67 Pink Floyd "Christmas On Earth" show in London, and at his very last concert. Apparently, he could not get the sounds he wanted from them.

In 1967, Buck Munger, now of L.D. Heater of Beaverton, Oregon, solidified a five-year contract (it lasted 14 months) between Jimi and Sunn after the Monterey Festival. He recalls Jimi "right off the boat, with banged up Marshall and Fender gear." Sunn supplied the entire Experience with anything they needed in exchange for Jimi's research and development input.

Jimi started with a cabinet Sunn designated as 100-F, with one JBL D-130 in the bottom and an L-E 100-S driver horn in the top. There was not much mid-range (Munger describes it as "almost a surfer sound"), and Jimi combined this with a stack of Marshalls to get a blend.

Later, the Sunn setup included up to five Coliseum PA tops, altered for guitar at 120 watts RMS each, with ten speaker cabinets with two JBL D-130 F's. "We then went to four 12" Emminence, at his request," Munger states, adding that Jimi convinced Sunn that the minimum acceptable power at that time was 100 watts RMS (they had been working with 60 watts).

The arrangement with Sunn, which worked well for bassist Noel Redding, did not satisfy Jimi. Part of the problem, according to Munger, was that the English RMS rating might be double the American one (even when a 200-watt English amp only put out as much power as a 100-watt American amp). "Jimi was used to the big numbers," Munger explains, "and when he turned his Sunn amps up, he got a lot of noise he didn't like." Sunn tried to solve the problem by putting on a dial that Jimi could turn up only to eight (though it would seem, on looking, to be at ten). Soon thereafter, Jimi went back to Marshalls.

This setup was humble in the beginning. Stickells says that Jimi and Noel shared one miked, 100-watt Marshall stack for their first album. This stack grew. Jimi came to use two 200-watt Marshall amps with four cabinets. At other times, he used three 100-watt and even three 200-watt heads, miked through PA systems and as many as six cabinets (with a seventh for monitor on Redding's side). Eric Barrett recalls that the group carried between a dozen and 18 tops and box upon box of speakers, which had to be changed daily after Jimi tore through them with his guitar. The grille cloth, however, was left hanging. Since Jimi performed with his amp settings nearly always on full, his systems wore out fast.

But his amps were given still greater power through the wizardry of a Long Island electronics brain, Tony Frank, who rewired and tuned up those 100-watt amps (which Barrett believes weren't putting out anything near that specification) so that they delivered 137 watts. Furthermore, Henry Goldrich states that the Marshall factory, after learning who Jimi was, began putting in somewhat heavier tubes and resoldering Jimi's amps so

TOM COPI

everything wouldn't fall apart. With all this power, it's refreshing to note that Les Paul remembers a phone conversation in which Jimi expressed to him a desire for a tiny amp, in those days preceding mini-amps.

As far as can be determined, Jimi primarily used Fender Rock 'N' Roll light-gauge guitar strings (.010, .013, .015, .026, .032, .038), though Mike Bloomfield insists that Buddy Miles insists that Jimi used very heavy strings on the bottom, a medium gauge on his *A* and *D*, a Hawaiian *G* string, a light (not super light) gauge *B* string, and a super light *E*. This was supposedly not just for experimentation, but something that Jimi did all the time because he thought it would keep the whole guitar in tune a little better. Bloomfield's information is not entirely secondhand, for he has tried some of Jimi's Stratocasters which Buddy now owns. Miles was not available for comment.

Jimi virtually always tuned his guitar down a half-step. In other words, his strings from lowest to highest were *E♭, A♭, D♭, G♭, B♭, E♭*. It's not entirely clear why he did this. However, tuning down a half-step makes the strings much more flexible for bending.

Jimi's principal distortion devices included the Dallas-Arbiter Fuzz Face, the Univox Univibe, and Vox wah-wah pedals. Stickells says that the Experience made it through the first tour with only two or three Fuzz Faces, contrasting with the two dozen units that were later carried. Similarly, at least a dozen Univibes (these simulate a rotating speaker) were always on hand, and two dozen wah-wah pedals. Barrett explains that this was necessary because "Jimi never would put his foot on a fuzz or wah-wah; he'd put his whole weight on it; they didn't last long." The wah appeared on the market towards the end of Jimi's first tour, and he quickly incorporated the pedal into his stock setup.

Other boxes and pedals included some made by Roger Mayer. He built, in Barrett's words, "quite a few little toys for Jimi; they didn't have names, just little labels to identify them." Most often used was a device called the "Octavia," especially built for Jimi, which changed the octave on the guitar (Barrett doesn't remember whether the jump was up or down) when Jimi stepped on the pedal. Most of the other devices were not used onstage, though Jimi on occasion used them in the studio, as he did nearly every device he brought home from anywhere. Numerous other individuals also presented him regularly with homemade equipment.

Miscellaneous units included The Bag (held like Scottish bagpipes); a Maestro Fuzz, which Mike Bloomfield saw Jimi use while he was with John Hammond, Jr.; and in 1967, 1968, and possibly 1969, Hendrix may have used a couple of Leslie speakers before the Univibe was developed. It could not be substantiated that Jimi used an Echoplex, or any of the equipment made by Electro-Harmonix, as has been suggested by various sources.

When Jimi walked onstage to begin a concert during the years of his greatest popularity, he could count on finding a Univibe, a Fuzz Face, and a Vox wah-wah plugged together into his Marshall amps. Beside them were at least five Stratocasters, a Les Paul, and his Flying V.

For picks, Jimi chose whatever medium gauge his hand came up with when he stuck it into the drawer at Manny's. Eric Barrett simply reports that on tour the Experience carried thousands of picks. They also packed hundreds of guitar straps, also from Manny's, to match Jimi's shirts. The after-hours jams that Mike Bloomfield mentions in his reminiscence were recorded, probably on two TEAC four-track machines bought at Colony Music in New York.

The range of interest that Jimi manifested with regard to guitaring equipment extended into other musical realms, for he not only collected everything imaginable for his own specialty, but also bought pianos, trumpets, saxophones, and other instruments — all of which he wanted to learn to play so that he could do an entirely solo album. "That," says Henry Goldrich, "is what the studio was all for."

Clues as to why Jimi preferred one brand or device over another are scarce. "He didn't express to anybody what he wanted," Eric Barrett explains, adding that, "his ear knew, and only his ears." The only scrap available comes from Mike Bloomfield, who states that he recalls Jimi giving him "a big lecture that Fuzz Face and Cry Baby were the only ones that really worked." Bloomfield was told by Hendrix that the Cry Baby gave the greatest range from treble to bass, the hugest wah effect, the fastest action, and had the most authentically vocal sound. Fuzz Face, Jimi felt, was the most distorted sounding of such units. The two plugged together gave permanent sustain and endless distortion.

It is impossible to determine for certain all the equipment and effects Jimi used in the studio and on records. We are left only with morsels: *Are You Experienced* and *Axis: Bold As Love* were both recorded (and mixed on a custom board) on four-track at 15 inches-per-second at the Olympic Studios in London. Jimi's guitar is a Stratocaster on the first album, except on the "Red House" cut, for which he used his old Hofner, which was in such disrepair that the pickups were stuck on with Scotch tape (he only used it a couple of times in performance before it was stolen). A Les Paul was probably used for "House Burning Down" on *Electric Ladyland*, while the black Strat was featured on *Band Of Gypsys*.

Eddie Kramer, Jimi's engineer from 1967 to 1970, feels that it is useless to approach Jimi's music in so analytical a manner. This is partly because Kramer's own approach was often too improvisational to capture, and partly because he does not wish to divulge studio techniques which he considers the finer points of his work. "I think the mystique should remain," Kramer states. "Analyzing it to the point that you want in your magazine is not a good idea. Part of the mystique is what I created with him in the studio, and I'd like to leave it at that."

And so, that is where we must leave it.

— Don Menn

Roadie's Nightmare

Jimi used tiny amps for clubs — assorted everything — but as soon as he started doing any kind of theater work, Chas Chandler got him a 100-watt Marshall top with two 4" x 12" cabinets. When I first joined, Jimi was traveling with just two cabinets and maybe two tops. Mitch Mitchell had a kit of drums. As we were going along, it got to be four cabinets and maybe then four tops. So, if Jimi had four, then Noel had to have four. Then it got to the point Jimi had six with three 100-watt tops on the top of those three and another one on the bottom pushing a slave on the other side for Noel to hear. So that resulted in Noel having six of these big Sunn amps with three 100- or 200-watt tops — I can't remember which — with another one at the side pushing one on Jimi's side. As soon as it got to that, Mitch said, "I can't hear my drums." So we started off getting him all this different stuff, and we eventually ended up with four of those big Altec A-7 cabinets that people used for PA systems stuck up right behind his head. He'd always say, "It's not loud enough! Give me more!"

Jimi had this thing — apart from the usual act of smashing up guitars I would build for him. If he had got everything out of a guitar that he loved, that you knew had to go out every night, it would be the first one he'd pick up, and you would have that guitar for maybe four or five months. When he figured he could get no more out of that guitar, that it had given him everything he could get, all of a sudden he would smash it, and I would go into a panic, because that was his favorite, and I'd think, "God, what's he going to use at the next gig?" Because that meant he had to start breaking in new ones, and it did take time to break them in.

If a string would bust, I would run out with another guitar, and we would change that in fractions of seconds. I would hold it up, he would take it off his neck, and I would slip the strap around his neck, and he would play this enormous chord. All of a sudden I would pull out one jack and go right in with another, and his hands would change down onto the same chord he was on. People very rarely heard a slump. I used to watch him constantly; I was always there from instinct: If I was going to hold that job I had to be the best. Otherwise, someone else would come along.

Some nights he'd be screaming, "Eric! This fuzz box isn't right!" So I would take out another one. He still wasn't happy with that. I took out another one. He still wasn't happy. So rather than go through 14, I would play a psychological game. I'd bring him back the very first one he had, and say, "This one is great; this one is brand-new." He'd plug it in, and say, "Now that's what it should have been the first time." Same thing would happen with wah-wah pedals. You'd take them back, change it three or four times, then give him back the first one he had, and he'd say, "Yeah! Now that's what I'm talking about!" Weird, but I think all musicians do things like that.

— Eric Barrett

Manny's Music & Jimi's Gear

Anything that was new, he bought," recalls Henry Goldrich. "Jimi always liked to be the first to use an effect." Henry should know. He and his relatives in the family-owned business served Jimi's equipment needs from 1964 until his death in 1970. Though Jimi obviously browsed in other music shops, the service and selection he found at Manny's 48th Street Musical Instruments Store in New York City led him to establish an open charge account there.

Jimi could rely on Henry to deliver eight or nine guitars by car on his way home, or ship a roomful of items ahead for a worldwide tour. Eventually, Goldrich equipped Electric Lady, Jimi's studio, from stem to stern. "Any kind of new toy or sound effect he bought immediately," Goldrich continues. "Whenever he walked in, he was good for $1,500 — $2,000."

Henry's father, *the* Manny, opened his shop in 1935, and it has survived everything from the tail end of the Depression to the crunch of high rises pressing on its rib cage, supplying a phenomenal roster of musicians — before and since Hendrix — with what is said to be the largest stock of musical merchandise in this country.

"Jimi used to buy three or four guitars every other week," Henry states. "But he lost them or gave them away. I'd see kids come in the store with guitars I'd sold Jimi the week before. If he liked a kid, he gave him his guitar, brand-new."

As a loyal customer before he was famous, Jimi never demanded preferential treatment after. Nevertheless, Henry used to keep the store open for him after hours because Jimi began to be hounded by admirers. He would come in once a week to hang out for an hour and a half and try out all the new instruments, distortion devices, accessories. Moreover, he'd take *all* of them home.

— Don Menn

Jimi's Favorite Guitar Techniques

TOM COPI

Trying to unscrew Jimi Hendrix' favorite techniques is as puzzling an undertaking as finding an adequate way to describe with words the difference between red and green. Mathematical equations may do that, but where are the *words* that encapsulate the perception of two very clearly differing realities? The problem is really even more complex. It's more like trying to verbalize the distinguishing qualities not of two colors but of every hue used in some wildly vibrant canvas.

We know that Jimi must have gone through certain procedures that always resulted in certain sounds. And it follows that since all those weird sounds were repeatable effects (most say he could conjure them at will), then it should be possible to list in tidy order the manipulations that led to each Hendrixian effect. After all, something causes something, and it ought to be easy to itemize what happens. So where are those one-through-ten lists that go with each item? Jimi never thought to write them down. Such an analytical logging was totally antithetical to his musical approach. He was too involved with creating new effects to chronologize the old. Nevertheless, there were a few highly noticeable movements that Jimi went through that seemed to have had some bearing on what sounds came out of his amplifiers. A few are sketched below, though they don't even represent the tip of the iceberg — scarcely a trickle down the side.

1. SHOWMANSHIP

Using tricks that go back a half century or more, Jimi revived and repopularized many of the old bluesmen's favorite high-stepping, upstaging show stoppers. He played his guitar behind his head or back, shoved the neck of his guitar between his knees. Most memorable of all, he played — actually played music — while holding the guitar to his mouth. It's not entirely a closed matter on how he used his mouth, or for that matter if he really used his teeth. Jess Hansen, a major Hendrix authority, says Jimi pushed forward with his front teeth moving his chin from his chest outward. Eric Barrett, Jimi's equipment manager, while conceding that no one really knows, thinks Hendrix did just the opposite, i.e. plucked with his teeth, moving his chin in towards his chest.

Chuck Rainey, who played with Jimi, believes that Hendrix was not using his teeth at all, but picked with his tongue. Innumerable photographs give credence to all theories, and observers abound who swear by their own pet explanations. Jimi himself said the idea came to him "in a town in Tennessee. Down there you have to play with your teeth or else you get shot. There's a trail of broken teeth all over the stage." Did it leave his gums sore? He advised others against trying it, but said he would never do it if it hurt him. Towards the later part of his career, Jimi discarded most of these maneuvers.

2. DESTRUCTION AS MUSIC

The sounds of a neck shredding or an amp flying apart; of a string popping, writhing, and melting away; of a dismembered pickup amplifying its own unravelling through a shattered speaker were sounds that Jimi did not invent, but nevertheless used to a particularly "musical" degree. They fit in well with his more aggressive, raw finales. Peter Townshend of the Who was doing this before Jimi, and he picked it up in art school. "Auto-destruction" was an offshoot of "happenings" staged in the early '60s. They were created by painters who used the everyday world not *for* a canvas, but *as* a canvas when they concocted events such as dropping a piano from a crane, filling the splintered wreck with hay, and then incinerating the whole mess. In the early part of his career, Jimi smashed many guitars, burned a few, and harpooned his speaker cabinets sometimes for show, sometimes out of frustration, and occasionally to create a raucous acoustical effect. It was all part of trying to get the most from his equipment, and when he could wring no more from it, he'd pound it out.

3. USING THE TREMOLO BAR

Jimi used the "wang" bar on his Stratocasters to wrench out numerous effects for which the device had not been originally designed. According to Mike Bloomfield, Jimi altered his tremolo bars to make them capable of changing a string's pitch by three steps. Eric Barrett says Jimi bent these bars by hand so that they would be close enough for him to use to lightly "bop" individual strings with the handle. He manipulated the bar in the usual ways with his picking hand, but also used less orthodox methods, vibrating it rapidly with his chording hand while tightening and loosening machine heads, pounding on the guitar's neck, or playing around with the tone and volume controls.

4. HAVING A FIFTH "FINGER"

Jimi got his wrist vibrato in every way imaginable. Primarily he used a push-pull action (moving the string back and forth across the frets) while slightly shaking his wrist. Eric Barrett recalls Jimi's incredible strength — he could bend the 1st string on a bass all the way to the top. Jimi also used his thumb extensively for chording. It was long enough to extend all the way around the neck and cover from low to high *E* strings. Jimi used his thumb mainly on the bottom three strings. For example, Mike Bloomfield describes how Hendrix, "Would play an *Em* triad on top, but use his thumb to play in *D* on the bottom strings." He would use his thumb going *along* (not always across) so that beginning on the 3rd fret on the bottom three strings he might play at one time a *G*, *D♭*, and another *G*. He used his little finger for runs and chords, but he would often hook it behind the neck of the guitar when using his thumb.

5. SLIDING TECHNIQUES

Though Jimi did not use a metal cylinder or glass bottleneck for slide, Jimmy Stewart remembers seeing him use his ring for slide effects. He would also grab the microphone stand and run it up and down the fretboard for bold, searing slide effects. For more raw, less defined sounds, he used his amp cabinets and his elbow (wiping the strings up and down).

6. PALMING THE PICK

Eric Barrett thinks that Jimi usually held his pick with his thumb and first finger. But Jimi seems to have performed occasional sleight-of-hand. Film footage of him playing clearly shows the pick vanishing as he begins strumming the instrument openhandedly. Many guitarists do this, and like them, Jimi may have palmed his pick either in his hand or grasped it with his fingers or thumb. Conceivably he could have devised some way to hold it secure with the band of his ring or even put tape somewhere to stick it on, though other films don't really substantiate this idea.

7. EFFECTIVE RETUNING

Jimi used to frequently change the tuning of his instrument midway through a selection. Aside from his fanatical attention to intonation, he did this intentionally to achieve wobbly on-off pitch variations. While cranking away at the machine heads, his line to the audience used to be, "Oh, well, only cowboys stay in tune, anyway." The only indication available that he may have used open tunings comes from Chuck Rainey, who distinctly recalls that in the King Curtis days Jimi used to tune to an open chord. Beyond this memory, Chuck could not recall the tuning, nor could anyone else when asked come up with a specific case indicating that Jimi played open tunings after he became more famous.

8. UTILIZING THE CONTROLS

The combinations are endless, but Jimi controlled his volume and tone almost exclusively from the body of the guitar (all amp controls were full on). This allowed him the usual range of possibilities, but he turned his lefthandedness to advantage. With a right-handed guitar turned upside down, the controls were above the strings. Therefore, he could pick the guitar and at the same time move the tone and volume controls with the heel of his hand to ooze in and out of a tone, or get a smooth, "rock" diminuendo.

In conjunction with other instrument parts, he also fooled with his toggle switch to achieve everything from a howling wind effect to machine gun blasts. Jess Hansen says Jimi would get a harmonic, flip the pickup switch, mess with the amp dials, shut the stand-by on and off and come up with the gunfire. Jimi also used to set his Stratocaster toggle switch in a little notch that can be found between the first and second pickups to catch both. This created a twangy sound such as is heard on "Little Wing," "Wait Until Tomorrow," and "House Burning Down." Hendrix also took out the back of his Stratocaster so that he could pull the strings and springs in back to get various "sprongy" sounds.

9. PLAYING THE NECK

Jimi used the back of his guitar's neck nearly as

much as the front. He would tap it lightly with the back of his knuckles up and down to bring out harmonics, or jar the instrument into setting up other vibrations that could be reprocessed and permutated. Tapping or tugging the neck, he could be gentle or merciless. Eric Barrett says Hendrix used to even grasp the neck and shake it back and forth to get a wild vibrato that was not possible either by hand or with the tremolo bar. In fact, Jimi used to wrench the neck back and forth so hard that it would sometimes come completely loose, leaving limp strings (and probably intonation problems that only someone like Jimi could deal with).

10. APPLYING ELECTRONICS

No one could unravel this with words or charts — probably not even Jimi. Obviously, years of experimentation with body placements, an extraordinary sense of equipment characteristics, a childlike willingness to play with possibilities that sounded "bad," an extraordinary intuitiveness and capacity to work on his feet with whatever started happening in his equipment, combined to help Jimi develop his unparalleled electrical inventiveness. As far as anyone knows, Hendrix did not have a textbook knowledge of equipment, though most who knew him insist that he could duplicate any sound he used on record.

A few tricks included getting feedback on two strings, then tapping the guitar with his ring, which set off a commotion that sounded like a five-alarm fire. He also often bumped his instrument with his hip to get a booming sound. He had his techniques so refined as to be able to get feedback going on a two- or three-string chord, coax and develop and alter that, all the while playing lead on the other strings. This facility is what made many musicians listening to his LPs wonder where the second or third guitar players with the group were, and why they weren't photographed on the album cover. It was inconceivable, at the time, to arrive at the actual conclusion — that there was only one guitar player.

* * * *

These are only some of the many and varied techniques that helped Jimi achieve the sounds he needed for self-expression. In the hands of lesser musicians, these are mere gimmicks; in the hands of a Jimi Hendrix, however, they are valuable tools of his craft — as necessary to him as properly trimmed nails are to Segovia or the right-hand mute is to Atkins.

— Don Menn

Michael Bloomfield Reminisces

The first time I saw Jimi play he was Jimmy James with the Blue Flames. I was performing with Paul Butterfield, and I was the hot shot guitarist on the block — I thought I was *it*. I'd never heard of Hendrix. Then someone said, "You got to see the guitar player with John Hammond." I was at the Cafe Au Go Go and he was at the Nite Owl or the Cafe Wha? I went right across the street and saw him. Hendrix knew who I was, and that day, in front of my eyes, he burned me to death. I didn't even get my guitar out. H bombs were going off, guided missiles were flying — I can't tell you the sounds he was getting out of his instrument. He was getting every sound I was ever to hear him get right there in that room with a Stratocaster, a Twin (amplifier), a Maestro fuzz, and that was all — he was doing it mainly through extreme volume. How he did this, I wish I understood. He just got right up in my face with that axe, and I didn't even want to pick up a guitar for the next year.

I was awed. I'd never heard anything like it. I didn't even know where he was coming from musically, because he wasn't playing any of his own tunes. He was doing things like "Like A Rolling Stone," but in the most unusual way. He wasn't a singer; he wasn't even particularly a player. That day, Jimi Hendrix was laying things on me that were more sounds than they were licks. But I found, after hearing him two or three more times, that he was into pure melodic playing and lyricism as much as he was into sounds. In fact, he had melded them into a perfect blend.

Jimi told me he'd been playing the chitlin' circuit, and he hadn't heard guitarists doing anything new. He was bored out of his mind. He was a real shy talker, and often spoke in riddles, though he could be quite lucid if pinned down. He explained that he could do more than play backup guitar in the chitlin' circuit. And though he was a rotten singer, he knew that he had a lot going on electric guitar. Jimi said he had never heard anyone play in his style.

We both performed around Greenwich Village for months, but I didn't know that Hendrix wrote his own music, and he never sang. He would mumble a song. Right around the time he was playing with John Hammond, Chas Chandler got hold of him and said, "You'll sing how you sing. Don't worry about it, man; you've got enough going for you."

There was no great electric guitarist in rock and roll that Jimi didn't know of. I could ask him about records that I knew had real fancy guitar parts, where the performer was ahead of his time or playing funky on a record that wasn't particularly funky. For example, Jimi knew all about a very early Righteous Brothers record on which there's a guitarist who plays very advanced rock and roll guitar for that time. There's another record by Robert Parker, who made "Barefootin'," called, "You Better Watch Yourself," that has a real hot guitar player with a style more like Hendrix than most session players. Jimi said it wasn't him, but that he knew the guy — somebody named Big Tom Collins. He knew every hot guitarist on record.

When *Are You Experienced* came out, it was fantastic. But I was even more impressed with Jimi's second LP, *Axis: Bold As Love*. It was fabulous, utterly funky. I'd heard the Who and Cream and much loud electric power music, but I had never heard a trio that really worked and was so danceable. Hendrix defined how a trio should sound. He had such an orchestral concept that *Are You Experienced* negated everything I had heard in the English lead guitar power trio field.

Jimi had been fooling with feedback, but when he heard the Yardbirds, he realized its huge potential. Hendrix would sustain a note and add vibrato so that it sounded just like a human voice. He used an immense vocabulary of controlled sounds, not just hoping to get those sounds, but actually controlling them as soon as he produced them. I have never heard such controlled frenzy, especially in electric music. Jimi said that he went to England to wipe them out, and he did.

When he came back to the U.S., he jammed a lot. He was in the habit, around 1968 or '69, of carrying two very good home recorders with him, and every time he jammed he would set these up so that, with the two four-track machines, he was getting eight tracks of recording. God knows who has these tapes, but Jimi was a massive chronicler of his own and other people's jams. I personally saw at least ten jams that he recorded. The Cafe Au Go Go in New York also had extremely good recording facilities, and I believe they recorded every time Hendrix jammed there; he did that countless times.

I don't think Jimi used anything but Stratocasters very much. If he used another guitar, that was probably because his wasn't around, or he just wanted to see what another was like, or — as in the case of the Flying V in the Hendrix documentary film — he was at a point where he didn't care about anything. I think the Flying V was something they stuck in his hands. He played real sloppy, and that was the only bad playing I ever recall seeing or hearing by Hendrix.

I never saw anything customized on any of his guitars, except he told me that his wang bar was customized on all of his guitars, so he could pull it back much farther than a whole step. He wanted to be able to lower it three steps. He had no favorite guitar; they were all expendable. Buddy Miles has some of his Strats, and all the ones that I've tried are hard to play — heavy strings and heavy action. I'm amazed that he could play as facile as he did.

Jimi's musical approach, as he explained it to me, was to lay out the entire song and decide how it should be — horns, strings, the way it would wind up. He would play the drum beat on a damp wah-wah pedal, the bass part on the bass strings of his guitar, and the pattern of the song with just the wah-wah pedal. Then he would flesh the pattern out by playing it with chords and syncopation. He was extremely interested in form. In a few seconds of playing, he'd let you know about the entire structure. That's why he liked rhythm guitar playing so much: The rhythm guitar could lay out the structure for the whole song. He would always say, "This is a world of lead guitar players, but the most essential thing to learn is the time, the rhythm." He once told me he wanted to burn Clapton to death because he didn't play rhythm.

Jimi would play a bass pattern, and then fill it in with chords. And at the exact same time he would play lead by making a high note ring out while using very unorthodox chord positions. He had a massive thumb, which he used like an additional finger, so his hand positions were unconventional for every chord.

Once we played a gig at The Shrine in Los Angeles, and we were backstage fooling around with our guitars. Hendrix was playing with his toggle switch. He was taking the toggle switch of the guitar, tapping the back of the neck, and using vibrato, and it came out sounding like a sirocco, a wind coming up from the desert. I have never heard a sound on a Hendrix record that I have not seen him create in front of my eyes.

I don't know how he kept the guitar in tune. If you jerk a wang bar, your guitar goes out of tune. But his didn't, apparently. He could bend it in tune.

Somehow, by tapping the back of his guitar neck (which he constantly did) and by using the bar, Jimi could control feedback. You would hear a rumbling start. He knew which note would feed back and what harmonic he was shooting for, and then he controlled it. Somehow, when he had all the notes open, he would raise the pitch level by using the bar and he'd get a higher note to feed back, or he would make the bass note feed back harmonically. He was listening for such things, and I believe he heard them on the English records, particularly by the Yardbirds and Jeff Beck. He was very modest. He never said he took feedback further than the Yardbirds. He said, "I fool with it, and what I'm doing now is the fruits of my fooling around."

You couldn't even tell what Hendrix was doing with his body. He moved with all those tricks that black guitarists had been using since T-Bone Walker and Guitar Slim — playing behind his head and with his teeth. He took exhibitionism to a new degree. He used to crash his guitar against his hip. It was a bold gesture, and he would get a roaring, fuzzy, feedback sound. His body motion was so integrated with his playing that you couldn't tell where one started and the other left off.

Many of his sounds were things that Jimi stumbled on, and a lot he shopped for. They became part of his musical language. It wasn't something he could just tell you how to do. You had to understand the whole way he heard sound, the way he wanted to feel sound and get it out to create music.

I remember going to his hotel room. He had a little Kay amp against the wall, and he had his guitar out. Immediately he was getting new sounds out of it. He never stopped playing. His guitar was the first thing he'd reach for when he woke up. We were bopping around New York once, and I said, "Let's find some girls." He said, "That can wait; there's always time for that. Let's play, man." He was the most compulsive player I've ever run into. That's why he was so good.

Melodically, he used two basic scales: The blues minor scale and its relative major. If he was playing *A* minor, he would go to *C* major and make it a major seventh scale. "All Along The Watchtower" is a perfect vehicle for minor or blues scale improvisation, while "Bold As Love," "Little Wing," and "The Wind Cries Mary" were perfect for major key explorations.

But it was no big thing for Hendrix to play melodies; he wanted to play like an orchestra. This is the crux of his music. It's not just lead guitar, it's orchestral guitar, like Segovia, Chet Atkins, Wilburn Burchette, Ry Cooder, and George Van Eps. Jimi Hendrix was the most orchestral of all. Have you ever heard "The Star Spangled Banner" on *Rainbow Bridge*? That's recorded like a huge symphony.

I recall Jimi saying that he wanted to get a band together that was not like the Experience, one with a lot of interplay and more equality, with guys he could learn from as much as they from him. With the Experience, he played bass half the time on record. He wanted a trio with percussion and a horn or two, with singers — more voices than his own. If anyone was a one-man band, it was Jimi. He'd tap his foot and would have a drum; that's all he needed. Perhaps the burden of being the whole orchestra was too much.

Hendrix was by far the greatest expert I've ever heard at playing rhythm and blues, the style of playing developed by Bobby Womack, Curtis Mayfield, Eric Gale, and others. I got the feeling there was no guitaring of any kind that he hadn't heard or studied, including steel guitar, Hawaiian, and dobro.

In his playing I can really hear Curtis Mayfield, Wes Montgomery, Albert King, B.B. King, and Muddy Waters. Jimi was the blackest guitarist I ever heard. His music was deeply rooted in pre-blues, the oldest musical forms, like field hollers and gospel melodies. From what I can garner, there was no form of black music that he hadn't listened to or studied, but he especially loved the real old black music forms, and they poured out in his playing. We often talked about Son House and the old blues guys. But what really did it to him was early Muddy Waters and John Lee Hooker records — that early electric music where the guitar was hugely amplified and boosted by the studio to give it the effect of more presence than it really had. He knew that stuff backwards. You can hear every old John Lee Hooker and Muddy Waters thing that ever was on that one long version of "Voodoo Chile" [*Electric Ladyland*].

I never heard Jimi play anything that sounds like jazz, though I have heard him play like Mahavishnu [John McLaughlin]. He learned to apply melodic ideas to permanent sustain, tied in with feedback from the Yardbirds and other English groups. I think he even mentioned Beck's "Bolero."

Jimi's lyrics and folkadelic clothes were all stone white, but he's as black as they come. He applied all of his techniques, which he mostly got from rock and roll and English groups, to black melody lines and bluesy scales. There's very little recorded of Hendrix playing blues, other than the two "Red House" cuts, but he was an unparalleled blues guitarist. However, I remember him saying that he found playing blues boring.

Though I watched Hendrix perform many times, I couldn't understand his hand positions or the chords he used. He could play left- or right-handed with equal facility. Sometimes, he didn't even re-string his guitar; he just played it upside down.

I feel that Hendrix was one of the most innovative guitar players who ever lived. He was the man that took electric music and defined it. He turned sounds from devices like wah-wahs into music. They weren't gimmicks when he used them. In fact, they were beyond music. They were in the realm of pure sound and music combined. Every time I ever saw Jimi play, I felt that he was an object lesson for everything that I should be and wasn't. But I could never say something like that to him, because he was a super-modest guy.

* * * *

I didn't see Jimi for a long while, and when I did, he had the stink of death on him. He smelled like he was rotting from the inside out. He had that rock star look that was fashionable then, the look of starving: no food, no sleep, very sallow. I couldn't talk to him because it was so shocking and horrible that I didn't want to confront that.

One of the traits of barbiturates is that you can taste them. If a capsule breaks before it gets into your stomach and lodges in your throat, it acts as an emetic and forces you to vomit. I'm sure that's what happened: A few capsules got caught in his throat, forced him to vomit, and he died. I'm positive he didn't commit suicide. But I'm also positive that if someone hadn't taken him in hand, he would have burned out anyway, because when I saw him before he died, he was a wreck. Too much of being a product was killing him. Maybe he didn't want to stop, or maybe he didn't know how. Ultimately, it's in the artist's hands. Obviously Jimi didn't stop.

— Michael Bloomfield

JIMI HENDRIX: A SELECTED DISCOGRAPHY

Officially released American solo albums (on Reprise, except as indicated): *Are You Experienced,* RS 6261; *Axis: Bold As Love,* RS 6281; *Electric Ladyland,* 2RS 6307; *Smash Hits,* MSK 2276; *Band Of Gypsies,* Capitol, STAC 472; *Monterey International Pop Festival — Otis Redding/Jimi Hendrix Experience,* MS 2029; *The Cry Of Love,* MS 2034; *Rainbow Bridge,* MS 2040; *Hendrix In The West,* MS 2049; *War Heroes,* MS 2103; *Soundtrack Recordings From The Film "Jimi Hendrix,"* 2RS 6481; *Crash Landing,* MS 2204; *Midnight Lightning,* MS 2229; *Nine To The Universe,* HS 2299; *The Essential Jimi Hendrix,* 2RS 2245; *The Essential Jimi Hendrix Vol. II,* HS-2293; *Jimi Hendrix Concerts,* 1-22306. **European solo albums:** *Isle Of Wight,* Polydor, 2302 016; *Experience Soundtrack,* Ember, NR 5057; *More Experience,* Entertainment Int., LDM-30 148; *Loose Ends,* Polydor, Super 2310 301; *Stone Free,* Polydor, 2343114; *Original Music From The Film "Jimi Plays Berkeley,"* Barclay, 80-555. **With Curtis Knight:** *The Eternal Fire Of Jimi Hendrix,* Hallmark, SHM 732; *What'd I Say,* Music For Pleasure, MFP 5278; *In The Beginning,* Ember, NR 5068. **With others:** Stephen Stills, *Stephen Stills,* Atlantic, SD 7202; Love, *False Start,* Blue Thumb, BTS 22; Little Richard, *Together,* Pickwick, SPC-3347; Isley Brothers, *In The Beginning,* T-Neck, TNS 3007; Lonnie Youngblood, *Two Great Experiences Together,* Maple, LPM 6004. **Anthologies:** *Woodstock Soundtrack,* Cotillion, SD3-500; *Woodstock Two,* Cotillion, SD2-400; *The First Great Rock Festivals Of The Seventies,* Columbia, G3X 30805; *The Guitar Album,* Polydor, 2679 026.

NEIL ZLOZOWER

Led Zeppelin's Jimmy Page

NEIL ZLOZOWER

A former session player and member of the Yardbirds, Jimmy Page formed Led Zeppelin in 1968 and became enormously influential through his playing on their first albums and tours. Two months after Led Zeppelin began, Page was interviewed by *Guitar Player* at the Fillmore West. The following feature was originally published in June 1969.

the artist

From the time Jimmy Page launched Led Zeppelin, it did what most groups dream of doing: It floated right to the top, first in England and now in the U.S. We caught Jimmy Page at the high temple of rock, the Fillmore in San Francisco, where he was making one of his first U.S. appearances. Although the Zeppelin had only been together two months, they were jamming as if they had been doing it for years.

Jimmy, who plays lead guitar for Led Zeppelin, worked two years with the much-lauded Yardbirds. At that time he became good friends with another Yardbirds veteran, Eric Clapton. "Eric and I did a lot of stuff at my house." he recalls. "We used to just get the tape recorder working and start playing. A lot of the tapes we did together came out on the media. However, at the time I was recording with Eric, he was under contract and so his company took possession of the recordings. It's interesting to see the progress Eric has made since then."

Jimmy started on the guitar about eight years ago: "I have always wanted to be an electric guitarist. I even started a paper route to get my first instrument because I didn't have any money. Well, I got one, and then I just started exchanging and getting better ones. I think the second one I had was a Fender Stratocaster, and that was the first good guitar I ever had. Then I got a Gretsch, and then a Les Paul with three pickups. The reason I don't use the Les Paul now is because I didn't feel that particular model was good for blues. It's called the 'fretless wonder,' and the frets are filed real fine, but it just doesn't happen for blues."

Jimmy says the best match he's found has been a Gibson guitar through a Marshall amp: "You get a Marshall with a Gibson and it's fantastic, a perfect match. I'm using Ernie Ball Super Slinky strings, although I usually sort of swap around on the gauges. You know, they have these custom-gauge things, and I usually have it a bit heavier around the third and sometimes a bit lighter. It depends on what sort of mood I'm in."

Once in a while when jamming, Jimmy will sit down behind a steel guitar. "We wanted to use a steel guitar in Led Zeppelin," he explains. "I have used one for about a month. It's frustrating to play it, though. You hear those country guys, and they can play it so damn well. It's such a complicated instrument for someone who doesn't have that sort of line to begin with, and it's a struggle for me to play. We used it in our album a couple of times, but

nothing really complicated. When I play, I try to do a bit of everything. I don't know if that's good. I guess it can be annoying." One of Jimmy's most dynamic sounds occurs when he draws a violin bow across the strings.

"Led Zeppelin's music never duplicates itself," he insists. "We might use the same pattern, but it's always changing. By now a tune may be entirely different from when we first started. The only thing which will remain the same is the first couple of verses. Although we've got cues when to cut in, the idea is to get as much spontaneity as possible. But to get yourself out of trouble, you've got certain keys you can use to come in. Otherwise it can be chaotic. Usually we just start the song off and then go in different tangents, change it four or five times, and then come back to the original song."

Jimmy wouldn't call what they do during rehearsal a practice. "We jam," he says. "Once we've got a number, everything is happy, but getting there is another thing. That is why it is so easy using an old blues number. You know it, and then you go on from there. I think most groups must have the same trouble.

"How original our work is depends upon how you want to classify it. You might say it's 80% original if you want to exclude the words. In fact, it would be 90% original, because our numbers would be ten or fifteen minutes whereas the original number might only be three minutes long. So basically we are making it up all the time."

Jimmy is establishing himself as one of the top rock guitarists. How high he goes is only limited by his creativity and ability to expand his technique.

— **Bob Kennedy**

Jimmy Page in 1977

NEAL PRESTON

During the eight-year lapse between stories, Jimmy Page recorded five Led Zeppelin albums, producing a rock classic with "Stairway To Heaven." Live footage of the band was released in 1976 as the film *The Song Remains The Same.* The interview that follows was done during Led Zeppelin's *Presence* tour and appeared as *Guitar Player*'s July 1977 cover story.

Led Zeppelin cut *In Through The Out Door* two years later, and continued on as a band until drummer John Bonham passed away in 1980. *Coda*, a Page-produced collection of tunes spanning Zep's history, was issued in 1982. During the same year Page also wrote and produced the *Death Wish II* soundtrack. At last report, the guitarist was organizing a band for a U.S. tour.

an introduction

Conducting an interview with Jimmy Page, lead guitarist and producer/arranger for England's premier hard rock band Led Zeppelin, amounts very nearly to constructing a mini-history of British rock and roll. Perhaps one of Zeppelin's more outstanding characteristics is its endurance, having remained intact (no personnel changes since its inception) through an extremely tumultuous decade involving not only rock but popular music in general. Since 1969 the group's four members — Page, bass player John Paul Jones, vocalist Robert Plant, and drummer John Bonham — have produced eight albums (two are doubles) of original and often revolutionary compositions with a heavy metal sound. For as long as the band has been an entity, their records, coupled with several well-planned and highly publicized European and American tours, have exerted a profound influence on rock groups and guitar players on both sides of the Atlantic. Page's carefully calculated guitar frenzy, engineered through the use of distortion, surrounds Plant's expressive vocals to create a tension and excitement rarely matched by Zeppelin's numerous emulators.

But the prodigious contributions of James Patrick Page, born in 1945 in Middlesex, England, date back to well before the formation of his present band. His work as a session guitarist earned him so lengthy a credit list (some sources cite Jimmy as having been on 50 to 90% of the records released in England from 1963 to 1965) that he himself is no longer sure of each and every cut on which he played. Even without the exact number of his vinyl encounters known, the range of his interaction as musician and sometime-producer with the landmark groups and individuals of soft and hard rock is impressive and diverse: the Who, Them, various members of the Rolling Stones, Donovan, and Jackie DeShannon, to name a few. In the mid '60s Page joined one of the best-known British rock bands, the Yardbirds, leading to a legendary collaboration with guitarist Jeff Beck. When the Yardbirds disbanded in 1968, Page was ready to start his own group. According to Jimmy, at the initial meeting of Led Zeppelin the sound of success was already bellowing through the amps, and the musicians' four-week introductory period resulted in *Led Zeppelin*, their first of many gold record-winning LPs.

the interview

Let's begin at the beginning. When you first started playing, what was going on musically?

I got really stimulated by hearing early rock and roll — knowing that something was going on that was being suppressed by the media. Which it really was at the time. You had to stick by the radio and listen to overseas radio to even hear good rock records — Little Richard and things like that. The record that made me want to play guitar was "Baby, Let's Play House" by Elvis Presley. I just sort of heard two guitars and bass and thought, "Yeah, I want to be part of this." There was just so much vitality and energy coming out of it.

When did you get your first guitar?

When I was about 14. It was all a matter of trying to pick up tips and stuff. There weren't many method books, really, apart from jazz, which had no bearing on rock and roll whatsoever at the time. But that first guitar was a Grazzioso, which was like a copy of a Stratocaster. Then I got a real Stratocaster; then one of those Gibson "Black Beauties" which stayed with me for a long time until some thieving magpie took it to his nest. That's the guitar I did all the '60s sessions on.

Were your parents musical?

No, not at all. But they didn't mind me getting into it; I think they were quite relieved to see something being done instead of art work, which they thought was a loser's game.

What music did you play when you first started?

I wasn't really playing anything properly. I just knew a few bits of solos and things, not much. I just kept getting records and learning that way. It was the obvious influences at the beginning: Scotty Moore, James Burton, Cliff Gallup — he was Gene Vincent's guitarist — Johnny Meeks, later. Those seemed to be the most sustaining influences until I began to hear blues guitarists Elmore James, B.B. King, and people like that. Basically, that was the start: a mixture between rock and blues. Then I stretched out a lot more, and I started doing studio work. I had to branch out, and I did. I might do three sessions a day: a film session in the morning, and then there'd be something like a rock band, and then maybe a folk one in the evening. I didn't know *what* was coming! But it was a really good disciplinary area to work in, the studio. And it also gave me a chance to develop on all of the different styles.

Do you remember the first band you were in?

Just friends and things. I played in a lot of different small bands around, but nothing you could ever get any records of.

What kind of music were you playing with the early English rock band Neil Christian & The Crusaders?

This was before the Stones happened, so we were doing Chuck Berry, Gene Vincent, and Bo Diddley things mainly. At the time, public taste was more engineered towards Top-10 records, so it was a bit of a struggle. But there'd always be a small section of the

NEAL PRESTON

audience into what we were doing.

Wasn't there a break in your music career at this point?

Yes, I stopped playing and went to art college for about two years, while concentrating more on blues playing on my own. And then from art college to the Marquee Club in London. I used to go up and jam on a Thursday night with the interlude band. One night somebody came up and said, "Would you like to play on a record?" and I said, "Yeah, why not?" It did quite well, and that was it after that. I can't remember the title of it now. From that point I started suddenly getting all this studio work. There was a crossroads: Is it an art career or is it going to be music? Well, anyway, I had to stop going to the art college because I was really getting into music. Big Jim Sullivan, who was really brilliant, and I were the only guitarists doing those sessions. Then a point came where Stax Records [Memphis-based rhythm and blues label] started influencing music to have more brass and orchestral stuff. The guitar started to take a back seat with just the occasional riff. I didn't realize how rusty I was going to get until a rock and roll session turned up from France, and I could hardly play. I thought it was time to get out, and I did.

You just stopped playing?

For a while I just worked on my stuff alone, and then I went to a Yardbirds concert at Oxford, and they were all walking around in their penguin suits. [Lead singer] Keith Relf got really drunk and was saying "Fuck you" right into the mike and falling into the drums. I thought it was a great anarchistic night, and I went back into the dressing room and said, "What a brilliant show!" There was this great argument going on; [bass player] Paul Samwell-Smith saying, "Well, I'm leaving the group, and if I was you, Keith, I'd do the very same thing." So he left the group, and Keith didn't. But they were stuck, you see, because they had commitments and dates, so I said, "I'll play the bass if you like." And then it worked out that we did the dual lead guitar thing as soon as [rhythm guitarist] Chris Dreja could get it together with the bass, which happened, though not for long. But then came the question of discipline. If you're going to do dual lead guitars riffs and patterns, then you've got to be playing the same things. Jeff Beck had discipline occasionally, but he was an inconsistent player in that when he's on, he's probably the best there is, but at that time, and for a period afterwards, he had no respect whatsoever for audiences.

You were playing acoustic guitar during your session period?

Yes, I had to do it on studio work. And you come to grips with it very quickly too, very quickly, because it's what is expected. There was a lot of busking [singing on street corners] in the earlier days, but as I say, I had to come to grips with it, and it was a good schooling.

You were using the Les Paul for those sessions?

The Gibson "Black Beauty" Les Paul Custom. [*Ed. Note: "Black Beauty," a term not officially adopted by Gibson, is often applied to stock black Les Paul Customs, both two- and three-pickup models.*] I was one of the first people in England to have one, but I didn't know that then. I just saw it on the wall, had a go with it, and it was good. I traded a Gretsch Chet Atkins I'd had before for the Les Paul.

What kinds of amplifiers were you using for session work?

A small Supro, which I used until someone, I don't know who, smashed it up for me. I'm going to try to get another one. It's like a Harmony amp, I think, and all of the first album [*Led Zeppelin*] was done on that.

What do you remember most about your early days with the Yardbirds?

One thing is it was chaotic in recording. I mean we did one tune and didn't really know what it was. We had Ian Stewart from the Stones on piano, and we'd just finished the take, and without even hearing it, [producer] Mickie Most said, "Next." I said, "I've never worked like this in my life," and he said, "Don't worry about it." It was all done very quickly, as it sounds. It was things like that that really led to the general state of mind and depression of Relf and [drummer] Jim McCarty that broke the group up. I tried to keep it together, but there was no chance; they just wouldn't have it. In fact, Relf said the magic of the band disappeared when Clapton left. [*Ed. Note: Eric Clapton played with the Yardbirds prior to Beck's joining.*] I was really keen on doing anything, though, probably because of having had all that studio work and variety beforehand. So it didn't matter what way they wanted to go. They were definitely talented people, but they couldn't really see the woods for the trees at that time.

You thought the best period of the Yardbirds was when Beck was with them?

I did. Giorgio Gomelsky [the Yardbird's manager and producer] was good for him because he got him thinking and attempting new things. That's when they started all sorts of departures. Apparently [co-producer] Simon Napier-Bell sang the guitar riff of "Over Under Sideways Down" [on LP of the same name] to Jeff to demonstrate what he wanted, but I don't know whether that's true or not. I never spoke to him about it. I know the idea of the record was to sort of emulate the sound of the old "Rock Around The Clock" type record — that bass and backbeat thing, but it wouldn't be evident at all. Every now and again he'd say, "Let's make a record around such and such," and no one would ever know what the example was at the end of the song.

Can you describe some of your musical interaction with Beck during the Yardbirds period?

Sometimes it worked really great, and sometimes it didn't. There were a lot of harmonies that I don't think anyone else had really done, not like we did. The Stones were the only ones who got into two guitars going at the same time from old Muddy Waters records. But we were more into solos rather than a rhythm thing. The point is, you've got to have the parts worked out, and I'd find that I was doing what I was supposed to, while something totally different would be coming from Jeff. That was all right for the areas of improvisation, but there were other parts where it just did not work. You've got to understand that Beck and I came from the same sort of roots. If you've got things you enjoy, then you want to do them — to the horrifying point where we'd done our first LP with "You Shook Me," and then I heard *he'd* done "You Shook Me" [*Truth*]. I was terrified because I thought they'd be the same. But I hadn't even known he'd done it, and he hadn't known that we had.

Did Beck play bass on "Over Under Sideways Down"?

No. In fact, for that LP they just got him in to do the solos because they'd had a lot of trouble with him. But then when I joined the band, he supposedly wasn't going to walk off anymore. Well, he did a couple of times. It's strange: If he'd had a bad day, he'd take it out on the audience. I don't know whether he's the same now; his playing sounds far more consistent on records. You see, on the "Beck's Bolero" [*Truth*] thing I was working with that. The track was done, and then the producer just disappeared. He was never seen again; he simply didn't come back. Napier-Bell, he just sort of left me and Jeff to it. Jeff was playing, and I was in the box [recording booth]. And even though he says he wrote it, I wrote it. I'm playing the electric 12-string on it. Beck's doing the slide bits, and I'm basically playing around the chords. The idea was built around [classical composer] Maurice Ravel's "Bolero." It's got a lot of drama to it; it came off right. It was a good lineup too, with [the Who's drummer] Keith Moon and everything.

Wasn't that band going to be Led Zeppelin?

It was, yeah. Not Led Zeppelin as a name; the name came afterwards. But it was said afterwards that that's what it could have been called. Because Moony wanted to get out of the Who and so did [Who bass player] John Entwistle, but when it came down to getting hold of a singer, it was either going to be Steve Winwood or Steve Marriott. Finally it came down to Marriott. He was contacted, and the reply came back from his manager's office: "How would you like to have a group with no fingers, boys?" Or words to that effect. So the group was dropped because of Marriott's other commitment, to Small Faces. But I think it would have been the first of all those bands sort of like the Cream and everything. Instead, it didn't happen — apart from the "Bolero." That's the closest it got. John Paul [Jones] is on that too; so is Nicky Hopkins [studio keyboard player with various British rock groups].

You only recorded a few songs with Beck on record.

Yeah. "Happenings Ten Years Time Ago" [*The Yardbirds' Greatest Hits*], "Stroll On" [*Blow Up*], "The Train Kept A-Rollin'" [*Having A Rave-Up With The Yardbirds*], "Psycho Daisies," "Bolero," and a few other things. None of them were with the Yardbirds but earlier on — just some studio things, unreleased songs: "Louie Louie" and things like that — really good though, really great.

Were you using any boosters with the Yardbirds to get all those sounds?

A fuzztone which I'd virtually regurgitated from what I heard on "2000 Pound Bee" by the Ventures. They had a fuzztone. It was nothing like the one this guy, Roger Mayer, made for me; he worked for the Admiralty [British Navy] in the electronics division. He did all the fuzz pedals for Jimi Hendrix later — all those octave doublers and things like that. He made this one for me, but that was all during the studio period, you see. I think Jeff had one too then, but I was the one who got the effect going again. That accounted for quite a lot of the boost and that sort of sustain in the music.

You were also doing all sorts of things with feedback.

You know "I Need You" [*Kinkdom*] by the Kinks? I think I did that bit there in the beginning. I don't know who really did feedback first; it just sort of happened. I don't think anybody consciously nicked it from anybody else; it was just going on. But Pete Townshend obviously was the one, through the music of his group, who made the use of feedback more his style, and so it's related to him. Whereas the other players like Jeff and myself were playing more single notes and things than chords.

You used a Danelectro with the Yardbirds?

Yes, but not with Beck. I did use it in the latter days. I used it onstage for "White Summer" [*Little Games*]. I used a special tuning for that; the low string down to *B*, then *A, D, G, A,* and *D*. It's like a modal tuning — a sitar tuning, in fact.

Was "Black Mountain Side" on Led Zeppelin *an extension of that?*

I wasn't totally original on that. It had been done in the folk clubs a lot. Annie Briggs was the first one that I heard do that riff. I was playing it as well, and then there was [English folk guitarist] Bert Jansch's version. He's the one who crystallized all the acoustic playing as far as I'm concerned. Those first few albums of his were absolutely brilliant. And the tuning on "Black Mountain Side" is the same as "White Summer." It's taken a bit of battering, that Danelectro guitar, I'm afraid.

Do those songs work well now on the Danelectro?

I played them on that guitar before, so I'd thought I'd do it again. But I might change it around to something else, since my whole amp situation is different now from what it used to be. Now it's Marshall; then it was Vox tops and different cabinets — kind of a hodge-podge, but it worked.

You used a Vox 12-string with the Yardbirds?

That's right. I can't remember the titles now — the Mickie Most things, some of the B sides. I remember there was one with an electric 12-string solo on the end of it which was all right. I don't have copies of them now, and I don't know what they're called. I've got *Little Games*, but that's about it.

You were using Vox amps with the Yardbirds?

AC-30s. They've held up consistently well. Even the new ones are pretty good. I got four in and tried them out, and they were all reasonably good. I was going to build up a big bank of four of them, but Bonzo's kit is so loud that they just don't come over the top of it properly.

Were the AC-30s that you used with the Yardbirds modified in any way?

Only by Vox. You could get these ones with special treble boosters on the back, which is what I had. No, I didn't do that much customizing apart from making sure that all the points, soldering contacts, and things were solid. The Telecasters changed rapidly; you could tell because you could split the pickups — you know that split sound you can get — and again you could get an out-of-phase sound. And then suddenly they didn't do it anymore. So they obviously changed the electronics. And there didn't seem to be any way of getting it back. I tried to fiddle around with the wiring, but it didn't work, so I just went back to the old one again.

What kind of guitar were you using on the first Led Zeppelin album?

A Telecaster. I used the Les Paul with the Yardbirds on about two numbers and a Fender for the rest. You see the Les Paul Custom had a central setting, a kind of

NEAL PRESTON

out-of-phase pickup sound which Jeff couldn't get on his Les Paul, so I used mine for that.

Was the Telecaster the one Beck gave to you?

Yes. There was work done on it but only afterwards. I painted it; everyone painted their guitars in those days. And I had reflective plastic sheeting underneath the pickguard that gives rainbow colors.

It sounds exactly like a Les Paul.

Yeah, well, that's the amp and everything. You see, I could get a lot of tones out of the guitar which you normally couldn't. This confusion goes back to those early sessions again with the Les Paul. Those might not sound like a Les Paul, but that's what I used. It's just different amps, mike placings, and all different things. Also, if you just crank it up to distortion point so you can sustain notes, it's bound to sound like a Les Paul. I was using the Supro amp for the first album and still do. The "Stairway To Heaven" [fourth untitled album] solo was done when I pulled out the Telecaster, which I hadn't used for a long time, plugged it into the Supro, and away it went again. That's a different sound entirely from any of the rest of the first album. It was a good versatile setup. I'm using a Leslie on the solo on "Good Times Bad Times" [fourth LP]. It was wired up for an organ thing then.

What kind of acoustic guitar are you using on "Black Mountain Side" and "Babe I'm Gonna Leave You" [both on Led Zeppelin*]?*

That was a Gibson J-200 which wasn't mine; I borrowed it. It was a beautiful guitar, really great. I've never found a guitar of that quality anywhere since. I could play so easily on it, get a really thick sound. It had heavy-gauge strings on it, but it just didn't seem to feel like it.

Do you just use your fingers when playing acoustic?

Yes. I used fingerpicks once, but I find them too spikey; they're too sharp. You can't get the tone or response that you would get, say, the way classical players approach gut-string instruments. The way they pick, the whole thing is the tonal response of the string. It seems important.

Can you describe your picking style?

I don't know, really. It's a cross between fingerstyle and flatpicking. There's a guy in England called Davey Graham, and he never used any fingerpicks or anything. He used a thumbpick every now and again, but I prefer just a flatpick and fingers because then it's easier to get around from guitar to guitar. Well, it is for me, anyway. But apparently he's got calluses on the left hand and all over the right as well. He can get so much attack on his strings, and he's really good.

The guitar on "Communication Breakdown" on Led Zeppelin *sounds as if it's coming out of a shoebox.*

Yeah. I put it in a small room, a little tiny vocal booth-type thing and miked it from a distance. You see, there's a very old recording maxim which goes, "Distance makes depth." I've used that a hell of a lot on recording techniques with the band generally, not just me. You're always used to them close-miking amps, just putting the microphone in front. But I'd have a mike right out the back as well, and then balance the two and get rid of all the phasing problems. Really, you shouldn't have to use an EQ in the studio if the instruments sound right. It should all be done with the microphones. But see, everyone has gotten so carried away with EQ pots that they have forgotten the whole science of microphone placement. There aren't too many guys who know it. I'm sure Les Paul knows a lot: obviously, he must have been well into it, as were all those who produced the early rock records where there were only one or two mikes in the studio.

The solo on "I Can't Quit You Baby" from Led Zeppelin *is interesting — many pull-offs in a sort of sloppy but amazingly inventive style.*

There are mistakes in it, but it doesn't make any difference. I'll always leave the mistakes in. I can't help it. The timing bits on the *A* and *B♭* parts are right, though it might sound wrong. The timing just *sounds* off. But there are some wrong notes. You've got to be reasonably honest about it. It's like the filmtrack album [*The Song Remains The Same*]; there's no editing really on that. It wasn't the best concert playing-wise at all, but it was the only one with celluloid footage, so there is was. It was all right; it was just one "as-it-is" performance. It wasn't one of those real magic nights, but then again it wasn't a terrible night. So, for all its mistakes and everything else, it's a very honest filmtrack. Rather than just trailing around through a tour with a recording mobile truck waiting for the magic night, it was just,"There you are — take it or leave it." I've got a lot of live recorded stuff going back to '69.

Is there an electric 12-string on "Thank You"?

Yes; I think it's a Fender or Rickenbacker.

Jumping ahead to Led Zepplin II*, the riff in the middle of "Whole Lotta Love" was a very composed and structured phrase.*

I had it worked out already before entering the studio. I had rehearsed it. And then all that other stuff, sonic wave sound and all that, I built it up in the studio, and put effects on it and things, treatments.

How is that descending riff done?

With a metal slide and backwards echo. I think I came up with that first before anybody. I know it's been used a lot now, but not at the time. I thought of it on this Mickie Most thing. In fact, some of the things that might sound a bit odd have, in fact, backwards echo involved in them as well.

*What kind of effect are you using on the beginning of "Ramble On" [*Led Zeppelin II*]?*

If I can remember correctly, it's like harmony feedback and then it changes. To be more specific, most of the tracks just start off bass, drums, and guitar, and once you've done the drums and bass, you just build everything up afterwards. It's like a starting point, and you start constructing from square one.

Is the rest of the band in the studio when you put down the solos?

No, never. I don't like anybody else in the studio when I'm putting on the guitar parts. I usually just limber up for a while and then maybe do three solos and take the best of the three.

What is the effect on "Out On The Tiles" from Led Zeppelin III*?*

Now that is exactly what I was talking about: close-miking and distance-miking. That's ambient sound. Getting the distance of the time lag from one end of the room to the other and putting that in as well. The whole idea, the way I see recording, is to try and capture the sound of the room live and the emotion of the whole moment and try to convey that across. That's the very essence of it. And so, consequently, you've got to capture as much of the room sound as possible.

On "Tangerine" it sounds as if you're playing a pedal steel.

I am. And on the first LP there's a pedal steel. I had never played steel before, but I just picked it up. There's a lot of things I do first time around that I haven't done before. In fact, I hadn't touched a pedal steel from the first album to the third. It's a bit of a pinch really from the things that Chuck Berry did. But nevertheless it fits. I use pedal steel on "Your Time Is Gonna Come" [*Led Zeppelin*]. It sounds like a slide or something. It's more out of tune on the first album because I hadn't got a kit to put it together.

You've also played other stringed instruments on records.

"Gallows Pole" [on *Led Zeppelin III*] was the first time for banjo and on "The Battle Of Evermore" [fourth album] a mandolin was lying around. It wasn't mine; it was Jonesy's. I just picked it up, got the chords, and it sort of started happening. I did it more or less straight off. But you see that's fingerpicking again, going on back to the studio days and developing a certain amount of technique. At least enough to be adapted and used. My fingerpicking is a sort of cross between Pete Seeger, Earl Scruggs, and total incompetence.

Was the fourth album the first time you used a double-neck?

I didn't use a double-neck on that, but I had to get one afterwards to play "Stairway To Heaven." I did all those guitars on it; I just built them up. That was the beginning of my building up harmonized guitars properly. "Ten Years Gone" [*Physical Graffitti*] was an extension of that, and then "Achilles' Last Stand" [*Presence*] is like the essential flow of it really, because there was no time to think things out; I just had to more or less lay it down on the first track and harmonize on the second track. It was really fast working on *Presence*. And I did all the guitar overdubs on the LP in one night. There were only two sequences. The rest of the band, not Robert, but the rest of them I don't think really could see it to begin with. They didn't know what the hell I was going to do with it. But I wanted to give each section its own identity, and I think it came off really good. I didn't think I'd be able to do it in one night. I thought I'd have to do it in the course of three different nights to get the individual sections. But I was so into it that my mind was working properly for a change. It sort of crystallized and everything was just pouring out. I was very happy with the guitar on that whole album as far as the maturity of the playing goes.

Did playing the double-neck require a new approach?

Yes. The main thing is, there's an effect you can get where you leave the 12-string neck open as far as the sound goes and play on the 6-string neck, and you get the 12-strings vibrating in sympathy. It's like an Indian sitar, and I've worked on that a little bit. I use it on "Stairway" like that; not on the album, but on the soundtrack and film. It's surprising. It doesn't vibrate as heavily as a sitar would, but nonetheless it does add to the overall tonal quality.

Do you think your playing on the fourth LP is the best you've ever done?

Without a doubt. As far as consistency goes and as far as the quality of playing on a whole album, I would say yes. But I don't know what the best solo I've ever done is — I have no idea. My vocation is more in composition really than in anything else. Building up harmonies. Using the guitar, orchestrating the guitar like an army — a guitar army. I think that's where it's at, really, for me. I'm talking about actual orchestration in the same way you'd orchestrate a classical piece of music. Instead of using brass and violins, you treat the guitars with synthesizers or other devices and give them different treatments, so that they have enough frequency range and scope and everything to keep the listener as totally committed to it as the player is. It's a difficult project, but it's one that I've got to do.

Have you done anything towards this end already?

Only on these three tunes: "Stairway To Heaven," "Ten Years Gone," and "Achilles' Last Stand," the way the guitar is building. I can see certain milestones along the way, like "Four Sticks" [fourth LP], in the middle section of that. The sound of those guitars — that's where I'm going. I've got long pieces written. I've got one really long one written that's harder to play than anything. It's sort of classical, but then it goes through changes from that mood to really laid-back rock, and then to really intensified stuff. With a few laser notes thrown in, we might be all right.

What is the amplifier setup you're using now?

Onstage? Marshall 100s which are customized in New York so they've got 200 watts. I've got four unstacked cabinets, and I've got a wah-wah pedal and an MXR unit. Everything else is total flash [*laughs*]. I've got a harmonizer, a theramin, violin bow, and an Echoplex echo unit.

Are there certain settings you use on the amp?

Depending on the acoustics of the place, the volume is up to about three. The rest is pretty standard.

When was the first time you used the violin bow?

The first time I recorded with it was with the Yardbirds. But the idea was put to me by a classical string player when I was doing studio work. One of us tried to bow the guitar; then we tried it between us, and it worked. At that point I was just bowing it, but the other effects I've obviously come up with on my own — using wah-wah, and echo. You have to put rosin on the bow, and the rosin sticks to the string and makes it vibrate.

What kinds of picks and strings do you use?

Herco heavy-gauge nylon picks and Ernie Ball Super Slinky strings.

What guitars are you using?

God, this is really hard. There are so many. My Les Paul, the usual one, and I've got a spare one of those if anything goes wrong. I've got a double-neck; and one of these Fender string-benders that was made for me by Gene Parsons [former drummer with the Byrds and the Flying Burrito Brothers]. I've cut back from what I was going to use on tour. I have with me a Martin guitar and a Gibson A-4 mandolin. The Martin is one of the cheap ones; it's not the one with the herringbone back or anything like that. It's probably a D-18. It's got those nice

NEIL ZLOZOWER

Grover tuners on it. I've got a Gibson Everly Brothers which was given to me by Ronnie Wood. That's like the current favorite, but I don't take it out on the road because it's a really personal guitar. I keep it with me in the room. It's a beauty; it's fantastic. There's only a few of those around. Ron's got one, and Keith Richards' got one, and I've got one as well. So it's really nice. I haven't had a chance to use it on record yet, but I will because it's got such a nice sound.

Do you have other guitars?

Let's see, what else have we got? I know when I come onstage it looks like a guitar shop, the way they're all standing up there. But I sold off all of my guitars before I left for America. There was a lot of old stuff hanging around which I didn't need. It's no point having things if you don't need them. When all the equipment came over here, we had done our rehearsals, and we were really on top, really in tip-top form. Then Robert caught laryngitis, and we had to postpone a lot of dates and reshuffle them, and I didn't touch a guitar for five weeks. I got a bit panicky about that — after two years off the road, that's a lot to think about. And I'm still only warming up; I still can't coordinate a lot of the things I need to be doing. Getting by, but it's not right; I don't feel 100% right yet.

What year is the Les Paul you're using now?

'59. It's been rescraped [repainted], but that's all gone now because it chipped off. Joe Walsh got it for me.

Do you think that when you went from the Telecaster to the Les Paul that your playing changed?

Yes, I think so. It's more of a fight with a Telecaster, but there are rewards. The Gibson's got a stereotyped sound maybe; I don't know. But it's got a beautiful sustain to it. I like sustain because it relates to bowed instruments and everything, this whole area that everyone's been pushing and experimenting in. When you think about it, it's mainly sustain.

Do you use special tunings on the electric guitar?

All the time. They're my own that I've worked out, so I'd rather keep those to myself, really. But they're never open tunings. I have used those, but most of the things I've written have not been open tunings, so you can get more chords into them.

Did you ever meet any of those folk players you admire — Bert Jansch, John Renbourn, or any others?

No, and the most terrifying thing of all happened about a few months ago. Jansch's playing appeared as if it was going down or something, and it turns out he's got arthritis. I really think he's one of the best. He was, without any doubt, the one who crystallized so many things. As much as Hendrix had done on electric, I think he's done on the acoustic. He was really way, way ahead. And for something like that to happen is such a tragedy, with a mind as brilliant as that. There you go. Another player whose physical handicap didn't stop him is Django Reinhardt. For his last LP they pulled him out of retirement to do it; it's on Barclay Records in France. He'd been retired for years, and it's fantastic. You know the story about him in the caravan and losing fingers and such. But the record is just fantastic. He must have been playing all the time to be that good — it's horrifyingly good. Horrifying. But it's always good to hear perennial players like Django, Les Paul, and people like that.

You listen to Les Paul?

Oh, yeah. You can tell Jeff [Beck] did too, can't you? Have you ever heard "It's Been A Long, Long Time" [mid-Forties single by the Les Paul Trio with Bing Crosby on Decca]? You ought to hear that. He does everything in one go. And it's just basically one guitar, even though they've tracked on rhythms and stuff. But my goodness, his introductory chords and everything are fantastic. He sets the whole tone, and then goes into this solo which is fantastic. Now that's where I heard feedback first — from Les Paul. Also vibratos and things, even before B.B. King, you know. I've traced a hell of a lot of rock and roll, little riffs, and things, back to Les Paul, Chuck Berry, Cliff Gallup and all those — it's all there. But then Les Paul was influenced by Reinhardt, wasn't he? Very much so. I can't get my hands on the early records of Les Paul — the Les Paul Trio and all that stuff. But I've got all the Capitol LPs and things. I mean he's the father of it all: multi-tracking and everything else. If it hadn't been for him, there wouldn't have been anything really.

You said that Eric Clapton was the person who synthesized the Les Paul sound.

Yeah, without a doubt. When he was with the Bluesbreakers, it was just a magic combination. He got one of the Marshall amps, and away he went. It just happened. I thought he played brilliantly then, really brilliantly. That was very stirring stuff.

Do you think you were responsible for any specific guitar sounds?

The guitar parts in "Trampled Under Foot"[*Physical Graffiti*]. [British rock journalist] Nick Kent came out with this idea about how he thought that was a really revolutionary sound. And I hadn't realized that anyone would think it was, but I can explain exactly how it's done. Again it's sort of backwards echo and wah-wah. I don't know how responsible I was for new sounds because there were so many good things happening around that point, around the release of the first Zeppelin album, like Hendrix and Clapton.

What's the most difficult aspect of recording a distinctive guitar sound?

The trouble is keeping a separation between sounds, so you don't have the same guitar effect all the time. And that's where that orchestration thing comes in: it's so easy. I've already planned it. It's already there; all the groundwork has been done now. And the dream has been accomplished by the computerized mixing console. The sort of struggle to achieve so many things is over. As I said, I've got two things written, but I'll be working on more. You can hear what I mean on *Lucifer Rising* [soundtrack for the unreleased Kenneth Anger film]. You see, I didn't play any guitar on that, apart from one point. That was all other instruments, all synthesizers. Every instrument was given a process so it didn't sound like what it really was — the voices, drones, mantras, and even tabla drums. When you've got a collage of, say, four of these sounds together, people will be drawn right in because there will be sounds they hadn't heard before. That's basically what I'm into: collages and tissues of sound with emotional intensity and melody and all that. But you know there are so many good people around like John McLaughlin. It's a totally different thing than what I'm doing.

Do you think he has a sustaining quality as a guitarist?

He's always had that technique right from when I first knew him when he was working in a guitar shop. I would say he was the best jazz guitarist in England then, in the traditional mode of Johnny Smith and Tal Farlow; a combination of those two is exactly what he sounded like. He was easily the best guitarist in England, and he was working in a guitar shop. And that's what I say — you hear so many good people around under those conditions. I'll tell you one thing, I don't know one musician who's stuck to his guns, who was good in the early days, and hasn't come through now with recognition from everybody. Albert Lee and all these people that seem to be like white elephants got recognition. I think he's really good, bloody brilliant. He's got one of those string benders, too, but I haven't heard him in ages. But I know that every time I've heard him, he's bloody better and better.

Do you feel that your playing grows all the time?

I've got two different approaches, like a schizophrenic guitarist, really. I mean onstage is totally different than the way that I approach it in the studio. *Presence* and my control over all the contributing factors to that LP, the fact that it was done in three weeks, and all the rest of it, was so good for me. It was just good for everything really, even though it was a very anxious point. And the anxiety shows group-wise—you know, "Is Robert going to walk again from his auto accident in Greece?" and all this sort of thing. But I guess the solo in "Achilles' Last Stand" on *Presence* is in the same tradition as the solo from "Stairway To Heaven" on the fourth LP. It is on that level to me.

— Steve Rosen

JIMMY PAGE: A SELECTED DISCOGRAPHY

With Led Zeppelin (on Swan Song): *Led Zeppelin,* SD 8216; *Led Zeppelin II,* SD 8236; *Led Zeppelin III,* SD 7201; untitled fourth album [sometimes known as *Led Zeppelin IV*], SD 7208; *Houses Of The Holy,* SD 7255; *Physical Graffiti,* SS 2-200; *Presence,* SS 8416; *The Song Remains The Same,* SS 2-201; *In Through The Out Door,* 16002; *Coda,* 90051-1. **With the Yardbirds:** *The Yardbirds' Great Hits,* Epic, PE 34491; *The Yardbirds' Greatest Hits,* Epic, LN 24246; *Over Under Sideways Down,* Epic, BN 26210; *Little Games,* Epic, BN 26313; *Having A Rave-up With The Yardbirds,* Epic, LN 24177; *Blow Up* (film soundtrack), MGM Records, SE-4447 ST. **With others:** Donovan, *The Hurdy Gurdy Man,* Epic, BN 26420; *Lord Sutch And Heavy Friends,* Atlantic, 2400 008; Joe Cocker, *With A Little Help From My Friends,* A&M Records, SP 4182; Cartoone, *Cartoone,* Atlantic, SD 8219; Jeff Beck, *Truth,* Epic, BN 26413. **Soundtracks:** *Death Wish II,* Swan Song, SS 8511.

Led Zeppelin's John Paul Jones

NEIL ZLOZOWER

Formerly a session musician, John Paul Jones co-founded Led Zeppelin in 1968. He was the first heavy metal bassist to be extensively featured in *Guitar Player.* This interview originally appeared as a companion piece to Jimmy Page's July 1977 cover story. Jones has kept a low profile since the demise of Led Zeppelin.

an introduction

John Paul Jones' ongoing vitality as a bassist, keyboardist, composer, and arranger has been carefully documented on record. From his early session work in the '60s with Donovan Leitch to his performance on the Led Zeppelin film soundtrack album, *The Song Remains The Same,* he has demonstrated a consistently solid and animated bass style. As one half of the rhythm section of the British hard-rock supergroup Led Zeppelin, his role on 4-string is a supportive one, but he is also responsible for classic lines on tracks like "What Is And What Should Never Be," "The Lemon Song," (both on *Led Zeppelin II*), and "Black Dog" (on the group's fourth untitled LP).

John's enthusiasm for music manifests itself in a constantly developing bass style, and one needs only listen to his work on the first *Led Zeppelin* album and then on a later release such as *Presence* to sense his growth as a player. This energy abounds in his words as well, and while he is generally regarded as the quietest member of the group, his thoughts and philosophies on music, the bass, and keyboard — once tapped — flow in a logical and intriguing dialogue. The 31-year-old native Londoner is a musician first and foremost.

Jones describes his parents as musical; his father was a piano player and bandleader. John Paul had one lesson on the bass and ascribes mainly to a philosophy he attributes to jazz bassist Charles Mingus: The best way to learn bass is to switch on the radio and play along with whatever comes on the air.

At 16, Jones left the strict English boarding school he hated. He remembers the only bright spot there to have been playing the organ at school prayers. With distaste he recalls that the only other musical training he had was given by a piano teacher who used the classic technique of whacking his students across the knuckles for their efforts.

the interview

What was the impetus behind your becoming a bass player?

I used to play piano when I was younger, and there was a rock and roll band forming at school when I was 14, but they didn't want a piano player — all they wanted was drums or bass. I thought, "I can't get the drums on the bus." Bass looked easy — four strings, no chords — so I took it up. And it *was* easy; it wasn't too bad at all. I took it up before guitar, which I suppose is sort of interesting. Before I got a real 4-string, my father had a ukulele banjo, a little one, and I had that strung up like a bass, but it didn't quite have the bottom that was required. Actually, my father didn't want to have to sign a guarantor to back me in the payments for a bass. He said, "Don't bother with it; take up the tenor saxophone. In two years the bass guitar will never be heard of again." I said, "No, Dad, I really want one; there's work for me." He said, "Ah, there's work?" And I got a bass right away.

What was your first?

Oh, it was a pig. It had a neck like a tree trunk. It was a solidbody Dallas bass guitar with a single cutaway. It sounded all right, though, and it was good for me because I developed very strong fingers. I had no idea about setting instruments up then, so I just took it home from the shop. I had an amplifier with a 10" speaker — oh, it was awful. It made all kinds of farting noises. And then I had a converted television, you know, one of those big old standup televisions with the amp in the bottom and a speaker where the screen should be. I ended up giving myself double hernias. Bass players had the hardest time because they always had to cope with the biggest piece of equipment. It never occurred to me when I was deciding between that and drums that I'd have to lug a bass amp.

What kind of music were you playing in that first band?

Shadows, Little Richard, Jerry Lee Lewis stuff. I started doubling on piano. We didn't have a drummer at first, because we never could find one. That happened to another bass player, Larry Graham, Sly Stone's bass player. He started off in a band with no drummer, which is how he got that percussive style. You've got a lot to make up for once the lead guitar takes a solo because there's only you left. You've got to make a lot of noise. We got a drummer after a while whom I taught, would you believe. I've never played drums in my life.

That must have definitely had an influence on your playing.

I suppose it must have. I don't like bass players that go *boppity boppity bop* all over the neck; you should stay around the bottom and provide that end of the group. I work very closely with the drummer; it's very important.

How long did that first band last?

Not very long. I found a band with a drummer. This band also came along with really nice looking guitars, and I thought, "Oh, they must be great." They had Burns guitars, so I got myself one, too — the one with the three pickups and a Tru-Voice amplifier. We all had purple band jackets and white shoes, and I thought "This is it; this is the big time." But as soon as I got out of school I played at American Air Force bases, which was good training, plus they always had great records in the jukebox. That was my introduction to the black music scene, when very heavy gentlemen would come up insisting on "Night Train" eight times an hour.

What was the first really professional band you were in?

It was with Jet Harris and Tony Meehan [bassist and

drummer formerly with the Shadows]; that was when I was 17, I suppose. And those were the days when they used to scream all the way through the show. It was just like now, really, where you have to make a dash for the limos at the end of the night — make a sort of terrible gauntlet. In the days before roadies you'd have to drag around your own gear, so we all invested in a roadie. We thought we owed it to ourselves, and this bloke was marvelous. He did everything: drove the wagon, lugged the gear, did the lights — the whole thing.

What kinds of bass were you using with Harris and Meehan?

Oh, I got my first Fender then. I lusted after this Jazz Bass in Lewisham, and it cost me about $250, I think. It was the new one. They'd just changed the controls, and I used that bass up until the last [1975] tour, and then she had to go. She was getting unreliable and rattling a lot, and I had to leave her home this time.

What followed your work with that band?

I got into sessions. I thought, "I've had enough of the road," bought myself a dog, and didn't work for six months. Then I did start up again. I played in other silly bands. I remember that Jet Harris and Tony Meehan band — John McLaughlin joined on rhythm guitar. It was the first time I'd met him, and it was hilarious. Here he was sitting there all night going *Dm* to *G* to *Am*. That was my first introduction to jazz when he came along, because we'd all get to the gig early and have a blow. Oh, that was something, first meeting him. And then I joined a couple of other bands with him for a while, rhythm and blues bands.

Do you remember the first session you ever did?

Not much of it. It was in Decca Number 2 [studio in London]. I was late, and I suddenly realized how bad my reading was. There was another bass player there with a stand-up bass, and I was just there to provide the click. It was nearly my last session.

Who were some of the people you were doing sessions with?

All kinds of silly people — I used to do calls with [British vocalists] Tom Jones, Cathy Kirby, Dusty Springfield.

The Rolling Stones and Donovan, too, didn't you?

I only did one Stones session, really. I just did the strings — they already had the track down. It was "She's A Rainbow" [*Their Satanic Majesties Request*]. And then the first Donovan session was a shambles; it was awful. It was *Sunshine Superman*, and the arranger had got it all wrong, so I thought, being the opportunist that I was, "I can do better than that" and actually went up to the producer. He came around and said "Is there anything we can do to sort of save the session?" And I piped up, "Well, look, how about if I play straight?" — because I had a part which went sort of *ooowooooo* [*imitates a slide up the neck*] every now and again, and the other bass player sort of did - *woooooo* [*imitates downward slide*] down below, and then there was some funny congas that were in and out of time. And I said, "How about if we just sort of play it straight; get the drummer to do this and that?"

How did the session go?

The session came off, and I was immediately hired as the arranger by [producer] Mickie Most, whom I loved working with. He was a clever man. I used to do Herman's Hermits and all that. I mean they were never there; you could do a whole album in a day. And it was great fun and a lot of laughs. I did all of Lulu's stuff and all of Mickie's artists. I did one Jeff Beck single, and he's never spoken to me since. It was "Hi Ho Silver Lining." I did the arrangement for it and played bass. Then we had "Mellow Yellow" for Donovan, which we argued about for hours because they didn't like my arrangement at all, not at all. Mickie stood by me; he said, "I like the arrangement, I think it's good." It wasn't Donovan — he didn't mind either — but he had so many people around him saying, "Hey, this isn't you." But he sold a couple of million on it, didn't he?

On most of these session you were playing bass?

Yeah, the Fender Jazz. It was a '61 because it was new the year I bought it. Amps were murder; amps were always murder. We were all right with Jet Harris and Tony Meehan because we used Vox amps, and I had the big T-60 which was, in fact, a forerunner of all these things we use nowadays with that big reflex cabinet and a little transistor top. It sounded great, but we had to have an arrangement with Vox to replace them every couple of weeks because they would not last any longer. Suddenly there'd be a horrible noise, and the thing would just sit there looking at you, so you'd just wheel another one on. Basically the problems haven't stopped; I find an amp that I love, and they've stopped making it. I can't win.

Was the "Hurdy Gurdy Man" session when you first met Jimmy Page?

No, I'd met Jimmy on sessions before. It was always big Jim and little Jim — Big Jim Sullivan — and little Jim and myself and the drummer. Apart from group sessions where he'd play solos and stuff like that, Page always ended up on rhythm guitar because he couldn't read too well. He could read chord symbols and stuff, but he'd have to do anything they'd ask when he walked into a session. But I used to see a lot of him just sitting there with an acoustic guitar sort of raking out chords. I always thought the bass player's life was much more interesting in those days, because nobody knew how to write for bass. So they used to say, "We'll give you the chord sheet and get on with it." Even on the worst sessions, you could have a little runaround. But that was good; I would have hated to have sat there on acoustic guitar.

How long did you do sessions?

Three or four years, on and off. Then I thought I was going to get into arranging, because it seemed that sessions and running about was much too silly. I started running about and arranging about 40 or 50 things a month. I ended up just putting a blank piece of score paper in front of me and just sitting there and staring at it. Then I joined Led Zeppelin, I suppose, after my missus said to me, "Will you stop moping around the house? Why don't you join a band or something?" And I said, "There's no bands I want to join. What are you talking about?" And she said, "Well, look, I think it was in *Disc.* Jimmy Page is forming a group" — he had left the Yardbirds — "Why don't you give him a ring?" So I rang him up and said, "Jim, how are you doing? Have you got a group yet?" He said, "I haven't got anybody yet." And I

JON SIEVERT

said, "Well, if you want a bass player give me a ring." And he said, "All right. I'm going up to see this singer Terry Reid told me about, and he might know a drummer as well. I'll call you when I've seen what they're like." He went up there, saw Robert Plant, and said, "This guy is really something."

What was your original name?

We started under the name the New Yardbirds because nobody would book us under anything else. We rehearsed an act, an album, and a tour in about three weeks, and it took off. The first time, we all met in this little room just to see if we could even stand each other. It was wall-to-wall amplifiers and terrible, all old. Robert [Plant] had heard I was a session man, and he was wondering what was going to turn up — some old bloke with a pipe? So Jimmy said, "Well, we're all here. What are we going to play?" And I said, "I don't know. What do you know?" And Jimmy said, "Do you know a number called 'The Train Kept A-Rollin'?" I told him "No." And he said, "It's easy, just *G* to *A*." He counted it out, and the room just exploded, and we said, "Right, we're on, this is it, this is going to work!" And we just sort of built it up from there. "Dazed And Confused" [*Led Zeppelin*] came in because Jimmy knew that, but I could never get the sequence right for years; it kept changing all the time with different parts, and I was never used to that. I'm used to having the music there. I could never remember — in fact, I'm *still* the worst in the band for remembering anything. And the group jokes about it: "Jonesy always gets the titles wrong and the sequences wrong." Even now I have a piece of paper I stuck on top of the Mellotron which says: "'Kashmir' — remember the coda!"

What were some of your early amplifiers?

I've used everything from a lousy made-up job to a great, huge, top valve [tube] amp. We started off in a deal with Rickenbacker where we had these awful, awful Rickenbacker amps; they were so bad. Our first tour was a shambles. For about a year I never even heard the bass. They said, "We've designed this speaker cabinet for you," and I said, "Let me see it. What's it got in it?" It had *one* 30" speaker! I said, "All right, stand it up there alongside whatever else I've got, and I'll use it." I plugged it in, and in a matter of five seconds I blew it up. I thought the bloke was having me on; I said, "There's no such thing as a 30" speaker!" And I had to take the back off because I couldn't believe it. Then we met the guy from Univox, and he came up with a bass stack which unfortunately didn't last the night. But while it was going, it was the most unbelievable sound I've ever heard. It was at the Nassau Coliseum in New York, I remember, and the bass filled the hall. It was so big, it couldn't have lasted. I don't think I'll come across anything that sounded like that. But as I said, three numbers and wheel the Acoustics out again. I used two or three 360 standard Acoustics for quite a long time; they served me well.

You used the Jazz Bass until just recently then?

Yeah. Oh, I got a hold of a very nice old Gibson violin bass [pictured in the little cut-out wheel on the cover of *Led Zeppelin III*]. That was nice, too; it's not stage-worthy, but it gives a beautiful warm sound. I don't like Gibson basses generally because they feel all rubbery; I like something you can get your teeth into. The violin bass was the only Gibson that was as heavy as a Fender to play, but still had that fine Gibson sound. I used it on *Led Zeppelin III*, and I've used it every now and again, usually when I'm tracking a bass after I've done keyboards for the main track. The one I have went through Little Richard's band and then through James Brown's band, and it arrived in England. In fact, I saw it on an old movie clip of Little Richard. It was probably about a '48 or '50 or something like that; it was the original one. Actually, I've also got an old '52 Telecaster bass. I used that onstage for a while, for "Black Dog" and things like that.

What is your bass setup now?

Rick Turner of Alembic made me an Alembic bass, and it's beautiful. It has standard Alembic circuitry and is extremely versatile: two pickups, with a hum-cancelling system. It runs from a power supply; it's power assisted somehow with a preamp, which fits into the guitar. I've got LEDs [for fret markers] all up the side — I love those — and it's got a full two-octave neck. In a shop, I came across an 8-string before this one, and when I found out it was Alembic, I rang up the bloke and said, "Look, what else do you do?" I think I'll get him to make me a fretless next. Last I heard, he was working on some idea with a stainless-steel fingerboard.

What does two full octaves mean to you as a player?

It gives you so much more room, and there isn't any position on the instrument that sounds off — you can use it all. I'm finding out all sorts of things; you could never get up there with a Fender.

Is it easier or harder to play than the Fender?

It's much more fun, and there's a lot more to do on it. When your intonation is true on all four strings all the way up, you suddenly realize you can play chords, and the notes are clear. It's a whole different way of playing. It definitely has changed my technique. I can now get above the 5th fret, which always has been somewhat of a mystery. I still use the Fender fretless because I need a fretless onstage. I don't particularly like the instrument, but it's better than any of the other ones they have.

Was the fretless hard to get used to?

No. You think it's going to be, but it's not. I also use a stand-up electric bass onstage; I think it's an Arco. There was a spate of them came out in the middle '60s — Italian-made basses — and I bought it for fun.

Do you play it on record?

No, it's nowhere near accurate enough, and it's too hard to play; you can't do anything with it. Since I've got a bit more power back in my fingers now, I can begin to go a little bit further up the neck. You couldn't use it for more than one number.

What kind of amps do you use?

The one they don't make anymore, GMT 600B [made by Gallien-Krueger], which has since been replaced by the 400B which bears no resemblance at all. But I'm going to ring them up, too, and ask if they'll please make me another of the old type, because it is excellent. It has a curious kind of shelving on the filter system. I think they call it "contour." It's very ballsy for a transistorized amp. Maybe the Alembic is a little too hot for it, but I might be able to work something out. This is just the head; I use Cerwin-Vega cabinets, which are excellent. I use just the one top and two cabinets, each of which I think has one 15" and one 10" speaker. It's loud, right? There's a lot of power, proper power.

You like solid-state amps for bass then?

Yes, I find them a bit tighter than valve amps, really. I don't think they're so good for guitar. The sound tends to spread a lot and you don't get the definition. I prefer more of a recorded sound onstage.

Your stage and studio equipment are the same?

Yes, although you really can't say that because in the studio I like to mix direct and amp. With the Fender, the direct was never that good, but the Alembic can go direct, and it sounds really good.

What settings do you use to produce the best response?

I usually set the amp in the middle. We have to run it a little lower than I like because, as I say, the Alembic is a bit hot. But that guitar is going to be more fun to record with, as far as settings are concerned, because there's a lot of variations in tone and all sorts of things you can do. I haven't used the Alembic for recording yet. I used the 8-string on *Presence*, but the 4-string was made after that. I'm still using the Fender on the live album [*The Song Remains The Same*].

Do you ever use a pick when you play?

Yes, when the situation demands it; on the 8-string it's awful messy with your fingers. On *The Song Remains The Same*, I use a pick to get that snap out of the instrument. It's fun; you play different. If I was just playing straight bass, I'd use fingers. When I first started, I always used my fingers.

What kind of a pick and strings do you use?

Herco gray and Rotosound wire-wounds. I got into them with the Alembic because I never used to like the round-wound strings. On the Fender I used Rotosound, but they were flat-wound, and I've never liked the string noise. But the Alembic just demands you use something a bit brighter; otherwise you're doing the instrument a disservice. I first put round-wound strings on the Telecaster bass because it demanded that. I tried flat-wounds on the Alembic, and sort of lost half the instrument. Plus the wire-wounds seem to fill out better if Jimmy's soloing; they make more of a guitar sound on the Alembic than a bass sound. But the Alembic's got enough low end that it fills out the spectrum. I think it's going to be all right.

You don't use any pedals or boosters?

No, I never have; what can you do with the bass anyway? You can go *wah-wah-wah*, or you can phase it and make it sound even muddier than it usually does. I think I'm more into the musical side of things; I don't use synthesizers because they always sound like synthesizers.

How has playing with Jimmy Page for the last nine years styled your playing?

That's hard. I play a lot looser than I used to. For instance, somebody like [Who bassist] John Entwistle is more of a lead instrument man than I am. I tend to work closer with Bonzo [drummer John Bonham], I think. But then again, I don't play that much bass onstage anymore, what with the pianos and the Mellotron. I'll always say I'm a bass player, though.

How do you develop a bass part?

You put in what is correct and what's necessary. I always did like a good tune on the bass. For an example, listen to "What Is And What Should Never Be" [on *Led Zeppelin II*]. The role of a bassist is hard to define. You can't play chords, so you have a harmonic role: picking and timing notes. You'll suggest a melodic or a harmonic pattern, but I seem to be changing anyway toward more of a lead style. The Alembic is doing it; I play differently on it. But I try to never forget my role as a bass player: to play the bass and not mess around too much up at the top all the time. You've got to have somebody down there, and that's the most important thing. The numbers must sound right. They must work right; they must be balanced.

Do you practice?

No, in a word. I fool around on piano, but bass I never practice. Although, again with the Alembic, I'm beginning to feel, "Wouldn't it be nice to have it in the room?" It really makes you want to play more, which is fantastic.

Who do you listen to?

I don't. I used to listen to a lot of jazz bass players once, but jazz has changed so much now it's hardly recognizable. I listened to a lot of tenor sax players: Sonny Rollins, John Coltrane, and all those people. Bass players? Scott La Faro, who died; he used to be with [late jazz pianist] Bill Evans. Excellent player. I liked the late jazz bassist Paul Chambers, and Ray Brown, and Charlie Mingus, of course. I'm not too keen on the lead bass style of some players. Paul McCartney I've always respected; he puts the notes in the right place at the right time. He knows what he's about.

There's nothing you'd like to do outside of Zeppelin in an instrumental context?

I always get the feeling I'd like to write a symphony. I like all music. I like classical music a lot — Ravel, Bach, of course. Mozart I could never stand, though to play it on the piano is great fun. If Bach had ever come across the bass guitar, he would have loved it. Rock and roll is the only music left where you can improvise. I don't know what's happened to jazz; it has really disappointed me. I guess they started playing rock and roll.

So you're able to continually experiment in Zeppelin and expand your playing?

Yes, absolutely. I wouldn't be without Zeppelin for the world.

— Steve Rosen

A SELECTED JOHN PAUL JONES DISCOGRAPHY

With Led Zeppelin (on Swan Song): *Led Zeppelin,* SD 8216; *Led Zeppelin II,* SD 8236; *Led Zeppelin III,* SD 7201; untitled fourth album [sometimes known as *Led Zeppelin IV*], SD 7208; *Houses Of The Holy,* SD 7255; *Physical Graffiti,* SS 2-200; *Presence,* SS 8416; *The Song Remains The Same,* SS 2-201; *In Through The Out Door,* 16002; *Coda,* 90051-1. **With others:** Jeff Beck, *Truth,* Epic, BN 26413; Donovan, *The Hurdy Gurdy Man,* Epic BN 26420; Donovan, *Sunshine Superman,* Epic, BN 26239.

Ritchie Blackmore with Deep Purple

Guitar Player covered Ritchie Blackmore for the first time in this July 1973 feature story. At the time, Deep Purple was touring the U.S. in support of their *Machine Head* album.

an introduction

Ritchie Blackmore, lead guitarist and co-founder of Deep Purple, was born in Weston-super-Mare, England. Emerging to fame in America in 1968 with the hit single "Hush," Deep Purple has appeared with the Royal Philharmonic at London's Albert Hall, faced 4,000 rioting fans in Stuttgart, and been smuggled out of a concert hall in Iceland in a paddy wagon.

Blackmore's first guitar was a secondhand Spanish type which he has since replaced with Fender Stratocasters and Gibson ES-335s. Recently his solos have been pushed forward in Deep Purple's overall sound, which has been recorded in normal studio settings as well as less orthodox places such as when their album *Machine Head* was made in a hotel corridor in Montreux, Switzerland.

the interview

Did you ever have lessons?

I had classical lessons for a year. That helped, because I learned how to use my little finger. A lot of blues guitarists play with only three fingers, so they can't figure out certain runs that require the use of their little fingers. Classical training is good for that.

Besides getting you to use your little finger, has classical training affected your playing in any other way?

I would say that it shows up most in the music I write. For example, the chord progression in the "Highway Star" solo on *Machine Head — Bm* to a *D♭* to a *C* to a *G* — is a Bach progression. In other words the classical influence is always there somewhat, but I don't intentionally use it that much really. I play a lot of single notes, and that's not classical.

How do you rate Steve Howe, as far as putting almost strict classical stylings into a rock context?

He's very good at it. I remember him from a long time ago, and he's always been good. But he's not the kind of guitarist I can listen to. He's very good at runs, but I don't like that type of playing much.

When you were first starting out, were you influenced by anyone in particular?

At that time everybody else was copying Hank B. Marvin and the Shadows. In the beginning Duane Eddy used to be my favorite. I also got into James Burton and Scotty Moore. Big Jim Sullivan was a big influence. He plays with Tom Jones now. He's very good, but he's kind of wasted with Tom Jones. Big Jim used to live practically next door to me. He'd only been playing about two years, but he was just about the best guitarist in England, straight away. I thought I was all right and learning pretty well until I saw him. I couldn't even understand what he was doing. So I used to kind of sit on his doorstep and wait. When he'd come out, I'd ask if I could come in. He taught me quite a lot of tricks. I think he used to get a bit fed up with me hanging around. But when you're around someone that good, your own standards are raised. It saves you a lot of trial and error.

Did you ever do much work in record sessions?

When I was about 17. Some of the work was a drag, but some of it was interesting. Session work makes you more strict. You can't hit notes all over the place. You've got to make each one really count. When you're recording, if you're not really clean in your playing, it sounds like a mess. You may think you sound fabulous onstage, but when you hear yourself played back on record, it's just disastrous most of the time. If you can play well in the studio, you can play well onstage.

You use three Stratocasters onstage. Are they mainly for breakdowns?

No. I use one of the brown ones mostly. The black one just happens to have a bit more of a distorted sound.

Are they modified?

Not much at all. I put the middle pickup all the way down, because it gets in the way of the pick. I only use the straight bass and treble positions. It wouldn't do me any good trying to use any of the special middle positions on the selector switch, because the way I play I'd just be knocking it out of position constantly. As it is, that black plastic cover keeps coming off, and I cut myself up all the time. I'm not into that Keith Richards trip of having all those guitars in different tunings. I never liked the Rolling Stones much anyway. I guess their popularity depends on something more than just their music. I don't use foot pedals and wah-wahs and fuzzes and whatnot. I used to, but I found that I couldn't get a good natural sound. It's impossible. When a wah-wah pedal's turned off, the sound is very thin. You'd always find that with Hendrix, for instance.

When do you use your Gibson?

The last time I used it was on the *Deep Purple In Rock* album, I think. I prefer the Stratocaster, because it has a more "attacky" sound. At first I couldn't quite get used to

NEIL ZLOZOWER

the Strat after the Gibson. The necks are quite different. But now I can't get used to the Gibson again. A Stratocaster is harder to play than a Gibson, too. I don't know why. I think it's because you can't race across a Strat's fingerboard so fast. With a Gibson you tend to run away with yourself. It's so easy to zoom up and down, you end up just playing physical shapes rather than really working for an original sound.

How did you come to use your tremolo bar so much?

I liked the way Hendrix used his tremolo, though I don't think I use it the same way. A lot of guitarists think that a tremolo arm is for someone who can't play a hand vibrato. But the tremolo arm gives a different vibrato altogether. It affects whole chords. I can do the old hand vibrato just fine, but I like attacking the strings and getting all those sounds. You can get a lot of aggression out with the tremolo arm. I've got a Bigsby on my Gibson, and it's a waste, because it's got too much leeway. You have to pull it back a half-an-inch before it does a thing. But the vibrato on the Strat reacts immediately. As soon as you pull on it, the strings start going back.

You do a lot of hammering-on, and frequently put your pick in your mouth and play with your fingers.

I play with my feet, also [*laughs*]. I use my fingers for different sounds and effects. But I actually play very lightly.

How did that light touch come about?

Years ago when I was playing in a big band, I noticed all these guys with banjo strings, so I decided to try them. When I did a solo they sounded fine, but when it was over I'd find that the strings would be out of tune. So I started playing lighter out of necessity. Playing a Fender is an art in itself, anyway. They're always going out of tune. But the way I play, I've got it pretty well under control.

How loud is your amp setting?

Full up. I've always played every amp I've ever had full up, because rock and roll is supposed to be played loud. Also, keeping the amp up is how you get your sustain. I turn down on the guitar for dynamics. I've also got my amps boosted. I know [amp manufacturer] Jim Marshall personally, and he boosted them for me. My setup is pushing out about 500 watts — I guess that's maybe 1000 watts in American ratings, but it's all distortion. The people at Marshall said it's the loudest amp they'd ever heard. I had an extra stage built onto it, and a couple more valves. That's why every two weeks things just tend to disintegrate. The speakers really get pushed out. I usually go through two, sometimes more, every two weeks. I only use one of my stacks. The other's just a spare in case I blow the other up.

Does that happen often?

Sometimes we have a run of bad luck where something slows up every gig. I've had it happen about six times continuous. You feel like giving it all up when that happens. Learning to play the guitar is one thing, but learning to play with a big amplifier is a different thing altogether. It's like trying to control an elephant.

But you can't get that power rumble without big amps.

Yes, but that's about all. I'd rather play a little amp anytime. I used to do the circuit with a little amp and played ten times better than I do now. I was fast and clean, but nobody took any notice except other musicians. Normal people didn't know what the hell I was doing.

What's that device on the drum case behind your amplifier?

A treble-booster with a variable control which gives me sustain. Hornby-Skues made it, but I had it slightly modified because I found that on some nights I had too much sustain and on others I didn't have enough. So I had a variable control put on. Actually, using a Stratocaster, I don't really need any treble boost. I use the unit mostly for sustain.

Do you use all of your stage gear in the studios?

The full whack.

When playing live, do you stick closely to your recorded solos?

I try. Unfortunately, I think the only one I can remember is "Highway Star." I can never remember what I do even in the studio.

What affects the quality of your performances?

Some nights I feel like I can do anything. Other nights I feel inhibited. It all depends on what I'm feeling. If I go onstage and think, "That guy down in the front row thinks I'm an idiot. He thinks I can't play the guitar," I seize up. But if just one person says, "You're great," I really get turned on to play. If I overhear someone saying something like, "This guy's useless; I'm not staying to watch," it doesn't do me a hell of a lot of good.

When do you feel you play best?

Actually, I can play best if we're having a jam session. The stuff we do onstage is always basically the same, so I like to jam now and then to keep in shape. The best I ever played this year was around Christmas at a jam in Hamburg, Germany, with some of my old friends who aren't very good players at all. I thought I played brilliantly, because I wasn't leaping around. I was just standing there with small amps.

You don't like leaping around on the stage?

I like leaping around onstage as long as it's done with class. Like Free; they're the best band in England. Paul Rodgers is a good singer and a brilliant mover. None of this jumping up in the air and doing the splits and all that. He just moves with the music, not like Pete Townshend who's gotten to the point that he waits until the photographers are well-aimed before he leaps. He's not very spontaneous.

Townshend, Page, Hendrix, Beck, and even Dave Davies in the Kinks all are supposed to have been the first to use feedback, fuzz boxes, etc. Who do you think was the first to really start getting into effects in a big way?

I've been on the scene for so long that I know all those people — or someone who does. Therefore, I knew pretty well who played on what and when and so on. The first fuzz box ever used on a guitar for a recorded solo was used by the Rip Chords about 1957. The first fuzz box solo ever played in England was by a guy named Bernie Watson, on a record in 1960 called "Jack The Ripper," by Screaming Lord Sutch. It was a B side.

When did you get your first fuzz box?

Around 1960. I used to have to push about 30 watts through a 3" speaker. But I'd have to kick the speaker in until I got a fuzz box sound. I tried getting a real fuzz box made up in about 1956. I told some electricians that I wanted a contraption to control fuzz and sustain, to overload the amp. But it's funny, the electricians said they were trying to get away from distortion. They just wouldn't have it. They thought I was stupid. Twelve years ago Jimmy Page had a volume pedal for violin sounds. Big Jim Sullivan was actually the first person in England to use a volume pedal, but Jimmy Page played on "You Really Got Me" by the Kinks. I know because Jon Lord, our organ player, played piano on that session and Dave Davies [younger brother of Ray Davies, leader of the Kinks] was nowhere to be seen. But Jimmy used to run around telling everyone that he played on certain records. I asked him if he played on "The Crying Game" — that was Dave Berry — and "My Baby Left Me." He said, "Yes, I played guitar on that." What he didn't say was that he played rhythm guitar on it. Big Jim Sullivan played the solo on "The Crying Game." He was livid when he heard what Jimmy was running around saying, because Jimmy had always used his guitar and everything. Jimmy played rhythm guitar because the lead guitar bit was a reading part and Jimmy couldn't read.

Who first used feedback?

Pete Townshend was definitely the first. But not being that good a guitarist, he used to just sort of crash chords and let the guitar feed back. He didn't get into twiddling with the dials on the amplifier until much later. He's overrated in England, but at the same time you find a lot of people like Beck and Hendrix getting credit for things he started. Townshend was the first to break his guitar, and he was the first to do a lot of things. He's very good at his chord scene, too.

Why do you suppose groups like Grand Funk are selling millions of records when other bands do the same thing much better?

Our main audience is about 18 years old. People that age don't really understand music that much. They're trying to understand it, but if they were really that musically hip they wouldn't even like us. They wouldn't like Led Zeppelin. They'd be into someone like [concert violinist] Yehudi Menuhin. America is so vast that I think people buy records mainly of groups they've seen, and I imagine that since they must have seen Grand Funk all over America, they buy their records. At the same time, though, I have never met one person who likes Grand Funk. On the other hand, there might be an increased interest in people like Pink Floyd. I really like some of Pink Floyd's stuff. Groups like Curved Air might start coming into favor. Some of their music is bloody good —classical, with Moogs and bombs going off. Some nights their music is a complete disaster, but other nights it works. It's chance music, like some of the stuff I play.

What do you mean by "chance music?"

If you hold your guitar against the amp, you might get a harmonic feedback or you might get nothing. But that's what interests me: playing with electricity. Like I can turn on some jazz guitarist, and he won't do a thing for me if he's not playing electrically. But Jeff Beck's great to listen to because he takes a chance, and when it comes off it's so emotional. When he gets feedback going right, it's like an orchestra playing instead of just a guitar with a lot of brilliant runs. Actually, the real art of chance music is knowing what to do if you don't get what you tried for. Like if a ballet dancer falls over, it's knowing how to get out of looking clumsy that counts. Beck takes a chance every night. Sometimes he's absolutely useless, and you wonder why he's got a name. Other times he pulls things off that sound like nothing you've ever heard before. He's one of my favorite guitarists. But taking all those chances is why he gets such bad reviews sometimes. The reviewers sometimes catch him on nights when it doesn't work. The kind of things that you do in that kind of playing are subconscious and depend on what type of day you've had and things like that. If I've read a lot, or if I've had a game of chess and my mind's working, I can play much better than if I've had a lazy day of sitting in a car or plane. But I also think there are good days and bad days, all having to do with the cycle of life. You know — 30 days forward and then ten days backward.

How do you like touring?

If you've only done it for a couple of years, it's all right. But when you've done it for about ten years like me, you end up feeling like you're always waiting for somebody or something. You wish that you could just come over here, play the 30 hours, and then go home. The whole day is a drag. You get up and wait at some stupid airport for some stupid plane, which is always late. It's like going into the army. You say goodbye to everyone and say, "See you again in three months," and then you come back a physical wreck.

Does listening to solos performed on other instruments help the beginning guitarist develop a personal style?

Listening to as many *guitar* solos as possible is the best method for someone in the early stages. But saxophone solos can be helpful. They're interesting because they're all single notes, and therefore can be repeated on the guitar. If you can copy a sax solo you're playing very well, because the average saxophonist can play much better than the average guitarist. Jimmy Page says he listens to piano solos. But I don't see how that helps, because a pianist can play about ten times the speed of a guitarist.

What advice would you give to a person who wanted to become a good rock guitarist?

I'd have a tendency to say, "Get a good guitar, and get a good tutor book." Really, the only way you can get good — unless you're a genius — is to copy. You'll never come up with your own gear until you've copied. That's the best thing. Just steal.

—Martin K. Webb

Blackmore's Rainbow

DAVID TAN

Deep Purple had come and gone, and Blackmore's Rainbow was evolving into a leading metal band at the time of Ritchie's September 1978 cover story. Rainbow has released two albums since then, scoring a Top-40 hit with "Stone Cold" from 1982's *Straight Between The Eyes.*

an introduction

When Ritchie Blackmore steps into the stage lights and begins to play, his 22 years experience and high adrenalin turn him into a self-described "aggressive bulldozer" of a guitarist. "I feel like I *own* the stage," he says. Indeed, his searing lead work with Deep Purple and his natural evolution with Rainbow have carried him onto the stages of four continents and his recordings into the charts time and again. In one year alone, Deep Purple sold over 14 million albums worldwide. Rainbow recently released their fourth album, *Long Live Rock 'N Roll*, which fuses the seemingly incongruous styles of classical, Renaissance, German Baroque, and heavy rock music. "I criticize my own work pretty harshly," Blackmore says, "yet I feel this is some of the best music I have ever been part of."

Ritchie's musical initiation began in 1956, when at age 11 he got his first instrument — a secondhand Framus Spanish guitar. He lived near guitarist Big Jim Sullivan, from whom, he says, "I learned quite a lot of tricks." By the time he was 17 Ritchie was working as a session guitarist, often sharing duties with Jimmy Page. He then joined Screaming Lord Sutch's band in London. Sutch, one of the most colorful characters in British rock during the '60s, modeled himself after American blues singer Screaming Jay Hawkins. "Working with him was terrifying, at first anyway," says Ritchie. "He did a stage act in which he'd dress up like Jack the Ripper. He had shoulder-length hair before anyone else, and every gig was an adventure. He taught me to get out and give it to the people."

After several years apprenticeship with Sutch, Blackmore tired of the British music scene and moved to Hamburg, West Germany. He became a regular at the Star Club, backing visiting musicians including Jerry Lee Lewis. In February 1968, Blackmore, organist Jon Lord, and drummer Ian Paice met in Hamburg and discussed the possibility of forming a group. They added bassist Nick Simper, who had also worked with Sutch, and vocalist Rod Evans to form Deep Purple. By the summer of the same year their first single — a hard rock version of Joe South's "Hush" — was released in the U.S. Following the success of their first album, *Shades Of Deep Purple*, the band toured the U.S. in October 1968. Though their first three albums received wide acclaim in the U.S., Deep Purple did not release any recordings in England until 1970.

In July 1969, Evans was replaced by Ian Gillan, who would later sing the title role in the recorded version of *Jesus Christ, Superstar.* Roger Glover took over as bassist. While the new lineup rehearsed, Jon Lord began working on a concerto for a rock band and symphony orchestra. On September 24, 1969, Deep Purple joined the Royal Philharmonic at Royal Albert Hall. The performance met with wide approval from both classical and rock reviewers, and was later released as *Deep Purple And The Royal Philharmonic Orchestra.*

Deep Purple spent a half-year working on *In Rock*, an LP that was successfully received in both the U.S. and England in 1970. Later that year the group toured Europe, and in May 1971 they made their first trip to Australia. The band scored further successes with their follow-up albums: *Fireball* in 1971, *Machine Head* (reportedly recorded in a hotel corridor in Montreux, Switzerland) in 1972, and *Made In Japan* and *Who Do We Think We Are?* in 1973. *Machine Head* and *Made In Japan* both achieved gold-record status soon after release. In 1973 Gillan quit the band, citing its "lack of progression," and he was soon followed by Glover. By 1975, Blackmore had also tired of his role in Deep Purple. "Things were getting a bit boring in rock and roll," he explained, and he began to seek new musical direction.

In spring of 1975, Blackmore teamed with former Elf vocalist Ronnie James Dio. Blackmore found that Dio shared his interest in medieval music, and many of the songs they began to write reflected this interest. Joining Blackmore and Dio was Cozy Powell, who had worked as a drummer for Donovan and Jeff Beck and had three solo singles to his credit. The musicians called themselves Rainbow. Their original bassist, Jimmy Bain, was replaced by ex-Widowmaker Bob Daisley, and keyboardist Tony Carey was replaced by David Stone. Shortly after its formation Rainbow traveled to Munich, West Germany, where they recorded *Rainbow*. With his new band, Blackmore claimed: "We're going to have much more emphasis on melody. In other words, everything isn't going to be hung on a riff."

Ritchie has recently begun to study the cello. When asked if he will soon be delivering cello solos in live performances, he answers: "Maybe when I'm 40. It'll take me that long to really play it well."

the artist

When did you first start playing guitar?

Basically I started when I was 11. I don't really have a musical background from my parents, but my father was a kind of mathematician, and he helped me with the notes in a purely mathematical way. I would show him some music and ask, "Why is this like this?" and he would work it out without knowing why, which I couldn't do at that age. And that's what I've been doing since I was 11.

Did you take any lessons?

Yeah, when I was 11 I took classical lessons for a year. I thought I had to start playing on the right foot and the right hand, and I felt I had to learn properly. So I took lessons for a year, and then I went my own way after that. You lose your identity unless you do it yourself. You've got to get off on the right footing, but after that you have to carry on with your own identity, which for me came later. I suppose my style originated from not being able to pick things up very easily. I used to play my own solos rather than copy other people's.

Did you find the guitar accessible?

No, I found it very hard at first. It was very difficult. The first six months were difficult and then it became very easy. Then after about three years it became very difficult again.

Was it some time before you got your first electric guitar?

It was about five years. The acoustic I was using was a Spanish guitar that had about 400 pickups and knobs and switches. And then I bought a Hofner, which was a very thin guitar. It was a great guitar; I wish I could find it today. It didn't have any f-holes; it was a solidbody. And then I bought a Gibson ES-335 when I was about 16, and I stayed with that one until I was 21 or 22, something like that. And then I heard Hendrix's sound, which hit me in the stomach, and I went for that. With the Gibson you really lose that identity — everybody sounds the same, I think, unless you're listening to one of the top-notch guys.

Did you play in bands with friends?

I played in a skiffle group, and there were about 20 guitarists involved and none of them could play. We were playing Lonnie Donegan stuff — "Rock Island Line" and things like that. But first I started playing off what you call a dog box; it's a piece of string attached to a broom handle which goes through a tea chest and gives you certain notes. And any one of the notes will do, as long as it goes boom. Then I progressed to the washboard with thimbles and things.

When did you begin studying with Big Jim Sullivan?

He was teaching me when I was about 12. My brother's girlfriend knew him and he would come over to the house; of course, after I heard him play I idolized him. I would always be around his house trying to learn different things. He was good because I could see how far I had to go to try and keep up. At first I thought, "Oh, no, I'll never make it if this is just the guy around the corner," but luckily not everybody was like him. It just so happened he lived around the corner. It was like having a genius around: You think everyone else is the same way.

What kind of things was he showing you?

He was teaching me classical — Bach, and things like that — and he was teaching me to read better than I was. He said to me once, "Whatever type of music you're going to play, you must stick to it; don't be a jack-of-all-trades." So I decided rock and roll was the thing. Which is ironic — he didn't practice what he preached. He plays country and western, classical — just everything very well, but of course people don't know him for anything. And so I started to rock and roll because I was excited by it.

What was the first band where your playing really had a chance to expand?

It was the Outlaws, which was a band that used to do a lot of sessions. Chas Hodges was on bass — he used to be with Heads, Hands & Feet. We stayed together for about two years and did a lot of sessions. That was a very good band. It was instrumental, and we didn't have a singer. I learned a lot from sessions; I did about four a day when I was 17 or 18. It was the same time Jimmy Page was doing sessions. If they wanted a rock and roll player they'd get Pagey or myself, because they had a lot of people who could read, but they didn't have too many people who could feel heavy rock music. All these readers didn't want to know about playing rock, whereas Jimmy and I didn't read too well, but we could just feel the sessions.

Whom did you do sessions for?

The sessions were for everybody, even for Tom Jones at times. But half the time they were backing tracks, so we didn't know who they were for. Occasionally we'd see the artists, but the people were really not well-known; they were well-known there but you wouldn't know them here.

You used the ES-335 for the sessions?

Yeah, and I had a system for getting a fuzz sound. This was the early '60s, and I hadn't seen a fuzztone, so I used a smashed speaker which was about three inches around and gave this fuzz-box sound.

What type of amplifier were you using?

A Vox AC-30.

That was virtually the only amp available then.

That's right, and they were the best, too. I've still got that Vox. It's encased in a Marshall cabinet.

You did sessions for how long?

I did sessions for about two years, and then I went to Germany after that and did sessions there and stayed there for quite a time, about three years. Then the Purple thing started.

You used the ES-335 for the early years of Deep Purple?

That's right, the first two years. I used it on the first two albums, *Shades Of Deep Purple* and *The Book Of Taliesyn.*

Your work with Screaming Lord Sutch was before Purple?

Yes, I forgot about that. The Screaming Lord introduced me to showmanship. Before that I used to play in the wings, and when I met him he pulled me out front and demanded I jump around and act stupid. My first impression of him was that I thought he was mad. In those days nobody had that kind of long hair; God knows how long it was. And he had his own act. But he had a fantastic band, an amazing band.

Who was in it?

Ricky Benson, who later went with Georgie Fame, and Carl Little, who the Stones wanted and he turned them down — he's been kicking himself ever since. And [pianist] Nicky Hopkins used to come along now and then, because we all lived around the same area.

How did that post-Sutch album, Hands Of Jack The Ripper, *happen?*

Sutch phoned me up and said, "Do you fancy playing tomorrow night?" I agreed and I came down with [keyboardist] Matt Fisher of Procol Harum, and we just did a night of playing. I saw the recording equipment and thought, "He's doing it again." And he said, "Here's $500 for playing tonight."

You started developing your stage routine with Sutch?

Yeah, that's right. He pulled me on the stage and I was slightly electrocuted, because he was touching the mike and me. After that I thought if he can get away with it, I

An early promo shot of Blackmore's Rainbow.

can do that, because I could see how well he was going down and how much money he was earning. I thought, "I can run around the stage and act like a maniac. Maybe I'll get paid for it, too."

Did you use a Marshall amp in the early days of Purple?

No, I was still using the Vox miked. It used to buzz like mad. I changed to Marshalls about eight years ago. I knew Jim Marshall. He was a drum teacher, and I saw the Marshall setup and liked the way they looked. The design I liked, but the sound was awful. So I went back to the factory and said, "Look, I want this changed and I want that changed." And I used to play in front of all the people that were there working. There would be women there assembling things, and I had the amp boosted to 400 watts. So I would be playing away right in front of all these people and they'd be trying to work. I'd go, "That's not right, more treble," and they'd take out a resistor. I had to play full blast or otherwise I couldn't know what it was going to sound like. The people hated me.

Did you change to a Fender Stratocaster for the third album, Deep Purple In Concert*?*

I think it was, yeah. In fact, the Strat I used belonged to Eric Clapton. I liked the sound of it; it was very sharp but impossible to play. The neck was so bowed; it was really bad. He just had one kicking around the house, and I picked it up and he said, "Take it away." It had a great sound for a wah-wah pedal because it was so sharp, but it was very difficult to play because it was so bowed. I thought it was an interesting guitar at the time, even though all the octaves were out.

You actually used that guitar on the third album?

Yeah, there are quite a few tracks where both guitars — the ES-335 and the Stratocaster — are used. But I can't remember what songs were with which.

Did you find it difficult changing from the Gibson to the Fender?

Yeah, the transition was really hard. I found great difficulty in using it the first two years. With a Gibson you just race up and down, but with a Fender you have to make every note count; you have to make the note sing or otherwise it won't work. It's more rewarding because with a Gibson nobody has an identity, as I said before.

Had you heard people like Eric Clapton and Jimmy Page using Les Pauls?

I was into Les Paul guitars when I first saw Albert Lee play. He's probably one of the best guitarists in the world. I first heard him play a Les Paul in 1960. That's when I wanted one. When it became popular and everyone had one, I dropped it. But I loved Les Paul and Mary Ford anyway; I had all of their records. I was into Les for about four years. Chet Atkins was the other guitarist that everybody was into, but his thumb thing got on my nerves a bit. I thought Les Paul was much better, and Mary Ford was better to look at.

Did you change to a Fender Stratocaster for the third album, Deep Purple In Concert*?*

Yes, I wasn't too impressed. I would like to someday meet Les Paul. It was like him, Scotty Moore, and James Burton who were my main influences. They were real guitarists, not posers.

What about the Green Bullfrog *album?*

That was me, Albert Lee, and Jim Sullivan. Ian Paice and Roger Glover were on it and whoever else was around at the time. Tony Ashton was on it, I think. It was awful, disgusting. It was done in a day and nobody knew what we were doing. I was embarrassed; I never heard that LP, actually.

It's interesting to hear when each of you takes a solo.

I was there with my stack, Albert was there with his little amp and Telecaster, and Jim was doing his finger-pick stuff.

So it was the Stratocaster and Marshall for the duration of Deep Purple?

Yeah. It was really hard at first, because they didn't match. It just looked right, especially the Marshall, so I thought I've got to make that amplifier sound right if it's the last thing I do. The standard ones are awful.

What did you do to change your Marshalls?

I had an extra output stage built on. I have no bass at all on the amp. They're an extra two valves [tubes] built into the output stage so there's more output. It's boosted to about 250 or 300 watts. I use the old 200-watt amps, which you can't get anymore because they don't make them.

Do you use 200-watt heads?

Yeah, which are boosted. They're the loudest amplifier in the world on their own. I'm not saying I play the loudest — it depends on how many you use. But one on its own is the loudest. I don't like to use a lot of cabinets. I think just two cabinets is enough; otherwise the sound is all around you. I like to keep away from the sound, and that's why onstage I play to the left of it and point it the other way. Then I can get a perspective of what's going on; otherwise all you can hear is yourself. And you tend to get feedback and overtones you don't want.

Did you initially use one stack and later add the second?

Yeah, I just have the other one as a reserve. It's on, but I'm not using it. It's just if I blow the first one.

Do you blow them very often onstage?

Yeah, all the time lately. I don't know why. It's the output transformer that blows up. It's like a finely tuned car; you can't expect it not to break down. I really push it.

Do you use the same guitar and amplifier setup in the studio?

Yeah. Actually I don't play in the studio, I have someone else who takes my place. Jim Page comes in [*laughs*].

Are there solos you played with Deep Purple that stand out in your mind?

The solo on "Highway Star" [*Machine Head*] was worked out; it's just arpeggios based on Bach. On *Machine Head* as a whole, in fact, there was some good stuff. The guitar solo on "Pictures Of Home" was good. But when I hear that compared to what I'm doing now, there's a big difference to me. It's much better now; I didn't have the control then that I do now. I think the solo on "Gates of Babylon" [*Long Live Rock 'N Roll*] is the best solo I've ever done. It is the best because it's the most intricate solo, yet at the same time it's not clinical. I was well pleased with that one.

Was that a spontaneous solo?

Yeah, that was spontaneous. And also it wasn't just 24 bars of just playing on *E*. There were so many weird chords involved that I could go back to my old way of playing, which is just to have the chords in front of me and play the solo, whereas now every time I go into the studio to play I know exactly what the song consists of. Usually it's just two chords, and I'm stale by the time I get in there. But we threw those chords around, and, in fact, David Stone, our keyboardist, helped a lot with that. They were strange chords — diminished, augmented —it was great. Because I love musical theory and I was well into that, I didn't have any problems with that side of it. I love playing a few augmented and diminished runs and not just the usual blues licks.

What did you think of the album Deep Purple did with the orchestra?

I didn't like it. I like proper classical, purist classical. That album was just a compromise. The orchestra was never playing at its best, and the best was certainly out of its depth. I like chamber music basically, medieval music moreso than big orchestrations.

What did you think of Deep Purple's two live albums, Made In Europe *and* Made In Japan?

I never listen to them; they're old, dead, and buried. I think both of them as live LPs are rubbish, but compared to all the live albums that are put out by other bands, I think they were brilliant.

What about Rainbow's live album On Stage?

That was dire when we did it. We had to have someone come in and salvage the tapes and get a better sound. They sounded awful. I don't know, there's something about being live that doesn't come across. I've got cassettes of us playing really well. As soon as the red light is on and we're recording, everything gets compressed and there's no way to get around it.

There was some good playing on Burn.

Yeah, that's because we had about a year off and I had the excitement to start again. Just before that I was ready to kind of leave myself. We were just working and flogging ourselves to death. I was sick all the time. Luckily we changed two members, and there was new blood. Then again, *Burn* was great, and *Stormbringer* became a bit funky, soully, smooth.

"Mistreated" on Burn *was a good song.*

Yeah. That was influenced by "Heartbreaker" [*Heartbreaker*] by Free. I get inspired by other people's songs and write something vaguely similar.

In fact, wasn't Paul Rodgers, Free's vocalist, supposed to join Deep Purple?

Yeah, that's right. He was for about a week. I think somebody was going to chop his legs off if he did leave, so he didn't. I think he was into a different type of singing, and he didn't want to follow Ian Gillan and all that screaming. Rodgers wasn't into that; he was more into blues.

It seems that Ian Paice really pushed you as a player.

Yeah, I used to have to look around at him some nights to get some sort of enthusiasm.

How is it different playing with drummer Cozy Powell as opposed to Ian Paice?

Ian plays more of a straight beat; Cozy always plays in front of the beat and he's pushing all the time.

Do you use a rosewood-fingerboard Stratocaster?

Yeah, I break the maple necks because they're so badly made. They should be broken. Now they're so badly made it's disgusting.

What year is the Stratocaster you're using?

I think it's about two years old. It's one of about ten that has a narrow neck.

What do you do to a guitar when you get it?

I do this carving-out business. I'll usually cover the Fender frets with tape or put in Gibson frets, and I'll sandpaper the wood down so it's concave so I can get my finger underneath. I have the action on my guitar fairly high so there's more control, but it's within reason. I mean, jazz players have it so high, and it's musical snobbery, really.

The Gibson frets have a wider profile than Fender's.

Yeah, they do. I do like big frets, but I've noticed in the last two years I've kept it to Fender frets.

Do you use Fender tuning heads?

No, I use Schallers. It's funny, I never saw anybody do it before I was doing it, and I did it years ago. Now everybody does it. I wonder why that is?

Do you change the nut?

No, because that's only good for sustaining a note open. Once you hit a note on the first fret, you depend on the first fret and not the nut. Although [drummer] Buddy Miles used to tell me Hendrix used a brass nut.

Do you rewire the guitars in any way?

No, but I sometimes insulate them with copper inside to stop the buzzing. That's about all, really. I don't use the middle pickup at all; I get rid of that one and rearrange the other two. I just have bass and treble — black and white, that's what I like.

How many springs do you use on your vibrato bar?

Four. And I have a friend who balances the arm. He loosens the screws at the very front of the tailpiece and sets the whole thing at a different angle so it is in perfect balance. It's amazing; you just can't go out of tune. I never thought it would work. I just used to bolt them down and forget about it. I pull and push the vibrato bar — it goes down a whole octave when I push it.

Do you try to get the settings between the three major positions on the toggle switch?

No, that's a little bit of a touch of gray in there.

What settings do you use on the guitar and the amplifier?

I never touch the tone controls on the guitar; they're always full up. But I will turn the guitar volume from full to half when I'm doing a quieter solo. On the amp everything is full up. No, actually I do have markings on the amp, but it's very hard to say because I can't compare it with anything. On some amps I have the presence completely up, and on some I have it completely off. And like I told you before, I have no bass. I use a lot of middle because I hate that screeching top; it's a little bit too penetrating. I use midrange treble. And the volume is on half; if it was full up it would just catch on fire.

Do you use the stock speakers in the cabinets?

Yeah, whatever they are.

Have you ever experimented with other speakers?

I've tried all types of different amplifiers, but they're a little bit too clear. I like a little bit of distortion which is controlled through my tape recorder. I built my own tape recorder. Well, I didn't build it, but I modified it from a regular tape recorder to an echo unit. It also preamps and boosts the signal going to the amp. If I want a fuzzy effect, I just turn up the output stage of the tape recorder.

Can you be more specific as to how it works?

I just keep it on "record" so it records, and it's like a continual echo because I couldn't get that echo with any echo machine. A continual boom, boom, boom, repeat. Most echo machines are awful; it's like you're in a hallway. The tape recorder doesn't interfere with the note you're playing.

What type of tape recorder is it?

I don't really know. I tried using a Revox, and it didn't work. I'd really be in trouble if somebody stole my recorder. I've been using it for the last four or five years.

How exactly is it hooked up?

There's a cord from the guitar into the tape recorder input, and the output stage just goes back to the amp. I can control the volume, too. I can have it loud with no distortion or vice versa. I have a little footpedal that I can stop and start it with. A lot of people think when they see the tape going the solos are recorded. Lots of people ask that. Some guy shouted in New York, "Turn the tape recorder off." Actually that inspired me. I turned it off and really whizzed around.

Do you use any other pedals or effects?

No. Well, I do use bass pedals. I've only been using them for about the last six months. When the band decides they don't want to play I can go do my own little set. It's very interesting because they're a challenge. Sometimes it works great and sometimes it doesn't, but that's the chance you take. They're so loud and so bassy.

What kind of picks and strings do you use?

I use tortoiseshell picks, one end squared, one end pointed. I have them specially made for me because you can't get them at all. I use tortoiseshell because plastic is too soft; I like them brick hard. I've used this shape ever since I was 11. I just cannot play with those round things everybody plays with because when you jump a string, you tend to hit the other string on the way. With this pick you can be more nimble. I use Picato strings; I've always used them. They're the best; Eric Clapton turned me on to these. He's now using Fender — I don't know why. The gauges I use are .010, .011, .014, .026, .036, and .042.

Are there certain keys you like to work in?

Yeah, I like *F#* and *Dm*. *E* is boring. I don't do too much in *C*; it's a little too obvious, too bright for me. *G* is a very resonant key. *F#* is more of a blues. *Dm* gives you the entire length of the neck to do nice open notes.

In the studio do you record rhythm tracks first and then solos?

I hate to do rhythm tracks; they bore me silly. That's why most of my rhythm tracks are very clinical. I'm so bored with just trying to get the thing right with the drums and the bass. I just love the part when it comes to putting my bit on there because if I mess it up it's just me. But I can't stand going through, "I've done my bit," and the bass player goes, "Oh, I messed it up." And you do it again and the bass player gets his bit right and the drummer messes up. Of course by the tenth time you start hollering at everybody and you mess it up. And that's it, you're over the top by this time. Everybody is stale. You become a combination of things — annoyed, stale, worried that you're not ever going to get it off. And it's so simple, it's something you'd knock off in one minute, but to get it onto tape is a pain in the ass. That's why I don't like recording too much. It's too clinical. A lot of people love it. They can edit their music and put it together and make it nice, but when they get onstage they're lost. My way of thinking is the opposite. I love to

ROSS MARINO

have that freedom of just going onstage and playing whatever I want to play at the time. I'll play the numbers which I'm supposed to play, but in the in-between parts if I'm feeling good I'll play something completely off the wall that I've never ever played in my life. In other words, I just lay back for the vocal and then I do my bit when it comes to the solo. I don't like to do intricate things in the backgrounds; I don't like to clutter. I like the foundation to be simple.

Do you use special miking techniques in the studio?

I have one speaker in the studio, and I have one in an echo chamber usually. And they're both miked up, but not very close. They're miked from about nine feet away because they're so bloody loud. I play near stage volume in the studio, because the amp only operates full out — it can't operate at half.

Do you practice?

Yeah, a lot. I have to. When I'm home I just play the cello and fiddle around, but when I'm on tour I usually practice for an hour-and-a-half before a gig. If I think it's going to be a good gig and I want to impress, I'll really practice. Otherwise I won't. But I'm always holding a guitar and fiddling with it. But that can be bad because you get really lazy, especially with a guitar like my old Spanish guitar with nylon strings. I tend to pick it up and just sit there strumming. It's like an artist and a paintbrush; you just shouldn't slap colors around very lazily. If you're going to play, you should play as hard as you can. It's hard to do because a guitar is such a great instrument just to sit there and fiddle with and sing old Beatles songs. That's the worst thing you can do.

Are there certain things you practice?

I don't practice specific things. I practice avenues of playing to try and lose myself in the guitar. I don't think you should be thinking too heavily about what you're playing. And lots of times when I'm playing the guitar, I don't really know what I'm doing or where I am. I'm just going up and down the guitar rather than looking at each note and thinking that's an *E* . And other times I stop completely and just go, "Ohhh" in frustration. It's whether I'm inspired. Being an extremist, I go from being totally uninspired to very inspired.

Do your speed and accuracy come from practice?

Yeah. I think it's because I also use four fingers and most other people just use three. When I first started I was taught to use my little finger, and of course I have ever since. Jeff Beck uses four; he was obviously taught the right way. It's funny, if you don't learn that in the beginning, you're lost. You must get off on that right away.

Would you like to put together a guitarist's album?

Not particularly, no. I wouldn't mind putting together a blues LP and just jamming with somebody like I did with Sutch. I often jam with my friends and I play much better than I do on record or anywhere else, because I haven't got the pressure. Just a 12-bar and that's it, no fancy frills. As soon as someone goes, "We'll record that," and the red light goes on, it's like "Oh, dear." My mind seizes up and I'm stale all of a sudden

How would you describe your right-hand technique?

It's up and down, always up and down. People like Alvin Lee play wrong because they play everything down. And it's so difficult to play like that. It's a very important technique to have. I often just sit in the dressing room and practice quick up and down strokes, just changing from one open string to another. And it's very difficult. The solo from "Highway Star" is that quick up and down stroke. The right hand doesn't really do much, but it sounds very fast. It's like with a violinist or cellist.

Jethro Tull is one of your favorite bands.

Say no more. Ian Anderson is a genius, especially with his later stuff. It's horrifying to think how he wrote that stuff. But if you talk to him, he goes, "Oh, I just count two." But you can't count two over that, it's 9/5½. Their guitarist, Martin Barre, and the rest of the group have memories like computers to remember that. Admittedly I wouldn't like to be in that band playing the same thing every night, but I love to go and see them. I see them at least four times a year.

Are there any bassists you admire?

John Glascock is a brilliant bass player, the best in the business in rock. Rainbow was after him, but we couldn't get him. If you get him on his own, he's great, a natural. Timmy Bogert is great. Jack Bruce is a great bass player and vocalist.

It seems that the bass players and keyboardists you've worked with have never been quite up to your level.

That's right; that's true. Rainbow is a three-piece band, really, and always has been and always will be, I guess. Bob Daisley was the best bass player we could find, and we looked for ages. There are not a lot of people who want to play straight rock. It seems that when the very good guys come along, they're into this very hip jazz thing. It's very limiting and challenging to play rock, as you know. You've got set chords. You can't throw in any augmenteds, whereas with jazz you've got the whole scale. But it's worth it once you find the answers in rock and you come up with a good song. To me there's no chance involved with jazz — you've got so much there to deal with. It's a musician's music; I like to play to people.

You think your playing has changed since the days of Deep Purple?

Yeah. I was listening to some of Purple's stuff and I thought I was better than that. It's very, very sketchy and clinical. At the time it was the best I could do, because we had three weeks to get an LP together and there were so many egos involved. But I go through the same sort of things as Jeff Beck; I'm never happy with what I'm doing. And I can't get really excited talking about myself. And that's why I can't talk about somebody else even to slag them. That's why I don't do interviews — what can you say about yourself? I do this, and I do that. "Yes, our new LP is great and we're touring." Everybody comes up with the usual crap — "With this new LP of ours we're going in a new direction." We're not going in any direction. We're just going along. If people don't like it, it's too bad. I certainly wouldn't change to suit the radio play that's gone down in the last three years — all the Fleetwood Macs and Eagles and all that business.

You don't like that kind of music?

Not at all. I like intensity and drama. If I'm going to listen to relaxing music, it's medieval or classical or it's up-front more. There's no in-between.

DAVID TAN

Are there any other projects you're involved in?

I haven't wanted to do any other projects, but I'd like to do some work with the band Carmen. It's flamenco style, but on rock. It'd be interesting to throw some wild solos in their stuff. I don't get inspired by many bands, but they're really interesting.

Do you take much heed in what critics say about you?

I never read reviews, because if they say it's great, then you go, "No, they're wrong." If they say it's rubbish, then that's fine with me. You have to believe in yourself. I listen to friends who are fans. If a fan comes up to me and says, "I like your music, but that's a bit. . . ," I'll listen; that's my critic. But people who write, I don't listen to. They're just out to get a name for themselves.

Do you like playing with other guitarists?

Not particularly, no. I think one guitar is enough unless you're into that frame of mind where you can work out very good harmonies, which I'm not into. I'm just a spasmodic guitarist. I'm into self-extemporization; I'm not into working things out too much. That's why I don't play with other guitarists.

Do you think your current playing is as good as it's ever been?

I think it's much better. That's one positive thing I can say about it.

— Steve Rosen

A SELECTED RITCHIE BLACKMORE DISCOGRAPHY

With Deep Purple (on Tetragrammaton): *Shades Of Deep Purple,* T-102; *The Book Of Taliesyn,* T-107; *Deep Purple In Concert,* T-119; (on Warner Bros.): *Deep Purple And The Royal Philharmonic Orchestra,* WBR 1860; *In Rock,* WS 1877; *Fireball,* WB 2564; *Machine Head,* BS 2607; *Made In Japan,* 2WS-2701; *Who Do We Think We Are?,* BS-2678; *Burn,* W 2766; *Stormbringer,* PR-2832; *Made In Europe,* PR 2995. **With Rainbow** (on Polydor): *Rainbow,* Pol-6049; *Rainbow Rising,* OY 1-1601; *On Stage,* OY-2-1801; *Long Live Rock 'N Roll,* PD 1-6143; *Difficult To Cure,* 1-6316; *Down To Earth,* 1-6221; *Straight Between The Eyes,* Mercury, SRM-1-4041. **With others:** Lord Sutch, *Hands Of Jack The Ripper,* Cotillion, SD 9049; Albert Lee and Big Jim Sullivan, *Green Bullfrog,* Decca, DL 75269. **Anthologies:** *Castle Donnington,* Polydor, 1-6311.

Tony Iommi
Black Sabbath

A founding member of Black Sabbath, Tony Iommi was interviewed during the *Sabbath/Bloody Sabbath* tour for this October 1974 profile. The band has released over a half-dozen albums over the ensuing years, *Live Evil* being the most recent. In 1978 Tony produced an album for Quartz. An interesting footnote: Sabbath co-founder Ozzy Osbourne, who quit the band to sing solo in 1978, was instrumental in introducing Randy Rhoads to the rock world.

the artist

Black Sabbath lead guitarist Tony Iommi stands well over six feet tall and plays like he has six fingers on each hand. Not bad, since several years ago Tony hacked off the ends of his middle and ring fingers on his right hand. A left-hander, he consequently had to completely alter his playing. Struggling with various types of plastic tips that he placed at the ends of the fingers, he has since gone on to become one of the more stylistic players on the rock scene today.

Tony always had an interest in music, though. His first aspiration was to be a drummer. After realizing that he couldn't afford a drum kit and that an accordion just wasn't what he wanted, he fell in with the guitar. "I got a guitar for a birthday present," he states, "and things just went on from there: I got a better guitar and a better guitar."

His first substantial electric guitar was a Watkins that ran through a small Watkins tube amplifier. During these early years of his playing, Tony would frequently get together with friends and jam, but nothing ever came about until he auditioned with Jethro Tull and scored the lead guitarist position. This was during 1969, following Mick Abrahams' departure and preceding the band's appearance in the Rolling Stones' "Rock 'N' Roll Circus." Tony was with Tull for the filming of the show only, and immediately left the band after the project was finished.

"It just wasn't right," he explains, "so I left. At first I thought the band was great, but I didn't much go for having a leader in the band, which was [flautist] Ian Anderson's way. As we are now in Black Sabbath, there's no leader. Everyone does their own part. Not only that, the communication between the band wasn't too friendly."

Originally, Iommi had left Sabbath to join Tull, but swiftly returned to his former band. His first guitar with Sabbath was a Fender Stratocaster (year unknown) which was plugged into two Marshall 4 x 12 cabinets powered by two 50-watt amplifiers. As the band grew in popularity, they started adding more cabinets, until they were offered an attractive advertising arrangement by Laney amplifiers in England. Since that time Tony has been using six 4 x 12 Laney cabinets which are fed by four 100-watt amps. They are channeled by plugging Y-cords into the "normal" outputs (they have "treble" and "normal" sockets) of the four heads. For treble boost he uses a Rangemaster unit which has been re-worked (extra tubes, boosters) by the band's roadies.

After using the Fender for several years, Iommi has changed to Gibson and now uses an old (year also unknown) SG. One major alteration has been the replacement of the stock pickups with specially built low-feedback units. Tony thought that the standard Gibson pickups fed back uncontrollably. Though the sound they produced was more than satisfactory, the searing screeches that accompanied that sound made the pickups impossible to use. The new ones cut down on the feedback, but don't totally stop the unwanted noise. Other changes include the application of polyurethane to the neck to give it a lacquer-like finish which resists corrosion of the wood and helps prevent the frets from wearing away. The frets themselves have been filed down, and new metal tuning pegs replace the original plastic ones.

Because he's always experienced difficulty in tuning his Gibson, Iommi has had several different bridges constructed. His current bridge raises the strings to a higher position than usual, but it has brought the open strings and 12th fret octaves into almost perfect sympathy. The bridge's height also prevents the lightweight strings he uses from constantly rattling against the fretboard. "It's sort of an experimental guitar," Iommi says. "Everything that can be done to a guitar has been done to this one. That's probably why I like it, because I've got it exactly as I want it, apart from still having trouble with tuning."

The change from Fender to Gibson came one night when the band was playing in Germany, and one of the pickups went out on Tony's Stratocaster. Grudgingly, he snatched the Gibson which he kept onstage for such emergencies, and since that time has never returned to a Fender of any model. The Gibson neck and fretboard appealed to him more than the Fender, as well as the ease with which he could bend notes. He now owns several Gibsons, including an old Les Paul SG with three pickups, a newer model SG, and a Junior which Leslie West gave him as a present. Among his collection of acoustic instruments are a Gibson J-50 and an expensive Guild guitar, though he confesses that the disarray throughout his entire house prevents him from really knowing what he owns.

All his guitars had to be switched around to accom-

NEIL ZLOZOWER

ROSS MARINO

modate his left-handedness. Tony now realizes that when he first started, he could have probably just turned a right-hand guitar around and played it upside down. But he didn't, and now must either buy a left-handed guitar, or alter any instrument he purchases to fit his needs. To add to his southpaw problem, Tony must also contend with the amputation he suffered years ago. "You see, I can't use right-handed instruments now," he points out, "because I snipped the ends of my fingers off, and on a reversed Les Paul you've got to get right up to the end of the guitar to hit the strings. Not many people know about the accident. It happened years ago when I was doing electric welding. One day I had to cut this sheet metal before I welded. Somebody else used to do it, but I had to do it this day because he didn't come to work. And it was a faulty switch or something: *Thhhht!* I pulled it out, and it just gripped the ends and pulled them off."

As fate would have it, the day of the accident was Tony's last day on the job before he was to have left for Germany with a rock outfit. Feeling completely lost, he decided to give up the guitar until a friend brought him a record of Django Reinhardt. After hearing what the brilliant gypsy guitarist did with just two fingers, Tony again took up the instrument, and slowly activated the two clipped fingers along with the two healthy ones.

"I had to start all over again," he recalls, "which was kind of a drag. I have to wear things now because the ends are so tender. It's helped me a little bit because now I use my little finger a lot."

The "things" Tony wears are like little plastic thimbles which fit over the ends of the two digits to make up for the loss in finger length and reach. He's tried various sorts of adapters, but hasn't really come up with any which are totally comfortable. Frustration at times over the accident, an ill-sounding guitar, and a poor performance used to bring out violent reactions. "I'd get annoyed and pick the guitar up and throw it and smash it," Iommi says.

But those days are over, and Iommi can look back calmly: "At first I don't think people realized how hard it was to learn to play like that. It involved a lot of determination, and a lot of hard work and practice. The accident happened over eight years ago, way before Sabbath or Tull. And when I joined Jethro, they even said, 'What are those things on your fingers?' When I told them, they were quite surprised to find I could play guitar with these. I've had to adopt a totally different way of playing because of these fingers. I mean, it's much easier when the flesh is there as it should be. Instead of, say, pulling a note, I have to sort of push it up to get a vibrato. These tips are a bit clumsy, and they slow me down and get in the way. I even have to wear leather on them to grip the strings. But it's just something I'll have to try and overcome."

Tony has also had to search for the right string that wouldn't clink or buzz when pushed with those fingers. By combining Ernie Ball light-gauge strings for the high *E* and *B*, and Picato light-gauge for the remaining strings, he's found a set that is comfortable for both chording and solo playing. Strings are changed twice a week and never right before a performance. Iommi feels that leaving them on any longer causes the strings to wear out over the frets, making them virtually impossible to tune.

A very percussive player, Tony hits the strings in his pick attack. He uses custom-made picks which are fashioned after normal Fender picks in shape, but which lie between the thin and medium weights in gauge.

Iommi explains that Black Sabbath tunes to a *D* onstage instead of the customary tuning to get more depth. "That's one of the reasons why I don't like using thick-gauge strings," he adds, "because when I bend the strings they'll rip my bloody fingers apart. On acoustics I like lightweight gauge strings as well, because I can get a nice sound from them."

Onstage, Tony uses no pedals at the present time, not so much from a religious dislike as for a pragamatic reason: He feels they do more harm than good. Because the band tours the United States so frequently, they must contend with the different systems of grounding. In England, their Laney amplifiers give maximum performance, but over here the different ground setup causes the stacks to hiss and growl and perform below average. Therefore, adding any sort of extra unit to the line causes extraneous buzzes. In England, Tony uses a wah-wah and a mini guitar Moog, but found that using them in America caused a significant drop in amplifier power and sound. The group is now searching for an American-made system which won't plague them with those problems.

In the meantime, to accommodate for the ill-performance of his Laney stacks in the U.S., Tony must set his amplifiers on full volume. The "presence," "middle," and "treble" are also on 10 with no bass on the amp whatsoever. The guitar volume is usually set on full because of the constant thundering chords he hammers out, and the three-way toggle switch ("rhythm," "middle," and "lead") is placed on the up position for chording and in the treble spot for soloing. In the studio Iommi uses these same settings, but only one 100-watt Laney stack. For a particular solo, though, occasionally he'll use a Fender amplifier. On record Tony delves into effects a little more than onstage, as on *Sabbath, Bloody Sabbath*, when he used a wah-wah, a Rotosound box (which makes the guitar sound like an organ), and various other boosters and phasers.

— Steve Rosen

TONY IOMMI: A SELECTED DISCOGRAPHY

With Black Sabbath (all on Warner Bros.): *Black Sabbath,* WS 1871; *Paranoid,* BSK 3104; *Master Of Reality,* BS 2562; *Vol. 4,* BS 2602; *Sabbath, Bloody Sabbath,* BS 2695; *Sabotage,* BS 2822; *We Sold Our Soul For Rock 'N Roll,* 2BS 2923; *Technical Ecstasy,* BS 2969; *Heaven And Hell,* BSK 3372; *Never Say Die,* BSK 3186; *Mob Rules,* BSK 3605; *Live Evil,* 1-23742.

Gary Moore

A solo artist with stints in Skid Row, Thin Lizzy, and Colosseum to his credit, Gary was on a U.S. tour when *Guitar Player* interviewed him for this September 1980 feature. Afterwards, Gary appeared on a project with Greg Lake and released a couple of albums and an EP under his own name.

the artist

Over half of Gary Moore's life has been spent with the guitar as its focal point. At 27, the native of Belfast, Northern Ireland, is one of Great Britain's best-known rock guitarists. Starting his career as a member of the late-'60s heavy metal trio Skid Row, Gary has in the past decade toured and recorded with Thin Lizzy, recorded with composer Andrew Lloyd Webber [who co-wrote *Jesus Christ Superstar* and *Evita*], and helped to resurrect the British jazz-blues amalgamation Colosseum. His debut solo album, *Back On The Streets*, contained the song "Parisienne Walkways," which was an English Top-10 hit in 1979; the same year Moore was chosen one of the top guitarists in the *Melody Maker Magazine* readers' poll. Currently, Gary is touring with his latest group, Moore (with bassist Tony Newton, drummer Mark Nauseef, and vocalist Willie Dee), and with them he has recorded one album, *G Force*.

The oldest of five children, Gary was constantly exposed to music through records. His mother sang on occasion, but the lad's real link to music was his father, who promoted ballroom dances featuring seven- or eight-piece bands throughout Northern Ireland. Gary first experienced the excitement of live music when he tagged along with his dad to some of the clubs: "I was bitten by the music bug when I was only five," he says. "And when I was six, my dad asked me if I'd like to get up with the band and sing a song. I said, 'Sure,' so he put me up on a chair — so that I could reach the microphone —and I sang 'Sugartime.' I really enjoyed that, so I went with my dad as often as he'd let me. As far as I was concerned, those bands were the *end*."

The desire to play guitar came to Gary when he was about ten years old, but only after his father asked him if he was interested. The boy was unsure that he would really be able to play; nonetheless, he said he was game. His reluctance was rooted in the bad experience he had with piano lessons when he was seven years old. "My teacher was too strong on discipline and not strong enough on music," he recalls. "After a few weeks of getting my knuckles rapped, I quit."

Gary's dad bought a £10 Framus acoustic with a cello-shaped body. "The body was about *this* big," Moore jokes, with both arms outstretched. "It was absolutely *huge*, and everyone used to laugh when they saw me with it. The action was so bad that there was at least a time zone between the strings and the fingerboard."

Young Moore set to work right away — without knowing how to tune his new instrument — and learned Hank Marvin's solo from "Wonderful Land" by the Shadows. He later found out that he was playing everything in the wrong positions, due to his mistuning of the instrument. A friend set him straight, and Gary began devouring songs by nearly all of the day's popular groups. "I found that I could play just about anything I heard," he says, "but my favorite songs were by the Shadows. After spending my first years learning their songs, I thought it was thrilling to hear them do my song, 'Parisienne Walkways,' on a TV show last year."

Because of his earlier experience with the piano teacher and his realization that his ear was a good guide, Moore never took guitar lessons. By the time he was 12, he was playing in bands, emulating the Beatles musically and by wearing matching clothes. He says, "Even though we were just kids, we worked hard at it, and won some local talent shows."

The need for amplification arose, and Gary's dad came to the rescue; he bought a £5 Hofner pickup to attach onto Gary's Framus. All the while, Gary was eyeing a flamingo pink Fender Stratocaster that was in the window of a local music store. He would spend hours in front of the shop, staring at the guitar, although he never went inside to try it.

Moore got his first electric when he traded the Framus toward a Vox Clubman, which he used for about six months. It, too, featured almost impossible action, as did his next instrument — a Rosetti Lucky Squire. "That one looked a lot like a Gretsch," he says. "It was a big hollowbody with painted-on f-holes. The strings were very stiff, and I didn't know any better; nobody ever let me play their guitars. When I finally got the chance to try someone else's, I just zoomed over the fingerboard. And here I had been learning Jeff Beck solos on those impossibly heavy strings. I don't feel too bad, though; I still have strong hands from playing on those awful guitars."

The Lucky Squire served Gary well until he was about 14. One night, after returning from a break between sets, he picked up his guitar, only to find the back had fallen off — apparently someone had treated it roughly during his short absence: "I said, Oh, well. It looks like dad's going to have to get me another guitar." Gary's next guitar was a 1966 Fender Telecaster that his father purchased on an installment plan. "I sort of conned him into getting it for me," Gary confesses. "He said that if I joined a show band called Dave And The Diamonds, he would keep up the weekly installments. I stayed with them a short while, and then I took the bass player and drummer and formed a power trio. So, at 16 I left for Dublin, and my dad was still making the payments. A while later I traded the Telecaster for a Gibson SG."

In Dublin, the band picked up Phil Lynott — later Thin Lizzy's founder and bassist — as a singer, but the band quickly evolved into a primarily instrumental ensemble, and Lynott quit. As a three-piece known as Skid Row, Gary and his associates gigged almost incessantly. They soon became popular enough to share the stage with big-name groups from England and abroad. After a concert with the old Fleetwood Mac, Gary was told by the emcee that Peter Green (Fleetwood Mac's guitarist then) wanted to meet him. "I couldn't believe it," Moore states. "He has been one of my big heroes ever since he was with John Mayall. So I met Peter, and we got to be good friends. He liked my playing, and convinced Fleetwood Mac's manager to sign us up and get things happening for us in England."

Gary and Peter Green got together occasionally to jam, mostly without amps in hotel rooms after gigs. "I was really over the moon abut it," Moore says. "Then in early '70, I was talking with Peter and he said that the band was driving him nuts — he wanted to quit music altogether. He was tired of all the ego-tripping and glamour, and he started getting rid of all his possessions that he associated with stardom."

Peter sold his sunburst '59 Les Paul to Gary for about $200.00, even though it was worth far more. And to Moore, Green's guitar was the ultimate instrument; he had admired it since he was 14. Gary sold his SG-style Les Paul in order to get the money to buy the guitar, and once it was in his possession, he never let it out of his sight. "I lived in a pretty bad area, and my apartment didn't even have a decent lock on its door," he recalls. "So I took the guitar everywhere I went. It's a really great instrument, and I still use it quite a bit."

In England, Skid Row recorded two albums with MCA Records: *Skid* and *34 Hours*. The first of the two, *Skid* entered the British charts at number 30 — encouraging to the band and the record company. But just as the group was picking up momentum in Britain, they were sent on a tour of the U.S. Consequently, their record dropped off the charts in the U.K. Gary reminisces: "We found that we did have a small following in the States, but we were also booked into some pretty weird places. We got to Los Angeles, didn't have any time to sleep, and had to play at the Whisky club that night. It was the first of five gigs there. And the place was packed with aging film director types trying to pick up on young chicks. There were soul dancers, and everyone thought we were too loud — they couldn't hear the glasses clinking together. We weren't that loud. I had my SG and a couple of Hi-watt amps and a Cry Baby wah-wah pedal. Luckily, San Francisco was more receptive."

Skid Row played three nights in San Francisco's Fillmore West, sharing the bill with Frank Zappa. Gary was impressed by the fact that Zappa's band did a different set each night, whereas Moore was relieved that they were able to hold together a solid hour of material. It was also Gary's introduction to more complex forms of music. "I had never heard anything like that before — kind of a jazz-rock style. Their phrasings and instrumentation were years ahead of people like John McLaughlin and Return To Forever. And although it wasn't the same type of music, it was certainly of the same quality."

Shortly after returning to England, Skid Row released a second album; this time the response was less than enthusiastic. Compounding the band's problems, they were booked into oversized halls, and were always being sent on tour in other places just as they were starting to make headway with audiences in one area. Realizing that the situation was deteriorating for Skid Row, Gary left in 1971 to form his own group, the Gary Moore Band. Plagued by personnel problems throughout its two-year existence, the Gary Moore Band produced one album, *Grinding Stone*, and broke up.

As if by fate, Eric Bell quit Thin Lizzy, leaving the guitarist's post vacant. Gary joined them for their 1974 tour. "We practiced for about six hours, and then went out on the road," he says. "After about four months of burning myself out with them, I left. I wanted to do something a little more rewarding musically, so in mid '74 I got in touch with [drummer] Jon Hiseman, who was talking about re-forming Colosseum. We got together soon after and formed Colosseum II."

At first, Colosseum II consisted of Moore, two members of the original Colosseum — drummer Hiseman and bassist Mark Clarke — keyboardist Don Airey, and vocalist Mike Starrs. As time passed, the group changed slightly, and Clarke was replaced by Neil Murray; Starrs left and wasn't replaced.

The material became progressively more complex —just the challenge that Gary had been looking for — but because he was showing up at many rehearsals drunk or high, the guitarist was starting to make too many mistakes, and in turn was making the sessions a waste of time for everyone. "Jon Hiseman tossed me up against the wall one day," Gary explains, "and said, 'Listen, if you keep doing this, you won't be working with me anymore. So straighten up or forget it!' He was older than me, and I really respected him — I looked up to him — and I took his advice. He scared me, and I've kept music and everything else separate ever since."

With a jazz-rock instrumental format firmly established, Colosseum II took to the road, amassing a large following in Europe, especially Germany. MCA Records released three albums by the band: *Strange New Flesh, Wardance,* and *Electric Savage*. And from 1975 to 1977, the record company was patient with the group's marginal album sales. But finally they began putting pressure on Colosseum II to produce music that was more marketable. It was then that Gary decided to leave the group.

Soon after his departure from Colosseum II, Moore once again found himself touring with Thin Lizzy — this time for three months — as a replacement for Brian Robertson, who had injured his hand. As the tour was winding up, he was asked to rejoin Colosseum in order to promote the *Electric Savage* album. After that tour in early 1978, the band broke up.

One project that Gary worked on with Don Airey and Jon Hiseman (as well as keyboardist Rod Argent and a number of other musicians) was entitled *Variations*. Written by Andrew Lloyd Webber, it included many tricky parts, all of which were written out in advance. Although Gary couldn't read the music, he had others play his lines, and by listening a few times he was able to learn his parts. "I was the only one on the entire session who couldn't read music," he says, "but in many ways it helped. I often had my parts memorized before others had finished reading through theirs. It wasn't *all* easy, though. There were some really hard sections that called for elaborate counterpoint and unison work between the bass and guitar."

Gravitating once more to Thin Lizzy in 1978, Gary not only toured with the group, but contributed to the entire *Black Rose* LP, playing dual leads with Scott Gorham. In sections where solos by individual guitarists were called for, the two guitarists tended to stay with tempos that they felt most comfortable with, thereby giving the music its most natural feel. Gary explains that it was sometimes advantageous to do some of the doubled lines himself: "On the song 'Black Rose' I did both parts because it would have taken longer to show him the lines than to do them myself. There were a lot of fast-moving thirds and octaves between the two solos, and it was hard enough for me to keep it together."

Moore is a firm believer in spontaneity in solos, citing the rhythm of the drums as an excellent sparkplug for explosive lines: "I prefer playing along with a good drummer on the rhythm tracks so that I can punctuate my runs according to his accents. And I make it a point to use modal lines and extensions, such as flat 3rds and 9ths — anything to make my solos stand out. I want to sound *different*, to express some individuality. To do so, I try to avoid the obvious notes as much as possible. After all, there are millions of combinations you can play along with any chord."

With Thin Lizzy, Moore used his '59 Les Paul and a Stratocaster with a couple of 100-watt Marshall amps. In the studio he also used an Ovation Custom Legend acoustic. His effects as well as his guitars have changed since leaving the group again in mid 1979 to pursue his own career. Onstage with the band he used a Colorsound Overdriver [distortion unit] and an Echoplex, choosing to keep his setup simple. Now he has a slightly larger array of effects, many of which were used on his *Back On The Streets* and *G Force* LPs. These include an MXR Flanger/Doubler, and MXR Stereo Chorus, a DOD Overdriver, and Eventide's Digital Delay and Harmonizer. He says, "It's only natural to want to expand the range of sounds that one can get from a guitar, but at the same time you must keep the guitar sound from being lost entirely. I love the sound of the guitar straight through the amp, so I try to use my effects sparingly."

Besides his sunburst Les Paul, Gary has a Les Paul Junior and a Gibson ES-345. He also has a pair of Strat-type guitars made by Charvel out of extremely heavy hardwoods. One has a bright red metal flake finish; the other has a leopard-skin pattern on it. "The leopard-skin one is made out of purple hardwood," he explains, "and therefore weighs almost as much as a bass. It's worth it, though, because it gives a great sustain."

On all of his guitars Moore uses Ernie Ball strings gauged [high to low] .010, .013, .017, .030, .042, and .052. And with every one of his guitars he uses either Fender heavy or Herco gray nylon picks — sometimes in conjunction with his fingers.

Because of his associations with rock and jazz-rock bands over the years, Moore has been categorized differently almost every time he has appeared on record or stage. He believes that typecasting any artist is a terrible imposition on their talents. "Say if you're a rock guitarist and suddenly everyone calls you a jazz-rock player, where do they put your records?" he asks. "Usually in with the jazz albums! And there you are, in with John Coltrane and Charles Mingus. It's an honor, but most of the people looking for the album by someone who has always been called a rock player won't look in the jazz section of a record store. It's a problem everywhere, but unfortunately that's the way it is."

Just as other styles of music have interested Gary Moore, so have other instruments and their exponents. He has listened extensively to keyboardists such as Chick Corea and Jan Hammer, citing their technical abilities and high degree of training as reasons enough for guitarists to be interested in different approaches. "Keyboard players tend to be better trained than most rock guitarists," he says, "and they also have ten fingers to produce notes with. Listening to other instrumentalists will surely make you a better player. But if you only listen to other guitarists, you'll end up sounding like everyone else. You need variety."

— Tom Mulhern

GARY MOORE: A SELECTED DISCOGRAPHY

Solo Albums: *Back On The Streets*, Jet (dist. by CBS), NJZ-36187; *Corridors Of Power*, Virgin, V2245; *Grinding Stone*, Cosmos, 9004. **With Moore:** *G Force*, Jet, 229. **With Skid Row:** *Skid*, Epic, E 30852; *34 Hours*, Epic, E 30913. **With Colosseum II:** *Strange New Flesh*, Bronze (dist. by Warner Bros.), ILPS 9356; *Wardance*, MCA 2310; *Electric Savage*, MCA 2294. **With Other Artists:** *Black Rose*, (w. Thin Lizzy), Warner Bros., BSK 3388; *Nightlife*, (w. Thin Lizzy), Vertigo, VEO-2002; *Peter And The Wolf*, (w. Robin Lumley and Jack Lancaster), RSO, RS-1-3001; *Variations*, (w. Andrew Lloyd Webber), MCA, MCF 2824.

■AMERICA TAKES UP THE GAUNTLET■

NIEL ZLOZOWER

Leslie West with Mountain

GEORGE POLAKOFF

Fueled by Leslie West's unforgettable playing on songs such as "Mississippi Queen," Mountain climbed to the top of the American metal heap in the early '70s. Leslie appeared on the cover of the April 1972 *Guitar Player.*

the artist

There is no mistaking Leslie West onstage. Hulking but easygoing, he is Mountain's dominant instrumental voice, and everyone in the band knows it. His forcefully visceral guitar playing provides the counterpoint for bassist Felix Pappalardi's schooled sophistication. Not a bad combination. As a booking agent in Los Angeles puts it, "Mountain is the first band in years that can get people off in the same magical way that Cream did."

Mountain has made the big time, so West can afford to relax a little by fooling around with his dog and four cats in the backyard of his country home in Woodstock, New York, or watching wrestling matches on TV with his wife in their London flat. But things haven't always been that easy.

West was born on October 22, 1945, in an Army hospital in Queens, New York. His father owned a rug cleaning company, and Leslie lived comfortably until his parents were separated. He spent a lot of time in the streets, but he was sparked with ambition when he saw Elvis Presley's notorious appearance on the Ed Sullivan show in the mid '50s. He wanted to learn to play the guitar like Elvis, so his grandfather bought him an old tenor guitar in a pawnshop. He learned three chords and played "Heartbreak Hotel" in a seventh grade talent show. But that wasn't the beginning of a professional career. "Playing three chords isn't really playing the guitar," he says.

After having attended more than ten private schools, West discontinued his formal education at the end of tenth grade. He tried making jewelry for a while and worked at odd jobs. With the proceeds from his bar mitzvah, he was able to put together the money to buy an electric guitar, and not long afterward he saw the Beatles in New York on their first tour. That inspired him to form the Vagrants, his first professional band. At that time he was playing a musty, scratched Telecaster. But to go along with his professional status, he wanted a shiny, new guitar, so he traded the Fender in on a Kent, a decision he has regretted ever since.

The Vagrants played the usual club tunes, like "Respect" and "Midnight Hour," in the usual clubs. They filled out their gigs by working "sweet sixteens" — private birthday parties given by parents in honor of their teenage daughters. The band was paid an average of $100 to perform at the parties, but, Leslie recalls, "It came out to about $3 a man after we got finished paying for the dinner jackets and everything."

During one stretch in a New York club, West and the Vagrants met the Rascals, who were playing a job down the street. "We thought we were better than the Rascals until we saw them live," West remembers. The Rascals introduced Leslie to an agent who helped the Vagrants put together two demo tapes and, ultimately, negotiate a contract with Atlantic. Cream producer Felix Pappalardi was called in to produce both sides of a single for the band. Later, West left the Vagrants and made arrangements for a solo album (titled *Mountain*) that Pappalardi also agreed to work on. Once the album was completed, Pappalardi left for England to produce a record with Cream bassist Jack Bruce. West decided that he wanted to get together more permanently with Pappalardi. As a result, Mountain (named after West's debut album) was formed in late 1969 when the bass player returned to New York.

"It wasn't until I saw the Cream live that my head really got turned around," says West. "The Vagrants were into smashing their equipment and playing games and trying to act like the Who. Then I saw Clapton, and that did it. I thought I'd better shit or get off the pot."

Unlike most rock guitar players who look for their roots in the blues, West was most influenced by Presley, Clapton, Keith Richards, and Peter Townshend of the Who, his all-time favorite band. He recognizes the importance of pop music and rock and roll in the formation of his own dynamic, hyper-amplified style. At a time when rock has turned in a mellow, lyrical direction, Mountain has kept the energy and drive of high volume, merging it with the subtlety of classical and jazz motifs.

When touring with Mountain, West plays three guitars — a Les Paul Junior, a Flying V, and a Plexiglas Dan Armstrong. He had the Flying V dismantled and a Les Paul pickup installed in place of the old treble pickup; he uses the leftover space as an ashtray. If the Les Paul Junior gets wet from perspiring hands during a set, he uses the Flying V for "Mississippi Queen," Mountain's encore number. The Armstrong is strictly for bottleneck.

Because West liked the distortion provided by tube amplifiers, he used Marshall and Sunn amps early in his career. "I was over in Germany doing this TV show, and this guy had some amps there. I tried them out and gave him some advice about changing a few things, like the speakers," he says. Those amps, the Stramp brand, will soon be available on the market as the Leslie West Professional Series. Onstage and in the studio he uses two stacks of Stramp amplifiers to get a sound that he thinks is similar to Marshall amp distortion. West claims that one of the advantages of the Stramp amplifier is that it is less prone to "blowing up" than the Marshall: "My amps don't have a ground switch. I can't explain it to you, but I have a funny feeling that is why they don't blow up. Those amps feel like little bulldogs."

The Stramp amplifiers have 100-watt brains and metal grilles to prevent the 12" Celestian speakers from being punctured. Interested musicians will ultimately be able to order Stramp amplifiers that will be exactly the same in all details as the ones used by West during live performances. Guitar players often order amps used by professionals because of the sound the professionals get with the equipment. What they don't realize, West says, is that the equipment has been modified, and they wind up with amplifiers from the factory that don't sound the same.

Much of West's sound comes from his hands: "When I use a pick — and I use one most of the time — I try to bury it between my thumb and first finger and just let a

RONN GREENMAN
Mountain onstage: Leslie West with bassist Felix Pappalardi.

little bit of the corner stick out. I can make a string jump harmonics that way. Albert King does that without using a pick; he uses his thumb. It really is a great sound, because if I'm playing along like, say, on the *B* string and all of a sudden I want a note that will really stick out and be an important part of the phrase, I can make a note jump an octave. It is really effective." A good example of West's ringing harmonic technique is the last note of his solo in the middle section of "Theme For An Imaginary Western" [*Mountain*].

West rests the side of his right-hand palm on the bridge of the guitar or on strings that he is not picking, but his picking technique seldom allows his hand to remain in a stationary position for very long. Along with the pick, he occasionally uses his third finger for double picking, and says he wants to work on developing the use of his fourth finger to aid in multi-string picking. Leslie uses La Bella and D'Arco strings, though one of Mountain's roadies puts them on the guitars. The top three are La Bella extra light, while the bottom three are D'Arco .045, .035, and .028.

For Mountain's album *Flowers Of Evil,* West used a hammering technique with his left hand that produced what he describes as a "violin sound — like what Segovia does. You can do it in rock and roll too." He hammers on a string and then turns up the volume of the guitar. The metallic sound of the string rattling against the fretboard is never amplified, and Leslie can control the intensity of the whining sound by adjusting the guitar's volume knob. He created the instrumental prelude to "Pride And Passion" by tuning every string to a single note, or that note's octave, and then playing the instrument bottle-neck-style through an echo unit. "It sounds like a string section. I figured that if I can make a guitar sound like a violin, why not make it sound like a couple of violins?" The same technique on the low strings produces a cello sound. West says that he doesn't like to use echo units onstage because one of the by-products is a hissing sound at high levels.

During the guitar solo of the "Dream Sequence" cut on *Flowers Of Evil*, West sustains a single note for a long period of time without any noticeable fade. "The note catches, man," he says. "There is a feeling you get; you can feel as soon as you hit the note if it is going to go into that sustain. You can hold it for days if your guitar is wide open." To do this he combined a harmonic with the distortion produced by his guitar set at full volume. He claims he can get that same ringing sustain with his Stramp amplifiers set as low as 2 or 3.

West hasn't used a fuzz device in four years, and he gets vibrato strictly through the natural control of his fingers and wrist. "Vibrato is all in control; it's like a voice, you know. Some opera singers control their voice to get that slow vibrato. Eric Clapton has got about the best vibrato I ever heard in my life. Hendrix and Mick Taylor have beautiful vibratos, too. I'd take these guys over anybody else because they control the whole thing. Some guitar players hit a note and go into a vibrato that's really fast and intense with no control, and it sounds like an opera singer with a bad voice."

So far, West is satisfied with his role in Mountain: "On the *Flowers Of Evil* album I got into Felix's songwriting more. There are a lot of things I can learn from playing his tunes — things that are difficult and new to me." The chord structures and tempo changes of Mountain's music are often sophisticated and demand high levels of musicianship, as shown in the recurrent theme riffs that West plays in "King's Chorale." And he picks it all up by ear. When Pappalardi writes a tune that he wants West to learn, he makes up a simple lettered chord chart with the number of beats per chord. Within that context West is free to devise his own phrasing, and he is capable of compositions ranging from the classical lines of "King's Chorale" to the Claptonesque blues embellishments of "Crossroader."

"To tell you the truth, man, I don't know the names of the chords I play," Leslie says. "I got the chord book that *Guitar Player* magazine sent me, but it didn't do a bit of good. I can't read music; I can't even look at a chord positioning in a book and play it." But that never bothered West when he was getting his licks together. "I would listen to records or listen to someone play the guitar, and also watch somebody fingering the guitar. Then by feel I'd copy it by pretending I had a guitar in my hand. If you've got the will, you can learn anything."

—Fred Stuckey

MARK MAC LAREN

Leslie West's Guitar School

When Mountain splintered in 1972, Leslie West and drummer Corky Laing enlisted bassist Jack Bruce to form West, Bruce & Laing. The lineup lasted a year, after which Mountain briefly re-formed. West continued on as a solo artist in the mid '70s, touring and releasing albums until ill health forced him to retire. Little was heard from him until 1980, when he opened a Manhattan guitar school called Leslie West Guitar. In this October '80 feature, Leslie describes his playing techniques and views on teaching rock guitar. West toured with a reconstituted Mountain lineup in 1982 and 1983.

* * * *

Leslie West. To fans of late-'60s and early-'70s rock and roll, the name conjures images of "Mississippi Queen" and huge stadium audiences staring open-mouthed at the large-bodied, whiskey-voiced figure pulling raw, fast-fingered solos out of a Gibson Les Paul Junior. His voice, wicked vibrato, and distinctively clean, harmonic-laden leadwork were the instantly identifiable trademarks of two headliner heavy metal bands — Mountain, and West, Bruce & Laing. West became as well-known for his long improvisational jams with bassists Felix Pappalardi and Jack Bruce as he was for his extended, one-man-onstage showcase solos that blended violin effects, wide feedback, and blistering runs. Along with Pete Townshend, Jimi Hendrix, Alvin Lee, and Carlos Santana, Leslie was one of the guitar heroes who shared the stage at Woodstock in 1969, and his playing is preserved full-force on 15 albums. More than ten years after Woodstock and the rise of Mountain, Leslie has returned to his New York birthplace to open Leslie West's Guitar, a rock and roll guitar school located on the city's upper East Side.

For students, the school represents a rare chance to have one-on-one tutoring from a rock giant. For Leslie it has brought a new hold on life and a renewed energy for his art: "I was fed up with touring and that whole thing of fighting after having made all those albums. I didn't really want to go back and try to do it all again. Financially, no amount of money in the world could have been worth what I had gone through mentally and physically after Mountain, West, Bruce & Laing and all that stuff ended. I was killing myself between the touring, the drugs, the lifestyle — everything. I used to think that you had to be on the charts and happening to feel like you're right there. But I'm playing more now than I've ever played in my life. I'm getting calluses again, and I've learned a lot of different techniques and tricks.

"There are a lot of guitarists who have names, but I don't think there are too many who would all of a sudden do something like open a school. I don't know if their egos would allow it. But I found out that the only thing that was stopping me was being afraid of failing, because who likes to fail after you've been successful once? Then I asked myself, 'Okay, so if I fail, what's the worst thing that can happen?' And when I found out that the worst thing would be that it failed, it wasn't so bad. *Big deal!* I looked at it like a song, and I had a lot of songs that failed. I thought of all the things I learned and what it's taken to learn them, and the only thing that it's really taken for most of them is experience. The school's going great. I've got almost as many students as I can handle, about 40 a week. I've discovered that the more I learn, the more I've got to learn. And I've learned from so many of these kids."

At the time of his first *Guitar Player* story, Leslie had played on three Mountain albums — *Mountain Climbing, Nantucket Sleighride,* and *Flowers Of Evil* — in addition to his 1969 solo debut, *Leslie West — Mountain,* and appearances on *Woodstock II* and *The First Great Rock Festivals Of The Seventies.* Soon afterwards, he quit Mountain and formed the power trio West, Bruce & Laing with Jack Bruce (previously of Cream) and Corky Laing. The group's first album, *Why Don'tcha,* came out in late 1972. Two more records followed — *Whatever Turns You On* and *Live 'N Kickin'* — before they broke up in 1973. Leslie worked briefly with Leslie West's Wild West Show before reforming Mountain in 1974. The band released a double live LP recorded in Japan, *Twin Peaks,* and a studio effort, *Avalanche,* before their final demise.

West embarked on a solo career with the release of *The Great Fatsby* in 1975. He was back on the road soon afterwards with his own band and recorded *The Leslie West Band.* Mick Jones, currently lead guitarist for Foreigner, played second guitar on the LP.

West then gave up playing and moved to Milwaukee with his partner, Charles Gottlieb, for two years. "I went to clean out my mind and body," he explains. "I took a cure for drugs, and I didn't even want to see a guitar. Then I was in Atlanta and a guy brought me an Electra MPC guitar. All of a sudden I said, 'Wow!' It was a little bit different from the Les Paul Juniors I had been playing all those years, and it excited me about playing guitar again. That's what started me back. I started working for St. Louis Supply Company, developing the MPC and the Crate amp. I got involved with the end of the business I was never in before." Leslie began playing again, although he felt he wasn't ready to record. He moved to Santa Cruz, California, to start a band with guitarist Steve Marriott. The group fell through when Marriott rejoined Humble Pie, and West returned to New York City and began playing with the Davis Jaynes Band.

One night while performing with Jaynes, Leslie was approached by a fan who wanted to learn a few leads. This encounter led West to develop his idea for Leslie West's Guitar. He ran two small ads in New Jersey's *Aquarian* newspaper and New York's *Village Voice* announcing the creation of the school. Within a week he had received over 200 calls from interested students. Currently Leslie handles five or six private students a day. Here he shares his views on teaching rock guitar.

— Jas Obrecht

the dialog

The first thing I ask students is how long they have been playing. Usually kids who have been at it anywhere from two to five years are almost in the same category, and you need something to start with. I ask every student what his or her goal is right now and explain, "What you get out of this is what you put in. I can *show* you how to play guitar; I can't *teach* you how to play. I can teach you how to teach yourself." If they can't learn from me, they can't learn from anyone, since what I play isn't complex. I can only play simply. I still can't play lead with all four fingers of my left hand. I just use the first and third.

A lot of kids out there who can't read music are too intimidated to say that they only know this much or that much. There's no reason for it, and I always say, "Here, we've got no egos. Nobody cares how good or how bad you are. You're learning here. There's a big difference between being here and going for an audition. When you go for an audition the saying 'Opportunity needs preparation' really comes through, but when you come to my studio, you're coming to learn. It's a different story."

There's no reason to impress me, and it usually takes them the first session to get over the fact that they're relating to a recording or playing-on-the-road artist. As soon as that's out of the way, boy, we get into some serious playing.

The whole session is tape recorded on my Toshiba microsystem, and the student gets to keep the cassette after the class. Luckily, the machine is perfect for what I'm doing. Since it records stereo, the student comes out of one side and I am on the other. I use headphones with it, so we can get a perfect balance in the cans [headphones]. If the guy wants to hear himself louder than me, he can control that. I like to hear myself very low. If you overdrive the mike channels, you get the same effect that you get overdriving an amp — that distorted sound, only at a lower level. We can record two guitars, play it back, and learn how to add a bass line. You can even put on a prerecorded tape, like something by Eric Clapton, and play along with it to see where you're at. The students can use these tapes as their memories, so when they are with me they can just play instead of having to try to remember everything. When we are through I usually talk for about 15 minutes, and I open up the mike so they get this as well.

I've had to adapt to everybody, and I don't force what I know on someone. Everything is geared to the individual. Some people just want to improve so they're happier with themselves. Others want something specific. There's a guy and a girl in a new wave group who come over to learn how to write songs. The guy's playing was real limited — maybe four or five chords — but he knew them in a lot of positions on the neck. So I'm having him work on learning more chords, and I can't take the lessons as far as I could with somebody who's really into

PAUL NATKIN/PHOTO RESERVE

playing lead. Another kid came in and told me he was a cellist learning guitar. I worked with his vibrato more than anything else, since on a cello you go from side to side and on the guitar you usually go up and down.

Another guy is taking guitar and singing lessons. Now, I don't teach singing because I don't feel confident with it. When I have a guitar in my hand, I feel confident. When I'm singing, I don't. I thought that singing was something I had to do to go along with the guitar. What I can show him is how to use the guitar and his voice so they work together. I tell him not to cover up any of his vocals and to play in the holes, and I show him how to phrase his singing so it matches his guitar playing. One kid was having loads of trouble controlling the feedback on his guitar. Onstage that guitar is like a live animal, and when you open it up all the way, it squeals. So I took the kid to a studio, set up a couple of my stacks, and let him play through them for a couple of hours. And boy, he learned how to control it.

I will teach students anything I've learned as a guitarist. I wouldn't say, "Well, I ain't gonna show you how to do that." There are actually guitarists who won't show you their best licks because they're afraid. They want to keep them for themselves. If you can't come up with any more than those licks, who wants to learn them anyway? And everybody seems to want the quick way of learning. There is no quick way of learning to play lead guitar the way it should be done; I'm talking about the Mick Taylors, Eric Claptons, Jimi Hendrixes, and Peter Greens. And people don't understand that lead guitar does not necessarily mean one note at a time. Keith Richards rhythms are, to me, some of the greatest leads ever recorded. Same with Pete Townshend.

Lead guitar is sort of like a foreign language if you don't know it. And you could learn that language with a lot of different accents. Like in parts of London you have an accent, and in another part of England you have another type, and then you've got Liverpool and Cockney. Well, you can play the guitar with all kinds of different accents. I tell students to pick their favorite guitarists and listen to them before they go to sleep. If you listen to them over and over and over for a couple of weeks, you'll pick up the attitudes those guitarists have.

Right now Eddie Van Halen is the top. It seems like every kid wants to learn his licks. He's right up there where Clapton was years ago. The kids have a hero today. I have one student who does this Van Halen thing that sounds like a Bach organ fugue, and he said that his band told him that if he plays it in one more song, he's out. He sticks it in every song in the set. He asked me if I could show him another solo. I said no. First of all, I'd have to take my time to stop and figure it out, and I have better things to do than figure out someone else's solos. I did say I'd show him how he could come up with his own solo, and that's what we did. I have to have somebody who's receptive to this kind of idea.

There are four things I immediately try to teach about solo construction: the entrance, tone, building the solo, and how it's going to end. Keith Moon, who was the drummer for the Who, used to say, "Remember, mate, they remember your entrance and your exit. Everything else in the middle don't mean a goddamn thing. Just make sure your entrance is great and your exit is great."

While this isn't completely true, it says a lot. There really is a thought process to soloing. Whether it's an overdub in the studio or something onstage, playing a solo is all the same thing. It's something, a statement. It's a song within a song. It's not just, "Time for a solo — oops, stick in any bunch of notes." Even if it's a hole you're filling between words, it should be played with the thought that after you're finished, something else is going to happen. Try to make it so the end of the solo will help the next section along.

The control of the vibrato is the most important thing. Forget about the tone, taste, and what notes to play for the time being — the vibrato is still the most misunderstood part of playing rock guitar, especially among young players. A lot of kids think it comes from their third finger; most of it comes from the wrist. I try to show them how to use all three fingers at once — index, middle, and third — to push the string up because that's where the power and control are. The fingers behind the note aren't going to affect the sound anyway. I let them grab hold of my wrist for about two minutes while I pick a note once and stretch it and bring it back several times. I find most kids throw the vibrato in before they even hit the note that they want. Say you want an *A*. They'll hit an *A* note, but waver it so much they won't even get it. They'll get *A*♭ and *A*♯. Many people don't realize that between the note you are hitting and the note you are stretching to, there is a whole spectrum of notes.

The vibrato in the left hand is like the tremolo in an opera singer's voice. Singers don't use vibrato with every note; they let it come in gradually. It seems like kids see guitarists at concerts and right away think you've got to move your fingers on the string. Not only do they not play the lead notes right, but they'll even stretch barre chords using vibrato in their fingers! Then the chord doesn't even come out the way it's supposed to. And when you're using light-gauge strings, you've got to be *precise* in what you're hitting. If you slip off the string and it jumps into another one, with the amount of sustain people are using today, it just ends up sounding like noise. And that's where we get our reputation for noise.

I have an exercise for developing vibrato that I try to have them practice at least half an hour a day. You do it without turning on your amp or using your picking hand. Take one note and push it up with those three fingers at once for vibrato, going very slowly. Push it up and pull it down, trying to build it up until you can go from slow to a little faster, and then still faster, all without stopping. The reason I say to do it with no sound is that when a kid first starts practicing it, it's going to sound lousy if he uses his amp. Why listen to it if it sounds bad? Just do the exercise, and then after a week, turn the amp on. All of a sudden you'll say, "Wow!"

Another problem rock guitarists have is with positions. When they finally learn you can play a solo in different positions than the one they've been using for however long, they're amazed. Most people go up to the 5th fret to do an *A* lead, and then up to the 12th for an *E* lead. There are places all over the fingerboard for leads.

The other thing kids want today is to be fast: "How fast can I be?" With new students I play a very simple, slow blues progression. I'll say to them immediately, "Listen to it first," because usually they'll start playing right away. How do they know what changes I want to go to? The first thing they're rying to do is show me all they know in 30 seconds, as many notes as they can hit. I'll say, "Okay, however fast you're gonna play, cut it in half. If you're thinking of four notes, think two. And then divide that in half again." Everybody seems to want to learn something at the speed they can hear it, thinking that's the only way.

I can almost get somebody to want to practice just by showing him that there is that little ray of hope. A lot of kids will struggle and can't get anything to satisfy them. They'll sit there shaking their heads, "Oh, I can't get it," and then rush and rush. You don't have to play a lick as fast as you've heard it. Learn it slowly, and then finally do it fast. Like when the CIA wants to dissect a tape, they slow it down and listen to exactly what's there. Well, it's the same principle with learning a new lick. Take your time. That word "patience" is so incredible.

I had one kid come in who was nothing but fast. He missed every other note he was going for, real quick. I started showing him something and he said, "Now Leslie, you're not going to ruin my style." And I said, "What style are you talking about?" He said, "Well, I'm known for playing fast." I said, "Has anybody told you how fast you play?" He said, "No." "Has anybody told you how great you play?" "No." "Has anybody ever asked you to play them another song?" "No." I said, "Then what style are we talking about? You don't have a style. Just playing fast doesn't mean anything." So to calm him down I taught him a very simple melodic line from Eric Clapton's "Wonderful Tonight," from the *Just One Night* album. I wanted him to hear the beauty of a simple lick, how pretty it sounds.

Believe it or not, about 90% of the kids playing rock and roll today don't know about playing something soft. Not so much soft in volume, but soft meaning that it's a warm tone, like when you play with the front bass pickup as opposed to the treble pickup. The treble pickup has a hotter, more biting tone. The front pickup has what Clapton used to call "the woman tone," a belly tone. As loud as you play it, it's still a warm tone. You can get the woman tone by taking all of the treble off the bass pickup, opening the volume wide, and getting a good sustain out of the amp. It makes you play differently than when you use a biting tone.

Another misconception people have is about equipment. Young kids who are impressionable will go out and spend a lot of money on an instrument. Then they come in and see me using a relatively inexpensive guitar: I use an MPC and a Crate amp, which is a great sounding, inexpensive amp. Right away they go, "What's he using that for?" Then when they hear the sounds that come out of it with the octave divider module and all of that, all of a sudden it's, "Wait a minute — maybe I can sell this guitar, and where can I get one of those?" They then think it's the guitar. I'll take their guitar from them and play the same lick. Then we turn the effects and amps off and I say, "Okay, just let me hear you play two notes and use the vibrato." For them it's something like being in Yugoslavia. They have no idea what it is to play two notes and just stretch the strings to different pitches. You know, they think you've got to spend thousands of dollars to sound good.

For years I've gone to Manny's Music Store in New York City, and he's got a little yellow and white old Silvertone guitar — an old Danelectro model. Everybody from Eric Clapton to George Harrison has offered him a lot of money for it. He uses it to check out amps, and it just lies around. You can make that guitar sound *good*, and it's really a cheap little guitar. I use this example to explain to students that you don't have to spend thousands of dollars for instruments. That's not going to make you play better. What's going to make you play better is practice.

I try to work with all of my students to set up good practice schedules. You know, if a guy says, "I come home at 6:00 and lay down and watch TV, and then my old lady comes home and we eat dinner," I say, "Well during the time she's not there . . ." If she's like my old lady, she won't like loud music all the time. Even I don't like loud music after I play a show. When you're alone you should practice. Take advantage of that time, because when somebody hassles you, you can't enjoy it. You need to be alone. Every time you pick the guitar up, try playing something you couldn't do yesterday. Try attempting something that you've never learned how to do, even if it's a classical piece. If you spend a little time working on unfamiliar things, you have no idea what may come out of it. If you get one good thing out of 20 tries, isn't it worth it? It's a good way to start your practice session.

At the end of my lessons I try to give students a couple of licks and a chord pattern and tell them to work out a solo around the changes or write a song. I don't care how lousy it is or if they use a couple of my ideas, as long as most of it is theirs. Other times I'll lay down a rhythm track and have them work out a solo for it. Getting them to do this on their own seems to help a lot.

Things are going so well right now my partner and I are working on taking rock guitar lessons to video disks and videotape and going on cable TV. They used to have an early morning flamenco guitar class on TV in New York City, and I used to ask myself, "Now who the hell gets up for this class except a friend of Montoya?" Now I ask, "Why are there no rock classes? Why is that eliminated?" It seems that people spend more money promoting rock and roll products and gadgets, trying to sell more guitars and amps, and yet no one wants to get up and say, "This is one way of doing it." I wish to God there had been something like this around when I was learning guitar. I hope to change all this.

— Leslie West

LESLIE WEST: A SELECTED DISCOGRAPHY

Solo albums: *Leslie West — Mountain,* Windfall, 4500; *The Great Fatsby,* Phantom, 0954; *The Leslie West Band,* Phantom, 1258. **With Mountain:** *Mountain Climbing,* Windfall, 5000; *Nantucket Sleighride,* Windfall, 5500; *Flowers Of Evil,* Windfall, 5501; *Twin Peaks,* Columbia, 32818; *Avalanche,* Columbia, 33088; *Best Of Mountain,* Columbia, 32079. **With West, Bruce & Laing:** *Why Don'tcha?,* Columbia, 31929; *Whatever Turns You On,* Columbia, 32216; *Live 'N Kickin',* Columbia, 32899. **Anthologies:** *Woodstock Two,* Cotillion, 2-400; *The First Great Rock Festivals Of The Seventies,* Columbia, 30805; *The Guitars That Destroyed The World,* Columbia, 31998.

Ted Nugent and the Amboy Dukes

A midwest institution long before becoming a coast-to-coast headliner, Ted Nugent was one of rock's original wildmen. He fought it out with other guitarists in glass-shattering battles of the bands, and toured incessantly with the Amboy Dukes between 1968 and 1975. Nugent went solo and signed with Epic a year before this November 1976 feature.

the artist

Assuming a fledgling guitarist with a hollowbody electric one day decided to devote his efforts exclusively to the heavy metal mode, the first thing he'd probably do would be either to buy a new instrument or stuff the f-holes of his guitar with sponge to dampen the feedback at high volume levels. Ted Nugent had other ideas. Leaving the body of his hollow Gibson Byrdland stock, Nugent set out not to eliminate the resulting barrage of feedback, but to tame it into a harmonic spectrum of screaming overtones.

It's the kind of unique approach to the instrument that makes this hard rocker an explosive original in the many-membered academy of high-energy guitaring. An 18-year-old Nugent, with his band the Amboy Dukes, first overcharged the radio waves in 1967 with a hit called "Journey To The Center Of Your Mind" [*Journeys And Migrations*] and thrilled audiences with feedback and stunts such as playing guitar with his teeth. Subsequent years, though, were commercially lean. But Nugent kept playing — averaging 200 gigs a year — and while perfecting his art produced some of rock's fiercest licks along the way. A dozen albums and a new band later, the guitarist, now 27, is again earning the national recognition and acclaim that eluded him for years, mainly though the success of a recent solo album entitled *Ted Nugent.*

Born and raised in the Detroit area, Ted got his first guitar at nine, courtesy of a forgetful airline passenger. "It was an acoustic thing with palm trees and coconuts painted on it," he recalls. His aunt, a stewardess, found the guitar on a vacant plane and forwarded it to Ted when nobody claimed it in the lost-and-found.

"I think I was so young when I started playing, I really didn't realize what I was getting into," Ted states. "At that point in life you're kind of flopping around aimlessly, and whatever you happen to latch onto, you pursue. So while everybody else was playing football, I was playing guitar. When I really realized guitar would be my profession was when I saw Elvis Presley on the Ed Sullivan show. I also watched Rick Nelson on *Ozzie And Harriet* all the time, and when I saw that guy [James Burton] playing that Telecaster, well . . . ."

Starting at age 11, Ted took lessons for two years: "I knew how to hold the guitar, use the pick, read music, and name all of the basic chords." He believes one of the most important things he gained from formal instruction was the teacher's emphasis on using the 4th finger of his left hand. "You might as well use everything you got," Nugent says. "If you don't, you're just cheating yourself."

By age 12, Ted was playing lead in a basic rock and roll band, working regularly at school dances and similar events. His first electric was "a great big fat Epiphone with one pickup." Later he used a Fender Duo-Sonic.

Through his teens, Nugent was impressed by several guitarists. "Big influences," he begins, "were Lonnie Mack, Chuck Berry, of course, and later Keith Richards. Lonnie Mack used to do all these solo things. He was fantastic, and he used to bend notes like crazy before most people even knew there was such a thing. I also sat down with Rolling Stones records and played them lick for lick. Only with Keith Richards did I ever do that. I was so young, I had nothing of my own. I had to have something to play."

When he was 16, Ted moved to Chicago and began giving guitar lessons out of his home to earn money to buy his first Gibson Byrdland, a single cutaway designed in 1955 by Billy Byrd and Hank Garland. Nugent had been haphazardly toying with feedback with the Epiphone, but it was the acquisition of the Byrdland in 1964 and the formation of the Amboy Dukes shortly thereafter that led him to incorporate it into his repertoire.

"It's not too sociable to play high-energy on a Byrdland," Ted remarks, "but Jimmy McCarty, Mitch Ryder's original guitar player, played a Byrdland, and he was so sensational that I was bent on playing it. I was also bent on playing loud. To do that you either have to eliminate the feedback characteristics—by buying a different guitar—or learn to control it. I started putting the feedback to good use."

Mastering the hollowbody Gibson with as much as 400 watts on the other end of the guitar cord is no easy proposition, so Nugent through the years has refined his equipment design and playing technique to a science.

Ted made only minor changes on the Byrdland itself. He currently owns five of them that were built in the late '50s and early '60s, his favorite being a 1964 sunburst. All the guitars have two stock humbucking pickups. Nugent has adjusted all the pickup posts flush with the cover plate and brought both units up closer to the strings. "For some reason it sounds better that way," he explains. "Maybe bringing the entire pickup — having the second set of coils closer — somehow adds to the fullness of the response." Ted also has filed down all the saddles on the bridge so there is, as he describes it, "the least necessary groove left capable of holding the string. This gives the string more resonance, since it is touching less metal, and the bridge saddle won't slow the string down." The only other modifications have been the installation of Schaller tuning mechanisms and the use of a Gretsch strap holder for a toggle switch, which affords a more solid handle for quick pickup changes in mid-song.

Nugent's amp stacks are designed with high-decibel output and the Byrdland's feedback characteristics in mind. Four Fender Twin Reverbs are connected in parallel through a junction box. Three Twins sit on top of — and are individually wired to — three cabinets holding two 15" SRO speakers. The fourth Twin drives a cabinet holding four 12" speakers. The stock 12s in the Twins have been replaced with Model 12 SROs and reinforced with wood braces under the magnets. Without the additional support, they tend to tear away from the face

A '60s promo shot of the Detroit-based Amboy Dukes.

board because of the weight of the larger magnets and increased vibration. Ted says he prefers the SRO replacements because they can take continual punishment. And though he plays full-out, he's replaced only five speakers in five years.

Concert settings call for the treble, bass, midrange, and volume controls on the Twins to be on 10 with the bright switch on. Though this results in a near merciless volume output, the sound of the setup is remarkably crisp and clear. (Nugent, it should be noted, wears a rubber-wax combination plug in his one ear that faces the amp and recommends similar precautions to aspiring high-energy guitarists.)

As to controlling the feedback from the Byrdland, Ted says it took years of practice and experimentation. He has found that only certain notes and strings will feed back at certain locations in front of the amps. "When one note feeds back in a certain spot," he says, "it will occupy all the acoustic area of that note, and no other note will be able to get in edgewise. I can catch an *A*-note feedback, step to the side two inches, and another note will kick in."

Ted began discovering this pheonomenon when he wrote the song "Journey To The Center Of Your Mind," which began its guitar solo with a long overtone. "When I had to perform it every night," he recalls, "I had to find the point to catch that hum. I used to put tape on the stage to mark the spots." Now, he says, he has all the areas mapped out in his mind. The stack of 12" speakers is used similarly. If he desires high-note overtones and sustain, for example, he'll move between the stack of 12s and cabinet of 15" speakers.

The Byrdland, however, will feed back just about everywhere, so Nugent employs a few more tricks to keep it at bay. When he's in front of the amps and playing slow, he'll mute the strings he is not playing with his left or right hand. This keeps them from being set into motion by the speaker signal, which is the first step towards most feedback. This is not easily done, however, through the speedy solos Ted often tackles. During rapid-fire work, he therefore stands in front of the drums, to the right of and away from the amps, to get the guitar away from a direct speaker signal.

Nugent uses no accessories in concert or on record, preferring instead to get special effects from the guitar itself. By taking his right hand and pressing on the strings between the bridge and tailpiece, he can get a vibrato-arm effect. While doing this, he'll also lightly touch a vibrating string up on the neck, causing it to form a screaming, high octave at the desired fret. Nugent also uses the volume control knobs while simultaneously striking a string — much as Roy Buchanan does — to get a crying sound. Ted also likes to mute chords or individual notes during a passage, alternating from clear tones to a thumping that sounds like a pile driver. For a contrasting effect, Nugent cuts back on the volume knob about two notches, transforming the Byrdland's response from raunchy rock to a sweet and mellow jazz sound. "That's one of the reasons I like the Byrdland so much," he says. "It's so damn versatile."

Nugent continues: "All too often I get this thing that I'm all noise and feedback and can't really play. I have to play loud to get that feel and to set up the dynamics.

There's a place for noise, a place for feedback, a place to be soft, a place for everything. It's just a matter of doing it with taste. Look at Jeff Beck. He's no super speedster. But he has great taste, and that's what makes him so good. For example, a singer doesn't just go *wa wa wa wa*. He goes *wa Wa wa Wa wa WA WA WA WA*. He hangs onto the notes, molds and changes them with vibrato and volume. That's what I try to do with guitar notes, so you cover more of the sound spectrum. When you play lead, you should be singing, changing tones, making it lyrical. If you do that, it will never get boring for the listener or yourself."

On basic guitar technique: Ted says he tries to approach the instrument in an all-encompassing frame of mind rather than consciously dividing execution into sub-categories. "I don't like to look at guitar from lead and rhythm — separate — standpoints," he elaborates. "Playing guitar consists of all these things. You're a total fool if you only learn to play lead. Leads have to have rhythm. Everything is based upon the rhythm, that *feel*. You have to play rhythm to be able to get any kind of decent feel of how a lead should be during a song."

Nugent believes the aggressiveness and violent nature of much of his music is therapeutic for both himself and the audience. "Everyone," he asserts, "has a form of positive aggression in them left over from when we had to hunt to survive. In the synthetic world of today, no one has an avenue to expose that aggression — unless they shoot people or beat their wife. That's bad. I get it out of my system by hammering on my guitar onstage. Those who come to a Nugent concert get it out with me. And that's good."

Ted says most of his solos are improvised on the spot, but within the form of the song. "I believe once a song is written into a structure, you play that structure," he explains. "But when it comes time to jam during the tune, I do something different every night."

As advice to beginners, Nugent offers this: "Practice, practice, practice. Practice until you get a guitar welt on your chest — *if* it makes you feel good. If you find you're working and not playing, go play basketball or something. But if it makes you feel good, don't stop until you see the blood from your fingers. Then you'll know you're on to something. Music is supposed to make you happy.

"Myself, I'm just really getting into it now. I've got unlimited realms to cover — still learning. I can play fast; I can play slow. I can play mean; I can play sweet. Now it's time to do it all better."

— Steve Rosen

Ted Nugent Solo

Nugent's decision to go solo proved wise. By the time of his August '79 cover story, nearly all of his Epic albums had gone platinum. 1978 alone produced two million-sellers: *Weekend Warriors* and *Double Live Gonzo,* one of the most successful concert albums in CBS history. Nugent released four more albums on Epic before signing with Atlantic in 1982 for *Nugent.*

an introduction

Ted Nugent tours a city the way Godzilla toured Tokyo. He plays very fast, very loud. "People come to my concerts just to lose weight," he huffs. "I tell 'em to sit up *real close* — makes their ears bleed; it's good for them. One time a pigeon — and this is true — a pigeon flew in front of my speakers and just literally *disintegrated,* man, just melted."

Nugent, a native of Detroit, was born in 1949. For ten years he led his bands — various incarnations of the Amboy Dukes — on legendary marathon concert campaigns, mostly through the Midwest and South. He pushed himself and his musicians to the limit, blitzing town after town and leaving behind him a wake strewn with ransacked auditoriums, shell-shocked audiences, wasted groupies, cackling critics, and disfigured vehicle codes.

Ted's attire for these occasions included loincloths, animal pelts, teeth necklaces, war paint, and feathers. Regular features of the concerts included death-defying leaps from amp stacks, lectures against the hazards of drugs, the exploding of glass globes with his instrument's feedback, and open invitations to local hotshot guitar players to bring their axes up onstage and get slaughtered. Ted is a showman, and his fierce guitar duke-outs with Wayne Kramer (of the MC5), Mike Pinera (Iron Butterfly, Blues Image), and Frank Marino (Mahogany Rush) scored big with concert fans.

Ted is tall, and his lean, muscular physique and wild lion's mane of hair make for an imposing presence, to say the least, even without the snakeskin cowboy boots, the chipped-tooth grin, or the crazed stare. He is an outdoorsman who loves to hunt, and when he's in a wilderness area he often tracks, shoots, guts, and cooks his food. He favors the bow and arrow and decorates his home with the heads and antlers of his kills. He's also a collector of shotguns and a long-time member of the National Rifle Association: "I support everything they stand for," he affirms. He is especially proud of his efforts to help a group of hunters that successfully established new breeding grounds for the now plentiful wood duck, once an endangered species.

Nugent owns several souped-up, off-road vehicles, and he likes to go crashing over war-zone terrain, fusing together the vertebrae of hapless passengers. One four-wheel hot rod has an engine and suspension engineered to his own specs. It's equipped with a two-and-a-half-million candlepower light beam array on top. "If I signal to someone to dim their lights," Ted says, "the son of a bitch better dim them — otherwise I'll fire up those suckers on top and run him off the road. You can't look at those lights; it's like looking at the sun."

Looking at the sun is what Ted Nugent's image is all about. He is not one of the more self-effacing people you'll ever meet, and his descriptions of himself are reminiscent of Mike Fink, a mangy, likable Disney river rat who once bragged to Davy Crockett that he could outeat, outdrink, outshoot, outfight, outcuss, outrun, and outtalk any man alive. "It *is* amazing, ain't it?" says Ted, groping for undepleted superlatives and referring to his dazzling speed on the guitar. Concerning his phrasing, he beats around no bushes: "I would say I've got the best phrasing of any fucking guitarist in America." And commenting on his songwriting skills, he says, "Sometimes I ask myself — have I the right to be this good?"

Nugent stokes himself up with so much hot gas that he threatens at any moment to inflate like a Macy's Thanksgiving Day Parade balloon. But like the Cassius Clay of old, he has more than enough talent, savvy, and guts to back up the talk, and enough tongue-in-cheek humor and flair to avoid self-parody.

The weapons, Indian getup, guitar shootouts, howling feedback, dead varmints, and kick-butt concerts all add up to what Nugent describes as a lifestyle that has attracted as much press coverage as his relentless blues-rock boogie music, maybe more. But on more than one occasion Ted has complained that editors often extract all comments from his interviews except those that heighten his image as a mad-dog guitar savage. "They only want the crazy stuff," he said in a *Creem* magazine article. "I'm human. I'm intelligent. I know what's going on."

When Ted travels he takes the time to catch the chauffeur's name, to compliment the waitress, to thank the bellboy. A polite Ted Nugent may appear to be a contradiction in terms, but he is quite capable of transcending his image. He knows all about his reputation — he's been refining it and living it for 15 years. Sometimes he reveals his human side, perhaps articulating newly acquired appreciations of home and kids; other times he chucks huge globs of gonzo-speak at the rock music press, playing the bad hombre role to the hilt and relishing the outrage he causes among "serious" critics. In either situation he chooses his words carefully.

The up-yours cockiness that endears him to his millions of fans also causes some people to assume that he is insensitive, a bore, or unkind. In much the same way,

NEIL ZLOZOWER

ROSS MARINO

his brain-damage volume levels and let's-boogie stage raps make it easy for critics to overlook his musical talents, which are considerable, or his approach to the onstage manipulation of feedback, which is almost scientific. Besides, he's right about his speed — it *is* amazing. Though it sometimes sounds like he foregoes a guitar pick in favor of a ball peen hammer, he actually employs a number of innovative techniques, such as bending a string up to one pitch and then sounding a second note by slamming his pick into the string at a certain fret. He constantly and skillfully manipulates the controls on his guitar to increase the dynamic contrasts between volume levels and various tones, or to approximate bowed effects. And aside from the suicide speed runs, he can also play provocative melodies, drawing from influences far more diverse than his usual concert barrages would suggest.

Ted suffers almost total deafness in one ear, a self-inflicted casualty of too many concerts at too-loud volumes ("but it's well worth it, man"). But again, there is more to him than destructo decibelmania. Consider his guitar. Ted's Gibson Byrdland — a jazz model, of all things — was invented over 20 years ago. It has long been his trademark and is essential not only to his tone, but to his technique as well. Its construction differs substantially from the guitars used by almost every other high-volume rocker. For one thing it has a hollow body, which necessitates a trapeze tailpiece that hinges at the bottom rim, rather than the bolt-on stop tailpiece.

The hollow body helps encourage the feedback for which Ted is famous. And the several inches of string length between the bridge and tailpiece allow him to manipulate the strings behind the bridge, changing the pitches of various notes for the air-raid siren effects usually associated with the Fender Stratocasters of Jimi Hendrix, Eddie Van Halen, and Ritchie Blackmore. The same technique permits him to embellish arpeggiated chord progressions with melodic note-bendings similar to those of a pedal steel (e.g., the intro to "Alone," on the *State Of Shock* LP). Ted has demonstrated the Byrdland's suitability for rock, adapting it to things its inventors wouldn't understand and probably wouldn't like. He gets Strat-like vibrato effects with no vibrato, and without the tuning difficulties that so many vibrato users seem to complain about. All in all, it's an inspired example of mechanical improvisation.

The Motor City Madman goes way back to the Lourdes, a Detroit group he played with at age 14. He went to Chicago and formed the Amboy Dukes shortly after acquiring his first Byrdland in 1964, returning to his home base in Detroit. From there the Dukes hit the road, slugging it out for 150 or 200 concerts each year for much of the next decade, and recording nearly a dozen LPs, including *Survival Of The Fittest, Call Of The Wild,* and *Tooth, Fang, And Claw.*

An indefatigable performer and road stormtrooper, Ted has been playing essentially the same style for 15 years. He was a pioneer of feedback, equipment destruction, playing with his teeth, and other hallmarks of late '60s rock guitar, and it is ironic that worldwide acclaim came relatively late. His early career was marked by assorted ripoffs, financial mismanagement, and little notoriety outside the Midwest and South. His "Journey To The Center Of Your Mind" made it to #8 on the national charts in 1968 (though Ted earned no money from it), and some of the Amboy Dukes albums crept up toward midpoint on the national Top 100. In 1971 Ted began to make money and bought a farm.

In 1975 Nugent dumped the Dukes, went with new managers and a new record company (Epic), released the *Ted Nugent* LP, and turned his career around. *Free-For-All* was released in '76, followed by *Cat Scratch Fever*, which hit big the next year. *Double Live Gonzo* came out in 1977, and it was followed last year by *Weekend Warriors.* All five Epic albums have turned platinum — a million units sold or more. From these LPs came several hits, including "Stranglehold," "Dog Eat Dog," and the huge "Cat Scratch Fever." Ted increased his touring coverage, performing successful gonzolectomies on Japanese and Hawaiian audiences in '78. His most recent Epic album is *State Of Shock*, released in May 1979.

A story in *Guitar Player*'s November '76 issue covers in detail Ted's career up to the release of *Ted Nugent*, including his influences, equipment, background, and technique. In the following interview, he mainly discusses his guitar playing since that time. Aside from the new measure of success, his music has broadened. For one thing, the production of the Epic releases is superior to the old Amboy Dukes' albums, and Ted is even writing some ballads. Does this mean that Ted Nugent is mellowing out? Forget it. He still looks at an audience the way a brick looks at a stained-glass window, and he gives every indication that he will continue the guitar journey that has now consumed over half his life — cranking up to 10, ransacking audiences, disintegrating pigeons, blasting critters, squealing his kamikaze guitar solos up into frequencies best heard by aliens and bats, and flaming off into space toward the ultimate gonzo meltdown.

the interview

How does recording compare to performing onstage?

My turf is the stage. It has always been the stage. My recording process is merely a vehicle for the continuing Ted Nugent saga to perpetuate itself, unendingly. Boy, that's eloquent. Anyway, in so doing, I find myself continuing my rock and roll stage attitude in the studio. However, in the studio you are playing for microphones and tape recorders. My music is designed for the human ear and the uninhibited appreciation thereof. But I go into the studio and they start slapping on a whole array of different microphones — it looks like somebody's on an international newscast deciding whether they're going to push the atomic war button. The microphones cannot absorb what the human ear can absorb, and vice versa. My stuff is designed for the live human ear. I'll go in and play a guitar sound that is biting and thick-sounding, and the microphone just goes, 'Sorry, does not compute, reject, try something else.'"

What can you do?

Number one, I refuse to back down on this biting sound. I must have it. If I can't get the biting sound, I will pass. I will not record it. But it can be done. You just have to search out all the proper microphones, and I really wish for the readers and everyone else that I could tell you that I use this mike or that mike, but unfortunately I really don't give a flying fuck. I leave that to my engineers and my producer.

Do you use different kinds of mikes that you can mix at various levels?

Right, and I have an array of amps. I use a dozen different amps in the studio, and I try them all so that what my ear hears in the room is what I subsequently hear on the tape. For me, a really great recording amp is this old Gibson I have with a 12" speaker and tubes that glow and breathe fire. But I'm using strictly Fender Twins now, and this endorsement arrangement I have with Fender is great for me, because I crave Fenders. Half of the rhythm guitar parts and half of the lead parts in the studio are played through Fenders; the rest are played through that ancient Gibson, or various other sundry small amps — antiques that just scream.

When did you start the formal Fender amp endorsements?

About a year-and-a-half ago. I've always used Fenders, and not because I'm too lazy to try anything else. I've tried everything and I've had amps built to my own specs. Nothing sounds more like a guitar than Fender amps.

Do you mix the miked amp signals with the guitar recorded direct?

No, never, not with my guitar, although we'll do it with the bass sometimes.

Do you record live in the studio — that is, with all the parts being played at once?

Not really, but it does sound like it because we take care to make it sound like a real band concept. But my ability to keep my attention span up in the studio isn't really great, and after a few days I'm ready to go, so during the few days that I spend in the studio I will put down the guide track — not a keeper guitar, but a guide with the drums and bass — and then they will work on the song in my absence. They'll get everything around that, and then I will come in and put down a keeper guitar track. I just don't want to stay in the studio too long. There's no sunshine in there.

What can you do to keep the energy level up during a recording, when you don't have tens of thousands of people screaming at you?

I encourage people hanging out. You know, a lot of young chicks are always conducive to blasting, but for the most part I just get honestly and unbelievably excited whenever I play. Just as soon as I go in, I plug in and I just start blasting. And that's how all the songs really get written, too — just by plugging in and blasting. When I get in the studio and we've got a given composition that we're working on, I go in and I just start blasting out on it and just the whole rhythm of the song will inspire a solo or a nice progression. There's this relentless drive going on. As soon as I put a guitar in my hands I have no control. I mean, I just go nuts.

Do you ever splice takes together to make a solo?

No. I keep a solo, or I discard a solo.

How would you say your records have changed over the years, aside from production values? Have you changed playing techniques?

It's not a change in technique, but there is one other thing that I think has caused a change in my recorded sound. I can hold back my enthusiasm and be objective to a greater degree now when I'm listening to the recorded music. In the past I would get so excited just hearing my song on tape, it could be the shittiest performance in the world and I'd still think it would be good. By me being a little bit more discerning and also surrounding myself with people with excellent ears, such as Cliff Davies, my drummer, I can be a little more critical and objective.

And Cliff is your coproducer as well?

Right. Cliff Davies coproduces my albums, and I give him full responsibility for the final improvement that has taken place on my records, beginning with *Ted Nugent* and being really more obvious in the last couple of albums — definitely in *Cat Scratch Fever* and *Weekend Warriors*. Some of the early stuff was basically uncontrolled, but I take more control now, and I take more interest in criticizing my own sound.

How prepared are you before you go in the studio? How much do you have worked out?

I have almost everything worked out. I know definitively how the song is going to sound when it's all finished.

All the parts?

All the parts. The only things that are not burned in steel are the solos themselves. I know what the thrust of a solo is going to be. I may come up with these little phrases that I didn't analyze prior to going into the studio, but like I said, when I go in and plug in, the phrases are inspired by the rhythms of the songs. Once I play a killer that I really like, then I will stick to it.

Are many of them first takes?

The majority of them are first takes. Some of them I have to play around with.

How many tracks do you use?

We usually use a 24-track machine, but I use anywhere from two to ten tracks just for guitar. With just the one rhythm guitar part of the song I may use three tracks, with three different amps to get three different sounds, all blended together to sound thick.

What's the studio budget been like?

No budget. I don't care about the budget. The budget has been limited only by the fact that we go into the studio better prepared than most, not as prepared as we *could* be, but we rehearse most of the songs prior to getting into the studio, so once we get in we're recording final arrangements for the most part. We might be able to improve on a small part, but we really don't spend that much time, and budgets haven't been a problem.

Do you ever record a track of feedback, just so you can have the option of fading it in later?

Yeah. These poor guys on the mixing board — when I put the thing down there's this constant minute of squeal, and they're going, "What is he going to do with that?" When I stop playing my solo, they fade in that sound, and it really makes a difference. On the new *State Of Shock* album, there's a song called "Satisfied" where I do something that's just the reverse of that. I take the solo and work another part along with it, feeding back, and then we put a backwards guitar on it playing the song theme, and it comes out in reverse — the backwards part is mixed with the forwards part. It's a song that's in the thrust of "Stranglehold" [*Ted Nugent*].

Do you ever record guitar parts and then mix them way back in the distance, just for effect or atmosphere?

No, I don't think there's a real change between what you play with rhythm guitar or solo guitar. I believe all guitars should have a lead quality. Here I go, ranting and raving, but I very seldom do a traditional chord rhythm. All my parts, regardless of label, are important parts that should be up in the mix. There are no distant sounds. I believe that if the instruments are vying for top level, like they are on my records, you might as well not even bother with the little background fillers. You can get your level out of the real biting sound, and that's what I prefer.

Throughout your career many of your compositions have been thematic, double-tracked guitar songs. Were you influenced by "Beck's Bolero" [on Jeff Beck's Truth*]?*

Well, there's no question that "Beck's Bolero" had an impact on me. A lot of my instrumentals were probably motivated by my original hearing of that, though I had written some instrumentals with a bolero-type feel prior to my ever hearing Beck. I don't really know if there are other things involved. It's funny, because so many people think my playing is tasteless and unrhythmical and unmelodious and unphrased, which is ridiculous. I would say I've got the best phrasing of any fucking guitarist in America. I always do a passage that could be sung [*scat-sings a blues lick*]. I repeat it, and [*singing*] I-*work*-my-way-*up*-like-a-*vo*-cal-would-*do*. And anybody who can't see that is a fucking nerd, man.

Are you influenced by vocalists?

No, but I think your bringing up Jeff Beck is a major influence, though. On the *Truth* album alone he may have set a standard for phrasing on the guitar — taking traditional notes, Benny Goodman notes, or any of the notes and playing them in such a structure that they could be vocalized. Leslie West was also a master of that. I do the same thing to an extent. I also believe that a guitar solo or a guitar part shouldn't be restricted to that approach, but rather it should take advantage of that phraseology, in order to set up a real out-and-out attack of notes, a real screaming riff.

Do you visualize patterns?

I don't think about it, but my ears are those of a listener. I play the role of the creator and the listener, you know. When I perform the solo to "Need You Bad" [*Weekend Warriors*] in concert, my ears anticipate the notes that are on that record. Maybe there's a flair — whether it's creativity or uncontrollability I don't know. There is *something* that surfaces that will sometimes make me go beyond and throw in notes other than those that are on the original recording. I'm not limited by that, but other times it will hold me into a pattern so that there's an identification on what's going on in my head, and what's happening with the crowd.

Are there advantages to working with a small crowd compared to a big coliseum?

NEIL ZLOZOWER

Well, basically they both have their positives. I don't really know any negatives about either. A lot of people may complain about certain negatives, but I don't really agree with them.

What are the advantages of each?

The positive of the big giant gigs is just the multiplication of all those heads aimed in the same direction of rock and roll, and the intensity is magnified that many times, it seems. You've got hundreds of thousands of brains heading the same way, wanting to rock. How can you miss? I mean the intensity factor is unequaled. The advantage of a small club is the immediate proximity of the listeners to the band and the feedback you can get, eyeball to eyeball. Now, at a large concert you can also get that feedback, because the first ten rows are right there. Everything is intensified by the masses, but the closeness in small clubs has its own intensity, because everything is so hearable.

Are you satisfied with your concert tone? If you multiply the power enough times, can you get the sound you want, even outdoors in huge arenas?

Yeah, yeah. My sound man's name is Dansir. When people come to us and go, "Well, Ted, we checked out the coliseum, and we think you'll need 200,000 watts," Dansir and I say, "Okay, triple that and we'll take it." You've got to go in with overkill in mind, so that you never have to push what you've got.

The way your band is spread out, do you ever have any trouble hearing yourself onstage?

No, people in the next *county* don't have any trouble hearing me onstage. I wear earplugs. I use six Fender Super Twins [180 watts RMS each] and six Fender bottoms with two 18s in each, and that's a lot of speakers.

How are they wired together?

The guitar goes into a single junction box that has its own amp, so I don't lose the signal, and then I just plug the Byrdland right into that.

And that all goes to the PA?

No, only two of my amps go to the PA. The rest are just blasting — stage volume, no PA.

What do you do to warm up for a show?

I wake up. I'm always ready to play. I crave it. I usually just go in the dressing room an hour or two hours before we go onstage and just start blasting out. When I come onstage I've usually been playing for a while.

What kind of amp do you use in the dressing room for practice?

I use Fender Twins. I'll use a Boogie amp sometimes. I use Music Man. I use a Lab, Gibson Lab amps. They all sound good, small amps.

How large is your road crew?

The immediate crew is just about eight guys, and I consider them to be my family crew. There are two guys who work on the guitars full-time, and then there are assorted gonzo destructo dogs and deviates and scoundrels who just carry guns and look mean.

Do you take good care of your guitars onstage?

I'm not always as careful as I should be, but for someone who's as nuts as I am, I don't abuse them. I could never hurt them, like some guys. I guess that stems from the time when I had to buy them for a grand a shot — lots of cash.

Have you ever broken a guitar?

Well, a lot of times when I hit the guitar I'm amazed that I don't just shove my hand clean through the son of a bitch. And a lot of times I've put wooden posts in there to keep me from doing that. But for the most part I've never had any trouble. I don't need any reinforcement, and I definitely don't want to take away from the feedback. There's only one kind of feedback I can't stand, and that's the high-pitched squeal of a microphone feedback, and that you just learn to control.

Since you play so hard, do you have any special tricks to help keep your guitar in tune?

I just wrap the strings around the post three or four or five or six times, and then I stretch the fuck out of them before I start playing. I never really have much trouble with tuning. There are occasions where I get a bad batch of strings, and all of a sudden I'm plagued, but it's infrequent.

On the Byrdland, does the way the neck joins the body keep you from playing as high up the fingerboard as you'd like?

No, for some reason I do anyhow. I can just walk up there when I have to. It does get in the way, but it doesn't eliminate the access altogether. It's not as easy as if it were totally open, like on a double-cutaway.

Why do you remove the pickguard?

So I can wrap my fingers and rest them on the body itself. I was taught the pickguard was where you would rest your fingers, but I like to grip the little finger of my right hand down around the pickups as, I don't know, a semi-anchor point. I do use my fingers and my wrist; I don't move my arm when I play.

How many Byrdlands do you have?

I've had 18 at one time, and I've owned 21 different ones. I presently own 16.

How many do you take on the road?

Only three. Usually only two, but right now I'm in the process of testing and scrutinizing a lot of DiMarzio pickups, and one of my Byrdlands is a test vehicle for a lot of different DiMarzio pickups, trying to get that original humbucking sound that my real good Byrdlands have.

Do you have a particular favorite?

I love so many of them, and they're all stock. Nothing's been done to them, except I put a Gretsch guitar strap knob on my toggle switch so I can switch gears a little faster. But I've got a black one, a blonde one, and a really beautiful sunburst — they're all from the early '60s. I usually rotate with those.

You seem to hold the guitar up high.

I used to hold it real high, almost chin-level, but over the years it's dropped a little bit more. Now I don't have it down below my balls like a lot of guys, but it's down belly-level.

Do you position it in order to encourage feedback?

No, with the Byrdland being as light as it is, I can easily swing it around. It's a very comfortable guitar for me, I guess for no other reason than I've been doing it for so many years. I've been playing a Byrdland for 15 years probably. Even in the old days, swinging it over behind my head was just really easy.

Do you ever work with guitars other than Byrdlands?

Yes. I've been playing around with a Gibson Les Paul that I got from Billy Gibbons [of ZZ Top] down in Texas,

ROSS MARINO

who's a friend of mine and who I have vast respect for, even though he is one of the swines of the earth. I got the guitar through [collector] Tony Dukes, Mr. Duster himself. Tony's a fellow dog man, a dog chewer. He thinks he can outshoot me, but the guy is obviously a victim of his own manifestations of delusion. But I got this Les Paul from him. He told me it's a '58, and I do believe it's true. It may be one of the rare occasions when he's told the truth.

Have you recorded with the Les Paul?

Yes, I use it on "Alone," which is on the *State Of Shock* album. I also use the Byrdland, but the solo on "Alone" is the Les Paul. It's a different instrument for me to play, and a different song for me to do. I don't know if one was responsible for the other, but that Les Paul has a beautiful solo into this frenzied speed thing, and the guitar keeps this distinguished, clean, fat sound.

Do you use a pedal for any of your volume-shift techniques?

No, I just use the knobs on the guitars.

Some of the things you do sound like they'd be hard to do even if you had a vibrato.

It's amazing.

How do you do vibrato effects on the Byrdland?

I push down the strings with the heel of my right hand. There's about six or seven inches of string behind the bridge, and it works the same way a tremolo bar works. I've got it down. On a song called "It Doesn't Matter" on *State Of Shock*, I make sounds that are just like a Strat, waterfall things. It's intriguing how these things work out, and for me it was a case of do or die — I either get these sounds to come out of a Byrdland, or I just don't do them.

Do you find it possible to keep your guitar in tune while you're doing the string-pushing technique?

That's one of the amazing things. Yes, I do. It's just a touch. There's a touch there when you want one feedback note but you don't want the other ones to feed. There's a touch, a position in front of the amplifiers, a

NEIL ZLOZOWER

stance that you take onstage, a position of your right-hand fingers dampening the other strings while your left hand is holding a note. On the *State Of Shock* album there's a song called "Satisfied." I'll begin a feedback note in the *A* position, the regular barre chord at the 5th fret, and I go for an *A* note by pushing up the *G* note on the *B* string [8th fret] to an *A*. I quiver it and feed back and I allow my little finger to take hold of the *G* string, which is a dissonant *E* note at the 8th fret, and the *A* note is now feeding back like mad, and I start dropping it down. My little finger is catching the *G* string, and that dissonant *E* is feeding back at the same time. Then, I drop them in sort of a waterfall thing, and it's mind-boggling. It's during the solo, about eight or ten measures into it. It'll blow your mind.

Is the feedback one reason why you have to manipulate your guitar's controls so much?

Right, so I can summon silence at will. The Byrdland is such a feedbacker that it is constantly almost out of control. And unless I work the controls, I get all this noise every time I take my hands off. Sometimes I'll have one pickup turned off, and I'll use the toggle to cut to that pickup and have silence between the licks. That's why I'm hitting the switch constantly. I'll do any combination of settings, depending on what chord and what tone setting I desire prior to the break.

And you play with both pickups on as well?

Oh, absolutely. I use every conceivable setting short of mid-numbers; in other words, I never run a tone knob at anything other than full on or off. I'll sometimes use graduated settings on my volume, if I want to come down with the level or change it while I play.

Before a gig, will you walk around the stage to find spots where you can get certain notes to feed back?

The volume is so damn loud that I can catch the note seconds before it has to actually feed back, and just the out-and-out volume sustain will hold it for a couple of seconds while I get over there onstage to where the actual feedback takes over. It's a combination of feedback and natural sustain. It's funny, but feedback will eliminate natural sustain. In other words, the overbearing feedback from the amplifier can actually eliminate a note.

So that there's nothing left but feedback?

Right, and it may not be the note I want, so I may shuffle over to a different position on the stage.

Have you ever experimented with stuffing your guitar with rags to cut down on the feedback?

That'd be the worst. I mean, you should never mess with cutting down on any feedback, because that's what it's all about.

Have you ever tried a guitar synthesizer?

I goofed around with one in Kansas City or Omaha — someplace like that — and the thing sounded so disgusting that I just couldn't handle it.

You used to use effects, and then you were quoted as saying you were opposed to then.

I wasn't adamantly against effects *per se*, but for a time my ear just told me that playing without them was better. I think the last time I used a wah-wah was on *Survival Of The Fittest* back in 1970. But on *State Of Shock* I use a Cry Baby wah-wah on "Paralyzed," and a Ross flanger on "State Of Shock" and "Alone." So I'm not against an effect if the ears and the song call for it.

What are you currently using onstage in the way of effects?

I use the wah-wah for "Paralyzed." That's all.

So you're not running through a whole bank of pedals?

Oh God, no. That always made me nauseous, really. I like a guitar to sound like a guitar. I think certain lines, certain passages and guitar parts can be enhanced by different tricks, but it should still sound like a guitar.

Have you ever fooled around with wireless transmitters?

Yeah, they don't work on Byrdlands. And it's a shame, too, because I could use the increased mobility instead of being gaffed to the amps all the time. It just won't deliver the top end. It won't deliver the cleanliness that I'm used to, and *that* I have to have.

Do you use heavy-duty patch cords or phone jacks?

My electrician has come up with some good ideas. We had one cord made out of solid rubber, but he forgot to put the wires in and it didn't work too good — didn't break, but it didn't work [*laughs*]. No, I think we're using stock stuff.

Do you blow out speakers or amplifiers?

Yeah, I blow a lot of speakers. I don't have any trouble with the amps — the Fender Super Twins hold out real good.

Are the speakers stock when you get them?

Well, I'd like to get the old Electro-Voice SRO Series, but those are an endangered species and hard to come by. I think we still have them in my cabinets right now; I'd have to talk to one of my boys.

Do your cabinets require extra maintenance?

Yeah, just to make sure everything is in maximum efficiency, even if it just means hardware, you know, even if it just means tightening the bolts down. I have a real efficient road crew, and they take care of business even if it just means taking the speaker cabinets apart and making sure everything is perfect.

Do you ever play with your right-hand fingers?

When I drop picks I do, but I don't otherwise. I use a thumbpick sometimes.

Do you do a lot of up and down picking?

Oh, all of them, both ways. When I do honky-tonk rhythms I try to make them all down, for percussiveness.

How do you attack the string?

I catch it between my finger and the pick itself. I don't hold a regular pick traditionally at all. I use the round edge, and I hold them very shallow; I mean, I just barely touch them. I use a thin pick, but it doesn't really matter. There's no flex there anyhow, because only a little bit sticks out from the fingers.

What kind of strings do you use? They don't sound too skinny.

They're not. Going high to low, they're .010, .012, .016, .028, .034, and .046. I use Ernie Balls, Fenders — they're all good. I find Ernie's are pretty good. A lot of guys use real slinko jobs, but I end up pulling them three feet off the neck.

You seem to use your left hand's little finger a lot.

Yeah, I always use my little finger. Got that baby there — might as well put it to work.

Do you practice much?

I *play* a lot. I don't think of it as practicing, though I'm sure it ends up being that way.

You don't have any specific scales?

No, it's called blasting. But what I end up playing is usually very intricate stuff, like very fast things. But it's not from thinking about it. Most of my stuff comes from just being around the studio where the rhythm track is. I'll start punching out leads and come up with these obnoxious little notes that make it. You couldn't discover those notes with patterns in mind. They've got to just come fumbling out of you. I wouldn't know a scale if it hit me in the nose.

You don't think of, say, chord inversions?

I don't *think*, is basically it.

Do you compose licks or songs when you're away from the guitar?

Absolutely. On the airplane today I wrote three songs, and I couldn't wait to get my guitar. I don't know what their names are yet, but those things just tumble out of my brain.

Do you ever use any non-standard tunings?

Much to my chagrin, yes [*laughs*]. No, I don't really — not on purpose, anyway. In one of my rare moments of thought, I decided what I'd like to do is to put six .010s on my guitar, tune them normally, and play lead with *all* them sons of bitches, six little tiny strings that can be bent all around. I don't know whether I'd get the low ones low enough, but if they started getting out of control I'd go up an octave. That'd be real weird. I've got to try that soon.

Have you ever experimented with odd time signatures?

Even though I have a shitty sense of timing, I have a great concept of driving rhythms. These syncopated drummers [*laughs, looks at drummer Cliff Davies*] — their main goal in life is to lose you. Again, it's my status as a rock and roll fan; I like it so much that the rhythm patterns drive me wild. As soon as I plug into an amplifier, I usually just go for a big *A* chord and start hitting it into a nice rhythmical pattern.

Do you listen to other guitar players very much?

I don't sit down and listen, no. I listen to the radio a lot. I do a lot of concerts with other guitar players. I've got a lot of guitar player friends who I go listen to. I haven't liked the stuff Jeff Beck has come out with lately, but I know he's a monster. As I said before, I think his *Truth* album is one of the all-time definitive rock guitar albums. There are guys like Brian May of Queen, who I just think is fantastic. Billy Gibbons is one of the all-time greatest guitar players. I think Eddie Van Halen is just a fantastic guitarist. There are so many good guitarists now. Ronnie Montrose is a monster. Rick Derringer's a monster. Johnny Winter is a monster—so many great guitarists. I mean, this is a guitarist's world, you know. They're everywhere. In the old days I was influenced by Jimi Hendrix, and Beck, and Eric Clapton in the Cream days.

When did you start singing a lot?

Well, I'm still not a bona fide lead vocalist. I mean, I just can't vocalize. The ones I choose to do, I can do. If I tried to sing "One Woman" [*Weekend Warriers*] or "Stranglehold" or a song that calls for talented note-hitting, I would sound like a real doughnut. But if it calls

ROSS MARINO

for some balls and some screaming and spitting it out, I can do it better than anybody. Nobody else could have sung "Wang Dang Sweet Poontang."

Who is the other guitarist working with you now?

Charlie Huhn. Charlie is my lead vocalist and guitar player, and he's from Michigan, and he's got the kind of voice that my compositions call for. He's been with me over a year now.

Do you and Charlie do double-tracked leads in the studio, or do you play both parts?

Life ain't long enough for me to get in all the licks I want to, and when it gets to recording an album, there sure ain't enough time for me to get in all the licks I want to. I play all the guitars and some of the bass. I'll do the vocals that I really feel I must sing, but I'm the first one to admit it when someone else could probably sing it, traditionally approached, better than I could. If I really wanted to sell albums I would go for that all the time, but I could really give a cat's ass. If I feel like singing a song like "State Of Shock," it may not maximize the potential of the tune, but it sure makes me feel good, and that's what motivates me.

Your music hasn't changed that much, and yet your career has changed drastically in the last few years.

You betcha it hasn't changed that much. I was doing things with the Amboy Dukes in 1965 that had almost everything I'm doing now in them.

Why didn't people catch on 10 or 15 years ago?

I attribute it to a couple of simple things. The competition is massive, but you're not necessarily competing against other talent, or you're not really competing with what is wanted by the public *per se*. You're competing with the exposure thereof. I have worked harder than anybody, period. Just period. Because I dig it. I will not work harder today than I worked at the Cellar Club in 1965, because I was having fucking riots in 1965. I have not altered my approach one iota. So I am working as hard as ever.

What about your new record company?

That's the other thing. There's additional teamwork. The Epic records gave me a run with the competition, with their marketing and exposure. The real test comes when you got exposure, and then the music stands on its own. And obviously mine stands on its own. It's the best high-energy rock and roll on earth, and people crave that as much as I crave it, because I'm only one of them anyhow. I just happen to be able to do it.

What do you think about criticism of your music?

I really could give a fuck. I read it. And I've really dug it because some of them have really been behind me. I attribute that to the fact that they are probably rock and roll fans too, and as long as I can retain my cockiness and spirit I think they'll stick by me. When they stop, I could really care less. Anybody who likes what I do is fine, and anybody who doesn't is welcome to not like it. I just don't play for them. I play for my own ears, and everyone else whose ears prefer it. I don't claim to be the answer to the universal ear orgasm. I just am there. When you want to rock, I'll be there.

— Tom Wheeler

TED NUGENT: A SELECTED DISCOGRAPHY

Solo albums (on Epic): *Ted Nugent,* PE-33692; *Free-For-All,* PE-34121; *Cat Scratch Fever,* JE-34700; *Double Live Gonzo,* KE2-35069; *Weekend Warriors,* FE-35551; *State Of Shock,* FE-36000; *Scream Dream,* FE-36404; *Intensities In 10 Cities,*FE-37084. *Nugent,* Atlantic, SD 19365. **With the Amboy Dukes:** *Ted Nugent And The Amboy Dukes,* Mainstream [dist. by Roulette], MRL421; *Dr. Slingshot,* Mainstream, MRL 414; *Marriage On The Rocks — Rock Bottom,* Polydor, I-6073; *Survival Of The Fittest,* Polydor, 4035; *Call Of The Wild,* Discreet [dist. by Warner Bros.], 2181; *Tooth, Fang, And Claw,* Discreet, 2203; *Journeys And Migrations* (dbl. reissue), Mainstream, MRL 801. **Anthologies:** *California Jam 2,* Columbia, PC2-35389; *Volunteer Jam 6,* Epic, KE2-36438.

EUROPE'S METAL MASTERS

ROSS MARINO

Michael Schenker

PAUL NATKIN/PHOTO RESERVE

German metal master Michael Schenker debuted with the Scorpions at 15 and won widespread acclaim with UFO. He was interviewed for the January '81 *Guitar Player* during the Michael Schenker Group's first U.S. tour. A prolific artist, Schenker released *MSG* later in 1981, and *One Night At Budokan* and *Assault Attack* the following year. Chrysalis Japan issued a deluxe *Michael Schenker Anthology* in 1983. Schenker's influence as a metal guitarist continues to increase.

an introduction

Since his 1971 debut appearance in Germany with the Scorpions, Michael Schenker has earned a formidable reputation as one of Europe's premier heavy metal wizards. On vinyl with the Scorpions, UFO, and the Michael Schenker Group, his playing incorporates liquid screams, lightning-fast runs, a well-controlled vibrato, growls, and harmonics — all governed by a strong melodic sense that sings more of creativity than repetition. His talent as a songwriter has also contributed much to the success of UFO and the band that currently bears his name.

The younger brother of present-day Scorpion guitarist Rudolf Schenker, Michael was born on January 10, 1955, in Sarstedt, a town 25 kilometers south of Hanover, Germany. He took up the guitar at nine and two years later began performing with a band called Enervates. He then became a member of the Cry. "We were the youngest beat band in Germany at the time," he recalls. "Everybody was under 14 years old." At 15 Schenker and Klaus Meine, who went on to become the singer for the Scorpions, formed a lineup called Copernicus. In 1971 Schenker joined the Scorpions and performed on their album *Lonesome Crow*.

Meanwhile across the North Sea, singer Phil Mogg, bassist Pete Way, drummer Andy Parker, and guitarist Mick Bolton were trying to slug their way to recognition in the English metal scene as UFO. They recorded two commercially unsuccessful albums in Japan and were about to tour Germany in 1973 when Bolton quit. Without gear or guitarist, the band plunged ahead, borrowing equipment and the lead guitarist from their warm-up act, the Scorpions. Proving himself adept with thunderous power chords, virtuosic solos, and intimate melodic textures, Schenker was invited to join UFO full time.

Even though he couldn't speak English, from the start Schenker contributed much to UFO, co-writing most of the music on their 1974 release, *Phenomenon*, which yielded the hits "Doctor, Doctor" and "Rock Bottom." During the next three years he added incendiary electric parts and delicate acoustic guitar tracks to the albums *Force It*, *No Heavy Petting*, and *Lights Out*. Then, just before an important U.S. tour, Schenker vanished without explanation. UFO brought in Paul Chapman as a substitute and left for the States. Schenker eventually returned to the lineup, and after months of solid touring the group recorded *Obsession* and a live LP, *Strangers In The Night*. Finding it increasingly difficult to express his musical ideas, Schenker soon afterwards left the band for good.

He rejoined the Scorpions in 1979 as a favor to his brother and recorded a few brilliant solos for their *Lovedrive* LP. He went on a European tour with the group, but quit midway through after announcing his decision to go solo. The result was *Michael Schenker Group*, which was produced by Deep Purple's Roger Glover and features two former Jeff Beck sidemen, bassist Mo Foster and drummer Simon Phillips, as well as keyboardist Don Airey and singer Gary Barden. Michael wrote or cowrote all of the tracks, and with the new lineup his playing takes on a livelier dimension than ever before. At the time of the following interview, Schenker was opening dates on the East Coast for Molly Hatchet. His touring band includes Gary Barden, drummer Cozy Powell, keyboardist Paul Raymond, and bassist Chris Glenn.

the interview

When you first started on guitar, how many hours a day did you spend playing?

When I was nine, it wasn't too serious. I never actually counted the hours then. But when I was 15 or 16, I started to play a lot more. Sometimes it was like four hours a day; sometimes I didn't practice at all for two days, and then I'd do eight hours straight. So I think I would average like four hours a day.

What did you think was most important to learn?

To be able to play without thinking, like a routine. But at the same time, I felt it was very important to play fast as well as slow, and with a lot of feeling. If you play fast, always use a melody, even if you are doing catchy lines and fast runs. That's what I was always after.

Did you ever study music?

No. The way I picked it up when I was nine was through my brother. He was already playing the guitar, and he had to go to work. I was going to school then, so he asked me if I could try and find out some riffs, like from Beatles songs. And I did that, and he gave me a Deutsche mark for each song. When he came back from work in the evening, I showed him the part. Then I became interested because it was fun, and it was exciting that I actually had something together. It just happened that I figured things out for myself.

Have you played electrics from the start?

No, I think I started on an acoustic guitar; that was the only thing we had. I got my first electric when I was 11, and it was my brother's guitar. Whenever he bought a new one, I got his old one.

Which guitarists had the strongest influence on you?

I think the main influences were always the big people — all the famous groups, famous guitarists. A very long time ago it was Hank Marvin of the Shadows, and then Jimmy Page. Leslie West is one of my favorites. There were quite a few solos by Jeff Beck and a few by Jimmy Page and Eric Clapton that I copied.

What is your philosophy of soloing? What do you think a solo should do?

What I do is just play a lead break which really comes from the heart. It's catchy and doesn't get boring. It has got the right length and build-up. And I try to use something new, like some original kind of vibrato.

Are most of your solos spontaneous?

If I play slow songs, I always work out a nice melody, except for "Tales Of Mystery" [*Michael Schenker Group*] — the lead break there was spontaneous; I was improvising. But usually I work out the solos in slow songs. The solos in fast numbers like "Rock Bottom" [*Strangers In The Night*], "Lost Horizons," and "Armed And Ready" [both on *Michael Schenker Group*] are always improvised.

You often intertwine several modes and scales in your solos. Do you know what you are doing in musical terms?

No, I don't know what the different kinds of scales are. I just use my ear.

How do you construct solos?

After all these years, I just pick up the guitar and practice, and all of a sudden I'll play a little line. I try to remember this line and repeat it. I often try to make this a bit longer by using it over all six strings instead of only playing it for like five seconds. I go all over the place. Then I keep practicing it every day until it sticks in my head. I ultimately use it in a lead break when I think it would fit. Sometimes I look for nice melodies — just mess around and try to play a bit weird, but stay in kind of a melodic way. I connect it by trying it out faster and slower and seeing how it works best. Then once in a while I use it in the middle of a lead break. And by doing this, I find other nice little lines, and that's how you develop your own style. You use your taste to put the parts together.

Do you change solos onstage?

It depends on how catchy the lead break I improvised on the album was. If it came out catchy, I like to repeat it live. If it was something like the long lead break in "Lost Horizons," I improvise. But it always depends, and I compromise. I usually like to keep the catchy and short parts.

Have you ever constructed a solo before you had a song to use it in?

Actually, I think that's the way "Doctor, Doctor" came together. At first I had the melody line, and then I did the rhythm, and then the rest. The way that number came out was one day we were writing songs for *Phenomenon*, rehearsing and jamming in the studio. I remember like nothing was happening — you know, someone brought a newspaper and we were laying on the floor reading it. There was silence for like half an hour, and all of a sudden I just picked up the guitar and played this riff, and that's the way it came together. Usually it's the rhythm guitar that's the first thing in the song.

If somebody wanted to hear the essential Michael Schenker, what songs would you recommend?

Oh, it's so difficult. On all the albums I've done in the past, there is a lead break in each song. To be honest, I can't remember all of them, and if I would say something now, I would probably forget about some important lead break. I wouldn't be able to tell.

Have there been times when you surprised yourself?

Oh yeah, many times, especially when I was younger. When I was 18 and did my first album, it was like magic.

Can you reproduce everything you've recorded?

Oh, yeah! This is because I keep practicing. I make sure that I keep all the little bits I like that are part of my past. It's the same as roller skating or ice skating or whatever you do: If you stop practicing, you lose it eventually. Like Jimmy Page — he's lost it.

How often do you practice, and what do you work on?

It changes. If you reach a certain standard, like you've been practicing for years and years, then you get to a point when you get fed up with all this stuff. You think you are much more clever now than you were before, and you get into this kind of weird stuff, like Jeff Beck does. I don't want to end up there, because I like rock too much. So if you reach a certain level of technique, you should stop practicing too much. Practice less and think more, because the people won't understand if you play too fast, if you play too clever. I think it's important to be very good, but if you are extremely fast or flippy, it doesn't really mean you're playing extremely good for the people. You're either performing for the audience or for yourself. If you are playing to yourself and just want to satisfy yourself, there is never an end in this kind of profession. But in rock I like to keep it straight. I like to be extremely fast and use a lot of melody. I just like to be a tasteful guitarist, so that people can understand what I'm saying. When I practice, I don't play anything for myself. What I play at home is exactly what I give the audience.

What keeps most guitarists from getting the speed you've achieved?

Speed is absolute, and you can only get it if you practice. Many people are too lazy to practice. Your hands are stiff if you don't. It's the same as running: To be fast, you have to practice. There's no other way. There's also talent in playing like Paul Kossoff, who played slow and kind of nice and had a good vibrato. Jeff Beck plays slow and absolutely tasty, which is his talent. Even if he never rehearses, he will probably always be a tasteful guitarist, unless he goes a bit too mad with the weird style he has got at the moment. But to be able to play fast, you need a lot of practice.

Can you transfer the notes you hear in your imagination to the guitar?

I'm not sure if I could do it straight away.

What are the most difficult songs in your repertoire?

I don't know. If you want to play them all good, they're all hard.

What do you think about when you're playing onstage?

I don't think I think anything. I'm just completely concentrating on the notes I'm playing. All I see is strings and hands; the left hand is reaching for different notes, and the right hand is hitting strings.

What makes you play your best?

All I need is seeing the people out there going mad and asking for the music and the group. That's enough. That's what gives me the power and the concentration to play, to give my best.

Does your emotional state at the time have much of an influence on the way you phrase or the notes you choose?

No, because the power of the audience and atmos-

phere is so strong. Well, I don't know. The tour I recently did in England was my first tour for a year-and-a-half, and it was also the first tour without any alcohol or any drugs. It was absolutely amazing. Before, I always used to play after at least three or four bottles of beer, because I thought I could never be onstage without alcohol or drugs. I've been without alcohol or drugs for nine months now, and I feel so much better than I did before! I think I play much better — everybody's noticed that. So I'm pleased with the way everything turned out, that actually alcohol is bad. You only *imagine* you feel better, but you don't, really.

In the two years between the Scorpions' Lonesome Crow *and UFO's* Phenomenon, *your style and tone changed dramatically. What do you attribute this to?*

I think if you only play for five years and don't really have a style together, and then practice a lot in one year, you change a lot. As soon as you find a style, then you never change for the rest of your life, preferably, but you still build on it.

When you first joined UFO, was it hard to communicate with the other members of the band due to the language barrier?

Yeah. I couldn't speak any English! But I had my girlfriend, who became my wife; we are separated now. She helped me out by translating if I had something important to say. I worked with UFO six hours a day, and the rest of the day I was talking German, so it took me a long time to learn English. A few months ago I went to school just to get a bit more into English, and I think it helped a lot.

When you were the only guitarist in UFO, how did you manage to play both the rhythm and harmony parts of "Doctor, Doctor" onstage?

Well, I changed the harmony a bit to be able to do it with two fingers of my left hand. You can actually use one finger if you play only one harmony. If you play two harmonies, you use two fingers — one for each riff. I just did the harmony with two fingers and bent the strings and did the runs at the same time. I used only my plectrum in the right hand — no fingers.

Was it your idea to add a keyboardist to the group around the time No Heavy Petting *came out?*

Yeah, I always liked keyboards, but I think the guy we had then was too much into keyboards. It was a good thing when we changed to Paul Raymond, because he plays guitar and keyboards and can switch.

Were there any after-the-concert overdubs added to Strangers In The Night?

We couldn't redo too many because the drum mike was picking up the guitar onstage, and we couldn't redo the drums. If we had overdubbed, we might have picked up the old guitar part on the drum track. You might get a song where it didn't pick up too much and you are able to control it, but not many. So most of those were actual live solos.

At the time you quit UFO, was the band too limited for what you found yourself able to express?

Yeah. The first time I left there were stories about me joining the Moonies and everything, because I didn't say anything when I disappeared. I was a bit errant and went on holiday and got myself straightened out. Two months later I had to get in touch with the manager, and they tried to talk me into rejoining, which I did because I was feeling okay again. The second time I told them two months in advance that I was going to leave. I'm happy with whatever happened in the past. I think it was just right and everything worked out perfectly. The good and the bad things — I think they're all important, forever. It could have maybe been better if I would've had different musicians; you never know. You can't say "If . . . ," you know. You make mistakes; you learn from them. But it's not good to go like, "Oh, I would have done this different and this different." It's the past, and you can't change it anyway, so you just try from now on to make it different and to look for the right musicians straight away — the ones you like — so you don't have to change all the time.

When you appeared with the Scorpions on Lovedrive, *many people thought you had rejoined the band. Was this ever part of the plan?*

No. When I did it, it was a favor. My brother asked me to do it. Matthias Jabs was a bit lost because he had just joined the group, and his lead breaks were a bit too technical and without feeling. So they did about three lead breaks, and I came over and did five. The record jacket only mentions that I did three lead breaks because the other two were a combination of my own leads and a bit of Matthias' and my brother's. I can't remember which cuts they are.

Some listeners have compared your style to that of Ulrich Roth, your original replacement in the Scorpions. Have you ever played with him?

I think I jammed with him once in Germany, a long time ago.

Is your new rhythm section giving you a lot of ideas for soloing?

Oh, yeah. It's like a train, a machine full of energy. Cozy [Powell] plays it on his bass drum, and the way he builds up his parts on the drums gets me into building up at the same time, which really makes it steam with high energy. It's really great.

Have you ever done any sessions outside of UFO and the Scorpions?

No, for some reason I never have. I don't know why. I think I was never really interested in appearing on too many different albums or with different groups. I just wanted to stick with one group and make the best of that one.

You have a unique tone with a very penetrating midrange. Do you record with a wah-wah partially depressed?

I think on *Phenomenon* I recorded a lot with a wah-wah. On the second album I did half and half. On *No Heavy Petting* I used a different guitar, and I think I used the wah-wah quite a lot. On *Lights Out* I used a Pignose instead of my Marshall on almost the whole album, and I didn't like it. So I went back to the Marshall for *Obsession*, which was again a combination of some leads played with a wah-wah, some without. On the live album I did almost every lead break with the wah-wah because it made the tone sing more. It's a bit more sustained. You can just set the pedal on treble, or you can put it in the middle or on low, and you'll get a different sound. You can change it if you want a different tone while you're playing a lead break — it's up to you.

What guitars did you use for Lonesome Crow?

I think that was with a Gibson Les Paul and a Marshall.

What did you use for the first UFO albums?

A 50-watt Marshall and Gibson Flying V's. The Flying V I'm playing now is the one I've always used. It could be about a '68 or a '70. It has been broken about ten times. Twice it has been in a thousand pieces, and somebody just managed to rebuild it completely perfect. It's even better than it was when I bought it new. I used it on *Phenomenon, Force It,* and some, I think, on *No Heavy Petting* and *Lights Out*. I also used it on *Obsession*, and I'm sure it was on *Strangers In The Night* and *The Michael Schenker Group.*

Aside from the repairs, has the guitar been modified?

No. It even has the stock pickups.

What other guitars do you possess?

I have another Flying V that is about a '62. I've only got this one spare, just two Flying V's. I don't even have an acoustic. I think it's very important to not have many guitars. It's better to stick to one and play it all the time so you get used to it and it gets used to you. You repeat — some people always play on *E*; some people always play on *A*. Everybody prefers certain chords. You play the same things over and over, and by doing this the guitar gets used to your kind of vibrato and how hard you press. Everything just goes very smoothly, and that's why a guitar sounds better after a while. When you get it new, it's stiff; it's not used to your kind of technique. As soon as it gets used to your technique, it starts singing and vibrates very gently and warmly.

What kind of strings do you use?

Fender Rock And Roll, from .009 [high *E*] to .040 [low *E*].

MARK LAITA

Do you ever have trouble staying in tune?

Not lately, for some reason. I did when I joined UFO. I always spent like a minute between each number to retune my guitar. I think it's because I didn't change my strings every night. Maybe that's the answer: Since I've been changing strings every gig, it just stays perfectly in tune. I bend the strings a lot, stretch them out as much as I can. I just play the guitar for an hour or two before I go onstage so the strings get played in a bit.

How is the action on your guitar?

It's actually getting quite high. I think I used to play much lower than I do now. It has something to do with the bridge. If it's a touch too low and I bend the *B* string, it goes dead. So I have to have a certain height to the *B* string so it still sings if I bend it on the 18th fret or wherever.

Do you take care of your instrument while you're on the road?

No, I don't do anything. On the last tour somebody cleaned it every night. If I'm on my own at home, I never do anything to it.

Do you always use standard tuning?

Yeah, I tune it the regular way.

Is your amplifier modified?

No. It's just a 50-watt Marshall.

What devices do you have onstage besides the wah-wah?

None. I don't have a pedalboard, just the wah-wah. I like to play straightforward without any special effects, so nobody can say, "Oh, it only sounds like this because he has this machine." I like the image when you've got the amplifier, the guitar, and one wah-wah pedal, and anything else is up to you. I have always liked guitarists who go this way instead of like Jimi Hendrix and all those guys who try to copy him, using a lot of phaser. Lately the mixing guy has been putting in the Harmonizer once in a while, just in case it gets too boring because I'm using quite a lot of treble pickup. There used to be a time when I played for one hour with only the treble pickup. Now I play the bass pickup for a while, and like three times in the whole set we'll put the Harmonizer in for a short part of the lead break. That's all I use, and I much prefer that.

How do you hold your pick?

I hold it with my thumb and the two fingers next to it.

Do you consciously follow any picking formulas?

If I play fast, sometimes I try to hit the string each time you hear a note or each time something changes. Then other times it's nicer to only hit the string once and let your left-hand fingers fly all over the strings, so it's different. It depends on what kind of taste you've got and what you want. Keep changing while you're doing a lead break — you only get it interesting if you use different techniques and nice melodies in one break. It's difficult to describe, actually.

How do you hold the pick to get harmonics?

I hold it so that the part that shows is very short. I hit the string with the plectrum, and then at the same time I hit it with my thumb a bit.

Does your vibrato come more from your wrist or your fingers?

Wrist, I would say.

Do you anchor any part of your right hand when you play?

Yeah, I rest it on the bridge.

Do you usually use the little finger of your left hand?

Not very often. Only if I'm playing fast lead breaks.

Do you ever play slide? Some parts sound like it, but it's hard to tell.

Yeah, I do. It's a good thing that it's hard to tell, too. That's what Jeff Beck does as well. Sometimes I can't tell if he played with a slide or if he played normal. But that's good! I like smooth slide players. I don't much like the old-fashioned blues too much [*imitates Elmore James' version of "Dust My Broom"*] — it's the old fashion. I like the kind of slide where you don't open tune; you just play as if it were any other lead break, and you just use whatever comes to mind. You use the right kind of vibrato and try to play it smooth, so it doesn't always sound like slide, and people go, "How did he do that?" I like that kind of thing. I use a big, thick glass slide.

How do you set up in the studio?

It's with the Marshall and the guitar, and I just sit around the control room and play around with mixing them. I play the way I play live, full-volume. Most of my technique is in my hands.

Do you usually get your solo in the first take?

No, you must be joking. I'm never satisfied with the lead breaks I do, so I keep playing them over and over. They go like, "Oh, my, there was a good lead break," and I say, "No, I can do better than that one." Then I do another one, and another, until we end up with about ten. Then I just compromise and take the best one.

Do you splice parts together?

Yeah. Sometimes you play a lead break and like the first quarter is not so good, but the last three-quarters has so amazing of a buildup that it would be a waste if you would forget about it and do another one. So we try to replace the quarter on the front to make it perfect.

When you co-write songs with others, do you usually come up with the music?

It's always the same. I do the music, and the singer does the lyrics.

How do you compose?

If I've got an idea, I put it on a cassette. I do this for six months, and then I have maybe two cassettes together. Then if I've just got nothing to do sometime, I listen back to the cassettes and record the best parts on another tape. I leave this for maybe two months, when I listen to it again and do the same thing. So at the end I've got like ten really nice ideas, and I put them together and try to make sense out of them.

What do you think when you hear other guys playing licks that you came up with?

I think it's quite interesting because then I can tell where I am. When I started playing the guitar, I used to copy somebody else. Then there was a time when I tried not to copy, which is from the middle of my past up to now. Now it has come to the part where people have actually tried to copy me, so I look back and go, "Amazing! I'm actually where people like Jimmy Page used to be for me when I was young." So it just gives me a kind of idea of where I am at the moment.

Are there any newcomer guitarists who especially

impress you?

I think I'm quite interested in Eddie Van Halen. He plays funny, and I like that. I think it's original. He doesn't play a straight guitar, which is not important. He uses a tremolo arm and has his own runs and styles, and it's good. I like the way he has chosen. It's really flashy. We all have our own little style. Eddie has got his little style, I've got mine, and all the good guitarists have got theirs. You can never say who's best, you know.

Are there times when you think you've reached your peak?

It's very difficult to say. I think it goes up and down. At the moment it's going up again. It's different because I'm doing it without alcohol and drugs, which gives me a slightly different style. If you're drunk, you play a bit more all over the place. You're not as precise. I think I'm going up again because everybody says I'm playing better than ever. We played the Hammersmith Odeon in London and the manager of UFO and drummer, Andy Parker, came backstage and said they couldn't believe it. They said I played so much better than I had with UFO, which is a nice compliment. I can't tell myself, because I can't remember how I actually played when I had a few beers.

Do you have any advice you'd pass along to young guitarists?

There's not much you can say. I think it's all experience: Some people have to go through shit to learn; some people never go through shit and they learn anyway. It all depends. The script of your life is already written for you, and there's nothing you can do about it unless you find out what life is all about, which means that you are a very wise person and can control your life the way you want to. All I can say is try to be wise!

— Jas Obrecht

MICHAEL SCHENKER: A SELECTED DISCOGRAPHY

With Michael Schenker Group (all on Chrysalis): *The Michael Schenker Group*, CHE 1302, *MSG*, 1336; *Assault Attack*, 1393; *One Night At Budokan*, WWS-67159. **With UFO** (all on Chrysalis): *Phenomenon*, 1059; *Force It*, 1074; *No Heavy Petting*, 1103; *Lights Out*, 1127; *Obsession*,1182; *Strangers In The Night*,1209. **With The Scorpions:** *Lonesome Crow*, Bomb,101; *Lovedrive*, Mercury, 3795.

ROSS MARINO

The Scorpions

Mainland Europe's leading heavy metal act since 1971, the Scorpions lost original lead guitarist Michael Schenker to U.F.O. in 1973. Ulrich Roth took his place for the next five years, touring the world and recording several distinguished albums. The German-based band auditioned over 170 players before hiring Matthias Jabs to share guitar duties with founder Rudolf Schenker. Conducted during the Scorpion's *Blackout* tour, this interview appeared in the May '83 issue.

The Scorpions at the 1983 US Festival: (L-R) bassist Francis Buchholz, guitarists Rudolf Schenker and Matthias Jabs, and singer Klaus Meine guesting on guitar.

an introduction

One of the first-generation European heavy metal bands, the Scorpions are proof that dedication, perseverance, and a strong direction may one day lead to success. Unaffected by trends and fashion, they've remained on a distinct heavy metal course for over a dozen years, delivering nine powerful albums. Like the Yardbirds (which produced Eric Clapton, Jeff Beck, and Jimmy Page in the '60s), the Scorpions have served as a testing ground for rock guitarists. Since its inception, the German band has introduced three of the most respected lead guitarists in the heavy metal vein: Michael Schenker, Ulrich Roth, and Matthias Jabs. The Scorpions have also been tremendously influential for many of today's top rock acts, including Iron Maiden and Van Halen, who covered Scorpions material early in their career.

Currently the band features two guitarists, 34-year-old songwriter Rudolf Schenker (Michael's older brother) and lead guitarist Matthias Jabs, who at 26 is the youngest member. With his roots in the blues, Matthias is a very talented player whose creativity and ability become more evident with each album. On their latest release, *Blackout*, Schenker supplies most of the solid, hook-laden rhythm that supports Jabs' melodic, aggressive lead work. Matthias' style ranges from the growling vibrato and blistering solo work featured on the title cut to the richly sustained harmony lines of "No One Like You." The brilliant teamwork of Schenker and Jabs has helped shoot the last few Scorpions albums high into the album charts. With *Blackout* making it to the Top 10 in the U.S. and Germany and all the way to #1 in France, the group continues to widen its audience. But it wasn't always so easy . . . .

Born on August 31, 1948, Rudolf graduated from high school in 1966 and immediately entered the working world in Hanover, Germany. Left with little time practice guitar, he hired his younger brother Michael at the rate of a Deutsche mark per tune to figure out material by the Beatles and, later, Mountain. In 1970, Michael, then 13, formed Copernicus with singer Klaus Meine. The group disbanded soon afterwards, leaving Michael and Klaus to team up with Rudolf and bassist Lothar Heimberg to form the Scorpions. The combination of these strong players earned the support of Germany's Brain Records, who signed them to the recording contract in 1971 that produced their debut album, *Lonesome Crow*, the following year.

The band's tour schedule in 1972 consisted of 136 gigs opening for acts such as Rory Gallagher, UFO, and Uriah Heep. The Scorpions worked on other projects as well, including writing the soundtrack for an anti-drug movie called *Das Kalte Paradies* [*The Cold Paradise*]. In April 1973 Michael left the Scorpions to join UFO. Coupled with other personnel problems, this caused the group to break up. After a short stint with Ulrich Roth's Dawn Road, Klaus and Rudolf convinced Ulrich to help them reform the Scorpions.

The new lineup, which included Francis Buchholz on bass, was signed by RCA Records in 1974. They recorded *Fly To The Rainbow*, only to face yet another change with the addition of Belgian drummer Rudy Lenners. The following year was monumental for the Scorpions, who embarked on their first tour outside of Germany as the opening act for Sweet. They attracted the attention of Dieter Dierks, who produced their next LP, *In Trance*, at his studio in Cologne. (Dierks has produced all subsequent Scorpions albums as well.) That November, the Scorpions made their concert debut in England, pulling in glowing reviews for their performances at London's Marquee Club. By 1976 they had achieved headline status throughout Europe and Japan, which pushed *In Trance* onto the best-seller list.

The reception of their next album, 1976's *Virgin Killer*, made it obvious to many that the Scorpions were on an unwavering path to superstardom. In Japan alone, the album went gold *one week* after release. As their popularity increased, so did the size of the venues they performed. The Scorpions returned to England in April 1977 for a far more extensive tour than those of previous years. Shortly after this, Rudy Lenners departed due to heart trouble and was replaced by current drummer Herman Rarebell.

Taken By Force was recorded towards the end of 1977, and in April 1978 the band embarked on a five-day, sellout tour of Japan. Portions of the Scorpions' two nights at Tokyo's Sun Plaza Hall were released as the two-record *Tokyo Tapes*. Despite the group's superstar status in Japan and Europe, Ulrich Roth quit at this time to pursue a different direction. He has since recorded two albums with Electric Sun.

Ulrich's departure left the band with the huge task of finding someone competent to fill his shoes. After holding auditions in London that drew over 170 applicants, the Scorpions hired Hanover guitarist Matthias Jabs and headed straight into the studio to record *Lovedrive* early in 1979. Coincidentally, Michael Schenker had just left UFO and was searching for a solid musical situation. He rejoined the Scorpions at Rudolf's suggestion, which left Matthias without a gig. Michael played half of the solos on *Lovedrive* and went on to tour with the Scorpions throughout Germany. After several "sick" spells, during which Matthias filled in, it became apparent that Michael had some personal affairs to straighten out.

Jabs took some time to contemplate the band's recent "musical chairs" and once again rejoined the Scorpions, who were soon whisked off to Japan. Opening for Ted Nugent afterwards, the Scorpions played for 68,000 fans on the first night of their American debut. The tour was cut short when they accepted an offer to headline England's prestigious Reading Pop Festival. A return tour broke the band in the U.S. and pushed *Lovedrive* into the charts for 30 weeks.

Completion of the next Scorpions album, *Animal Magnetism*, came in March 1980. This was followed by tours of the United Kingdom, continental Europe, and the U.S., where they were once again billed with Nugent. The band flew to southern France in March 1981 to record tracks for *Blackout*, but were disappointed to learn of Klaus Meine's vocal deterioration. Nodes were diagnosed as the cause of his illness, and an operation to remove them resulted in a secondary infection. After recuperating and consulting a specialist in Vienna, Klaus began voice training. Consequently, his performances on *Blackout* are his strongest ever. After the album's release, the band performed before sellout audiences in Germany, France, Italy, and the U.K. Beginning in June 1982, they headlined a tour of the U.S. and Canada, with Iron Maiden as their chief supporting act.

Currently at work on a new album, the Scorpions remain true to the heavy metal style they helped create in the early '70s. Although their music transcends most cultural barriers with its universal hard-driving rhythm, it should be remembered that Matthias Jabs and Rudolf Schenker speak English only as a second language and are much more articulate in their mother tongue. The following interview was conducted in English during the Scorpions' 1982 appearance in Oakland, California.

a dialog

The Scorpions have stuck to their style of music. They don't seem to change with the times like other bands who go from being hard rock to new wave to heavy metal.

Rudolf: Fashion is not for us. We love music.

Matthias: What you play best is what you can feel. Jumping on trends is bullshit. I couldn't go out and play some Cars-like stuff, you know [*starts to sing "Shake It Up"*]. For me, it wouldn't be right. It's good music for them, but not for me.

Are you playing your favorite kind of music right now?

Matthias: It comes close.

Rudolf: Yes. When you listen to our first and last album, you notice that our style has not changed. Between *Lonesome Crow* — our first album — and our latest album, we've just tried to get better. We want to be a very good group; it's important to us. We are happy that people like our music.

Do you feel that you're getting out 100% of what you want to deliver?

Rudolf: Look, if you're giving 100% all the time, then you leave no room to get better. You can only get better if you feel that you're doing, say, 90%. We like what we've done, but we like to keep getting better. We like our last album, *Blackout*, very much. It was a very painful album. Our singer, Klaus, had to have his throat operated on. I said, "Look, Klaus, take your time. Work very hard on yourself." Everybody in the group said the same thing.

So you feel strongly unified as a band?

Rudolf: Yes. We've had problems with other people who have worked with the band before. Some people's personalities were so strong, it worked against the group. It made it hard for us to work with each other.

Rudolf, you've always written a lot of songs but you don't take many solos. How would you describe your role in the Scorpions?

Rudolf: I am one-fifth of the band. Anyone in the band can write songs. The band has to choose which compositions are best. I'm not in the band to say, "This is my composition. Now play it!" When the band feels that a certain solo is right for me, they say, "Rudolf, play it!" and I play it. We don't sit and say, "I want to play this solo," or "That's my song; I have to play that solo." No! When I find a good solo line in a song and people like it, I do it.

Are you proficient on instruments other than guitar?

Matthias: No. I play a little bit of piano, though. Basically, I only play guitar.

Rudolf: I just play guitar.

Did either of you grow up in a musical household?

Matthias: Yeah. My mom and dad both played piano, and pretty bad! I started on guitar when I was 14. I got a very cheap acoustic guitar as a Christmas present from my parents. I got my first electric half a year later, and that was an Ibanez Les Paul copy. My first professional guitar was a '64 Fender Stratocaster. I progressed very fast after just one year of playing.

Who started playing guitar first in the Schenker family?

Rudolf: Me. I am older than Michael. The point is, when you live together and you start playing guitar, the younger brother usually likes to play along. I'd say to Michael, "Here's some cello parts. Find the right melodies and we'll play together." So Michael first learned guitar by listening to cello. And then we could play together. It's much more fun to have someone play along with you. When my brother and I would play together, we had a good feeling and very good communication. Even back then I was playing the rhythm parts and Michael was playing lead. I think the rhythm is the most important point. I like to play rhythm. To have a good basic rhythm is more important than having a bad basic rhythm and a good lead.

Did you ever study with teachers or from books?

Rudolf: No teacher. Some books in Germany gave us different chords.

Matthias: I learned from listening to records. I know something about the technical terms of the modes and scales I play, but I have trouble translating because there are different names in German than there are in English. In Germany, we have names taken from the Greeks. Strange names.

Did any artists inspire you to play?

Matthias: I started off listening to Jeff Beck, then Jimi Hendrix, and later on Allan Holdsworth. But I've stopped listening to them now. I don't listen to that much music anymore. I don't have the time. In the first years of playing, I practiced several hours every day and listened to a lot of records to get ideas, to get better. Technically, Allan Holdsworth is probably the best. He's a great guitar player. I don't like everything he's done, because sometimes it's just too strange, but overall I like it a lot. I've also listened to Eric Clapton and all of these old, famous guitar players. Now I listen to the radio, buy a few records and tapes once in a while.

Rudolf: I was influenced by the Pretty Things, the Yardbirds, and the Animals. I wasn't particularly a big fan of the Beatles, although they were very good composers. For me, the Beatles were too much pop. In terms of solos, I liked to listen to the Yardbirds — Jimmy Page more than Clapton. For me, Jimmy Page was very creative. Although sometimes he doesn't play all that well, his ideas are very, very good. For me, Jimi Hendrix was also very good. But as far as a feeling musician, it was Peter Green from Fleetwood Mac. He was amazing. I

NEIL ZLOZOWER

Marshall
Marshall
Marshall
Marshall
Marshall
Marshall
Marshall
Marshall

JON SIEVERT

saw one live concert in Hanover, my home town, and his playing was so full of feeling it was like you were on an LSD trip, you know? The emotion I felt from him was great.

Did either of you make any recordings before the Scorpions?

Rudolf: No. The same with Michael: We started with the Scorpions.

Matthias: Yes. The band was called Lady. We released one single on Germany's Polygram label. It's very hard to find. I don't know how many copies they released, and I only have one or two of these left.

Was Lady your first professional band?

Matthias: No, it was not a professional group. We made a 45, but it was not my style. It was pop metal. I wasn't that much into it. It was not this kind of music. It was close, but they had keyboards and all this stuff. It's hard to find good musicians in Germany. There are only a few bands a person can play with there. When they asked me to join the band, I had to take a chance. Lady did a lot of TV stuff, and I thought it would be a good experience to get some studio work. I was very young at that time; this was six years ago.

What was it like playing with Ulrich Roth?

Rudolf: We had a good feeling with Ulrich, but he had a different direction. I like Ulrich's guitar playing very much. He's a very good guitar player who is classically influenced. He's original. It's the same with my brother: He's a good guitar player, too, but Michael had a very big ego.

There is a rumor that when Ulrich was in the band, he often played both the rhythm and lead parts on songs he wrote. Is this true?

Rudolf: We are so different, Ulrich Roth and me. Sometimes he could handle my feelings, and sometimes I couldn't handle his feelings. If we both liked a song, then one of us would just say, "Do it!" It depended on the feeling. I didn't want to say, "I'm the rhythm player: I must do this song," or "I'm the lead player: I must do this song." No! The Scorpions have a style, and when Ulrich was in the Scorpions, then there were actually two styles. And that's not so good.

It must have been difficult to follow Ulrich.

Rudolf: It was very hard for Matthias to be the next guitar player after Ulrich Roth. Directionally, Matthias came from a normal band, a pop band, from Hanover. When we auditioned guitar players in London, 170 people were there. Paul Chapman from UFO turned out. It was important for us to have the right guitar player, you know — one that would fit the band. So we went to Hanover and asked Matthias to play with us, and he said, "Yes."

Matthias: They called me. I didn't actually know that they were looking for a new guitar player.

Did you have to audition?

Matthias: Yes.

Rudolf: We had known each other some years before, and he still had to audition.

Were you looking for a German guitar player?

Rudolf: No, no. That's not the reason. The person had to fit together with the Scorpions.

Matthias: I was smart enough to pick up all their songs in advance. I mean, if you're going to an audition, you'll probably play a few of the songs that they play and then add what you can do. I auditioned, and it was all right.

Were you a fan of the Scorpions before you joined them?

Matthias: Everyone around our home town knew this favorite local band. I wasn't a fan. I owned some of the albums. I knew them very well already. I liked them. Ulrich Roth was a good friend of mine even before he joined the Scorpions. We grew up in the same area.

Did you admire his playing?

Matthias: Yeah, sort of. He was the best at the time in this local area. But I think he's lost . . . . Well, I don't want to talk bad about him, but I talked to him about his direction, and he is convinced about what he is doing. I think he used to be much better when he was with the Scorpions, and he could have been better still. He's an excellent guitarist. But what he's trying to do right now, I can't understand. Nobody can understand. He could have been so great. Listen to his stuff: It's not for the people; it's for himself.

Is your approach to play for the people?

Matthias: Well, yeah, basically. But everybody plays a little for themselves. I try to play for the whole sound. I try to play what fits best for a song rather than just do some crazy, fancy lead stuff. That's what a lot of people are doing today — just fooling around. I try to play what the song needs. That's the most important thing for me.

Four months after you joined the band, you were replaced by Michael Schenker. How did you feel about this?

Matthias: Ah, what can I say? I didn't get mad. It was a different situation. It didn't feel that bad. The idea was not that far away because Michael and Rudolf are brothers, and I kind of understood it. Still, it felt strange.

Why didn't Michael stay with the Scorpions after playing on Lovedrive*?*

Rudolf: He had a very big problem with UFO. Michael was in a situation where he was drinking lots of alcohol and taking too many drugs. And in order to give his best onstage every day, it was way too much. So then he came to us after leaving UFO and asked if he could come back to the Scorpions. We said, "Great!" It was hard for Matthias, who said, "Okay, I'd like to leave this band." Onstage, Michael played with us in Germany and in France. His big problem was, he said, "I can't play onstage anymore." Michael told us to forget it, and called Matthias back and said, "Please play with the Scorpions." Matthias said, "Okay. I'd like to play with you until the Japanese tour, and then I'll see how I like it." After the English tour, Matthias said, "Okay, we have a good feeling." Matthias learned a lot from Michael; he saw many shows that we did with Michael. Matthias was very young then, and he learned a lot from watching him.

Let's discuss your equipment. Which guitars do you use most?

Rudolf: Gibson Flying V's with normal pickups. I have two Flying V's that were made in 1958, and two from the mid '60s. The rest of them were made in the '70s. I now own 18 Flying V guitars. Onstage I use my black and white V; it was made in 1974. In the studio, it depends. I use different guitars for different sounds. We use an Ovation for the acoustic tracks. On tour I bring four or five guitars, but I leave my '58s at home.

Matthias: A Gibson Explorer and an early-'60s, pre-CBS Fender Stratocaster with a Floyd Rose tremolo unit. Actually, I have four Strats. One is a '58; the other three are early '60s. All four of them are black and white. Two of my Stratocasters are modified, and two aren't. In one of them I use a Bill Lawrence pickup in the treble position and a humbucking pickup. In the studio I use my stock Stratocasters with three pickups, and live I use Strats that have one humbucking pickup. I also have two Gibson Explorers: One is white with black stripes, and the other is black with white tape. And I have a very light cherry sunburst '59 Les Paul Standard; it's curly maple. I used it on "No One Like You" for the lead solo. Everything about the guitar is original. It's one of the nicest Les Pauls I've ever seen.

Did you buy most of these guitars after you joined the Scorpions?

Matthias: Yeah, basically. I've had many nice guitars before, but whenever I wanted to buy a new one, I'd have to sell one of the other ones. Now I can keep some of them.

Do any of your guitars have special wiring or out-of-phase switches?

Matthias: No. I hate out-of-phase switches. On one of my Explorers I changed my stock Gibson pickup to another Gibson pickup. I don't know what the model is called. Other than that, though, those guitars are stock.

What guitar was used to do the nice vibrato bar wang on the song "Blackout"?

Matthias: That was my Floyd Rose Strat.

Do you prefer maple or rosewood fingerboards?

Matthias: Rosewood.

Rudolf: It's not important what kind of neck it is, as long as it feels good. If I play a chord and it gets into my body and into my heart, then I know the guitar is right.

What is your favorite amplifier?

Rudolf: It's an old Marshall 50-watt top, 10 or 15 years old. I keep that at home as well. Every 50-watt amplifier has a different sound. In the studio, I try to get the best sound possible, so I use my old 50-watt head. We both use Marshall 50-watt amps live.

Matthias: I use two 50-watt Marshall stacks for the normal sound, and I have one stack as a spare and one stack for the voice box.

Rudolf: If there's a real small hall where we're playing for fun, I just use one 50-watt Marshall.

What kind of effects do you use live?

Matthias: I use an Electro-Harmonix talk box, an Echoplex, and a Cry Baby wah-wah. That's it.

Rudolf: Sometimes I use a phaser; I don't know what kind it is. And I play a Vox wah-wah. The old Vox wah-wahs are fantastic.

Matthias: They're the best. I have between six and ten broken ones, so I have to use Cry Babys.

Do you use wireless systems?

Rudolf: Yes. I have a Schaffer-Vega wireless. It cost a lot of money, but I wanted to have the best. The Schaffer-Vega helps me to keep the sound I like.

Matthias: I have tried the Nady systems. The basic sound that they deliver is fine, but if you play fancy stuff where you need the harmonics, you don't get the power you need. You seem to lose a little of the bottom sound. I have spoken with John Nady, though, and we're going to try it again. I just use a straight cord now, and it's fine. Sustain and harmonic overtones seem to get lost with wireless systems.

Do you use your tone and volume knobs very much during a live performance?

Matthias: What is that [*laughs*]? I use the volume, but not the tone. I keep the treble on full. In the studio I do different things, but onstage I just ignore the tone knob.

Rudolf: Normally not.

Is there anything about your playing that is unique or revolutionary?

Matthias: I don't know if it's anything unique. Today, everybody's doing this fancy stuff. I don't know if it's unique or not.

Did Eddie Van Halen inspire your two-handed trills?

Matthias: Anybody in any bar can do this today, you know. Eddie was the first one to do it right, but I have heard it before that. Some of the classical players did it 50 years ago. He got it from them. Eddie probably does it the best, so what can you say? As long as it goes with the song, it's fine. But if you just fool around and it doesn't fit the song, it's bullshit. It wastes it.

Matthias, how do you do your effect where one picked note sounds like a chord?

Matthias: I hit one string, and by the way I use the pick in the right-hand position, I'm able to get multiple notes. I hold the pick real short, between the two pickups. The main effect is with the pick that you keep in your right hand. It's just by feeling. I first realized I could play this in the studio, but I didn't use it.

If you can expand this technique, it's quite possible that you could break some new ground.

Matthias: I hope to. I think I can do a lot about my

JON SIEVERT

tremolo technique as well — more than I'm doing now.

What kinds of picks and strings do you prefer?

Matthias: Gray Jim Dunlop picks. They're nylon. I use D'Angelico strings, the regular set beginning with a .009 high *E*. I switch between .009s and .010s, depending on the sound I'm trying to get. My Les Paul sounds a lot better with .010s. For the bottom lower notes, I like to be able to get a screeching sound, so I use the heavier set.

Rudolf: I use these kinds of picks [*holds up a small, thumbnail-sized pick with the Scorpions' insignia and his autograph stamped into it*]. For strings, I use a set beginning with a .010.

Do you ever use a slide?

Matthias: Yes. I used one on the song "Animal Magnetism."

What kind of strobe tuners do you use?

Matthias: In the studio, we use the Conn strobe tuner. We can't use it in America, though, because of the different voltage. So on tour we use the battery-powered Korg tuners. We don't keep them onstage, though. Our roadies take care of that. When a guitar is out-of-tune, we just give it back to the roadies and change guitars.

Rudolf: I tried to use the tuner onstage, but I got rid of it. It was just too much aggravation.

What size concert venue do you prefer?

Matthias: There's a certain size hall that is just perfect because you can put everything that you need and want onstage. It's between, say, 6,000 and 12,000. We need a certain size hall to put on the kind of show that we like to put on. I think we all like to play in small halls, too. In Europe, we've got small halls. They have theaters that have nice acoustics and nice atmosphere. For a change, we like to play at very large shows — like 50,000 seats.

Rudolf: I like a very large concert hall, but communication is important. In a club, you come off feeling fantastic just because of the communication with the audience. Three hundred people in a club can be right with you.

How do the Scorpions warm up for a show?

Rudolf: Sometimes Matthias and I play together.

Matthias: You basically just want to warm up your fingers. Because of the temperature, the roadies are always asking us for our guitars because they want to tune them for the stage. I would rather practice until the last moment, but I have to give the roadies the guitars. We each have one guitar roadie.

When you're off the road, do you rehearse much old material?

Matthias: We're moving on to new things. We never practice old things off the road.

How many hours a day do you practice when you're not touring?

Matthias: It depends. A couple of hours. It depends on the feeling: If it doesn't feel right, there's no reason to push it and to keep practicing. We can't say, "Okay, we're going in at noon. We're going to practice until 8:00 in the evening." It just doesn't work that way. It makes no sense.

Rudolf: It's not a question of how long you rehearse; it's that you're in the right mood while you're rehearsing.

Do you ever create material in the studio, or is everything worked out ahead of time?

Rudolf: Sometimes an idea can develop in the studio, but mostly we come up with things at the hotel or at our homes. We both have Teac 4-tracks, and I use a Revox A77 for echo.

Matthias: I'm going to get one of those Tascam 4-track Portastudios. The other stuff's just too big. There's too many little things. It's too complicated.

Do you work out solos before recording?

Matthias: On some songs, I just start playing. It feels right, and I keep it. When I go in the studio, I don't know exactly what I'm going to do on *every* song, but on a few songs I know pretty much exactly what I'm going to do. I always have a basic feeling for the song. It's just a matter of refining.

Do you do a lot of splicing when recording solos, or do you pretty much play live from top to bottom?

Matthias: I prefer to play the solo in one track. In rehearsal, I may play around with the beginning, middle, or end. Of course, this doesn't happen all the time, but I try to get it in one take on one track.

What is the Scorpions' recording process? Do you all go in at one time and play your parts, or do just a few of you record at a time?

Matthias: We do it both ways.

How many tracks did you use when you recorded your last album at Dieter Dierks Studio?

Rudolf: 32 tracks. Our contract calls for two more albums with Dierks.

Will you be staying with him after that?

Rudolf: We'll see. He's a producer, but we are a team. He's not a person to say, "Do this. Do this." We talk together and work together. He's not a producer to tell us what our style is; he's an engineer and a producer. When he comes up with an idea and we don't like it, we say, "No, we don't want to do that," and we don't do it. Normally, the producing is by Dierks and us.

From Animal Magnetism *to* Blackout *you seem to be playing a lot faster and taking much more of the spotlight with your solos, Matthias. Is this because you've been getting better?*

Matthias: No. On *Blackout* I could do what I wanted to. Last time, the producer was too much involved. He tried to tell me what was right and what was wrong. He didn't have faith in me 100%. I told him, "This time, I'd like to do what I want to do." I got to bring out what I wanted to say. That's why it sounds a lot better than it did before. If you feel right, then you can play the right thing. If somebody tells you what to do, it's bullshit, because you can't play something if you don't feel right about it.

There's a song on Blackout *called "When The Smoke Is Going Down" that features an out-of-tune lead guitar. Are you aware of this?*

Rudolf: I know! But the feeling is so good! Do you know Jimmy Page, all the wrong notes he plays? Of course I know it's out of tune; I'm not stupid! But the feeling is more important than the pitch or right notes.

Two other songs on that album, "No One Like You" and "You Give Me All I Need," have a very similar progression. Why did you put them back-to-back on the album?

Rudolf: No, that's a mistake. "No One Like You" is three years old, and "You Give Me All I Need" is only a year old. They're different! I'll tell you one thing: I think it's much better to try things different. When we look at all the songs, we try to find the right order to give people a good way to listen to the music.

What's the most important thing to keep in mind when composing?

Rudolf: The singer. I try to write in the direction that Klaus normally sings in. I write most of the melodies. When I write a song, I have a melody that goes along with the chords in my mind. I'll come up with an idea and a melody, and I'll sing something on tape. Then I'll play it for Klaus.

Have you and your brother Michael written many songs together?

Rudolf: Yes, of course! Most of the first album, *Lonesome Crow*, was written by my brother and me. Nothing recently, though. We may do something for fun sometime.

What do you think of Michael's solo albums?

Rudolf: The drummer isn't heavy enough. The second album has some really good ideas. I don't think the producer is so good, though.

You haven't written any material for the Scorpions yet, Matthias. Are you going to?

Matthias: You never know. I put a lot into the songs anyway. I think I have some good material.

Have you ever thought of adding keyboards to the Scorpions?

Rudolf: Every time we've tried keyboards, we've listened back and said, "No, that isn't the Scorpions sound."

What are your ideas for the next album? Do you have a title?

Rudolf: No. When you're on tour you get many new ideas, and we take these ideas home and work them out with the group.

Matthias: Even if you would say, "Okay, I have the best idea for a title," or whatever, you never know in a couple of months if it's going to change or not. You have to wait until the last moment, until you find the very best thing.

Do you plan to put out another live album?

Matthias: Yes, we should do one. Maybe not the next album, but soon. You never know when it will happen.

— **Mike Varney**

JON SIEVERT

SCORPIONS: A SELECTED DISCOGRAPHY

Lonesome Crow, Bomb [Canadian import], 101; *Fly To The Rainbow*, RCA, AFL1-4025; *In Trance*, RCA, AFL1-4128; *Virgin Killer*, RCA, PPL-1-4225; *Taken By Force*, RCA, APL-1-2628; *Tokyo Tapes*, RCA, CPL2-3039; *Lovedrive*, Mercury, SRM-1-3795; *Animal Magnetism*, Mercury, SRM 1-3825; *Blackout*, Mercury, SRM-1-4039. **Anthologies;** *Castle Donnington*, Polydor, 1-6311.

ROSS MARINO

Judas Priest

Arising from England's largest industrial city in 1973, Judas Priest staged a hard-fought battle for international recognition, achieving headline status after signing with CBS in 1977. Led by the fiery twin-guitars of Glenn Tipton and K.K. Downing, the band was in the forefront of British metal in the early '80s. This July '83 cover story interview was conducted by heavy metal producer Mike Varney during the *Screaming For Vengeance* tour.

K.K. Downing (L) and Glenn Tipton.

an introduction

There aren't too many groups that can boast of two accomplished guitarists who are equal in ability, each having a knack for captivating audiences with a combination of soul, finesse, and guitar histrionics. Hailing from England's largest industrial city, Birmingham, Judas Priest has just celebrated its tenth year in the business. Hot on the trail of heavy metal supremacy, the band comprises the double guitar assault of Glenn Tipton and K.K. Downing, charismatic singer Rob Halford, and the thunderous rhythm section work of bassist Ian Hill and drummer Dave Holland. These five workaholics have recently completed a grueling six-month U.S. tour in support of their latest LP, *Screaming For Vengeance*, which has gone gold and is drawing near platinum.

Judas Priest's original lineup — K.K. (Kenneth) Downing, Glenn Tipton, Ian Hill, Rob Halford, and drummer John Hinch — emerged in England's Midlands club circuit in 1973, playing a primitive fusion of blues and metal. The following year, U.K.-based Gull Records signed the band to a recording contract and their first album, *Rocka Rolla*, was released shortly thereafter. Although stylistically different from successive albums, this release enabled them to tour and laid the groundwork for a promising career. As they began to play larger venues in England and support major artists, word began to spread. This led to an invitation to perform at the prestigious Reading Festival, their largest gig up until that time. Gradually Judas Priest's music began to change, as did their drummers when Alan Moore replaced Hinch. As the band's reception grew stronger, so did their confidence, which gave them the impetus to record their next album, *Sad Wings Of Destiny*.

Their first U.S. release, this album marked a turning point in the group's musical direction. The blues influence was cast off in favor of more of a "death and destruction" theme that transcended the band's music and helped shape the dark image for which Judas Priest has become known. With songs such as "The Ripper," "Genocide," "Victim Of Changes," and "Epitaph," Judas Priest became a minor success, charting moderately in the U.K. and Japan, and modestly in the U.S.

It became clear to Judas Priest that their record label was incapable of supporting them any further, and they began to shop for a new contract. After careful consideration, they signed a worldwide deal with CBS Records and released their third album, *Sin After Sin*, in April 1977. Sporting a production by former Deep Purple bassist Roger Glover and amazing session drumming by Simon Phillips, they churned out metal anthems including "Sinner" and "Dissident Aggressor," as well as a heavy metal interpretation of Joan Baez' "Diamonds And Rust," which contributed to higher sales figures. Their first major U.S. tour, which opened in June, climaxed with two shows opening for Led Zeppelin at the Oakland Coliseum.

Released in February 1978, Judas Priest's fourth album, *Stained Class*, utilized the skills of veteran producer Dennis MacKay and new drummer Les Binks. Judas Priest were well on their way to establishing themselves as England's premier heavy metal band and were out to conquer the world, filling a void left by the demise of Deep Purple and the worldwide saturation of disco music. The intensive tour that followed encompassed 35 U.K. gigs in 35 nights, which prepared them for a three-month U.S. tour, during which they were seen by over a quarter of a million people. Then they were off to Japan for July and August, and returned to England for a mammoth two-month tour. Upon completion, they began preparation for their next LP.

Hell Bent For Leather included the band's first British Top-10 single, "Take On The World." Their third U.S. tour included several significant engagements, namely three sold-out nights at LA's Starwood club, a standing-room-only show at Manhattan's Mudd Club, and two sold-out nights at Toronto's El Mocambo. Upon returning to Europe, the band was elated to find that "Evening Star" had become the second British hit from *Hell Bent For Leather*. This soon became their best-selling LP, tripling the sales of *Stained Class* and breaking into America's Top 100.

Japan, where in the late '70s Judas Priest was ranked among the top ten bands, provided the recording site for their first live album, *Unleashed In The East*. Their debut project with current producer Tom Allom, this LP contains their hottest concert numbers: "Sinner," "Exciter," "Running Wild," and a splendid cover version of Fleetwood Mac's "Green Manalishi," to name a few. Recorded at the beginning of what observers termed "the new wave of British heavy metal," *Unleashed In The East* was issued during the middle of the band's ten-week 1979 North American tour, which included a month of dates opening for Kiss. At this time, the band announced the replacement of Les Binks by former Trapeze drummer Dave Holland.

The live album shot into the U.S. Top 50 and doubled the sales of their previous LP, partially because "Diamonds And Rust" broke as their first significant AOR single. The band continued on a month-long, sold-out European tour, performing in France, Germany, Holland, Switzerland, and Belgium. After taking a much needed Christmas vacation, they headed back into the studio with Allom to record their next LP.

When *British Steel* was released in March 1980, the musicians headed back out on the road for a 30-day, 30-show tour of the U.K., which had sold out nearly three months in advance. In the past the BBC had been reluctant to play Priest's abrasive heavy metal over the airwaves, but demand virtually forced them to add "Living After Midnight," and for the first time the band enjoyed airplay over BBC-TV with their "Breaking The Law" video. After a short European tour they headed for America, beginning with ten dates in Texas and working their way east. *British Steel* rocketed into the Top 40, surpassing the sales of the live album and all previous airplay.

With *Point Of Entry*, on sale by March 1981, Judas Priest was clearly riding atop the new wave of British metal. They received accolades from *Rolling Stone* and *Creem*, as well as from other periodicals that had previously panned them. Julian Temple produced two acclaimed videos of the Priest tunes "Hot Rockin'" and "Don't Go," which received an incredible amount of attention from emerging video clubs and cable TV broadcasters. After four months of extensive touring, the group began their latest LP in Spain and finished it in Florida.

Entitled *Screaming For Vengeance*, this record is representative of their conscious gradual departure from a quasi-satanic lyrical content toward a new reliance on less dark, updated subject matter that is more of the '80s. The music is as heavy as ever, but seems to appeal to a larger demographic group. It also demonstrates that the relationship between the band and Tom Allom is a magical combination that has produced one of the best-sounding heavy metal albums ever. Featuring a gigantic drum sound and fat, distorted guitars, the Allom-Priest sound is rapidly becoming much sought after by other groups and nearly defines "state of the art" for the heavy metal recording genre.

Judas Priest has one of the most intense and elaborate stage shows in the business, relying on tons of smoke and flashpots, a massive PA and lighting system, and an amazing double-tiered stage that holds the drummer on a platform high above the main amplifier line. Lead singer Rob Halford, decked out in traditional S&M regalia, uses two high ramps, stage left and right, to work the crowd into a frenzy.

Today Glenn Tipton and K.K. Downing serve as role models for many aspiring heavy metal guitarists. It's refreshing and encouraging to note the vast technical improvements both guitarists have made — both in tone and playing ability — since their first album. Glenn's pentatonic, blues-based riffs blend exceptionally with K.K.'s more abstract, gut-wrenching tremolo bar solo work. Tipton's slow, melodic solo on "Beyond The Realms Of Death" from *Stained Class*, for example, builds up to a fast and frenzied lead break by Downing, showcasing a brilliant cross section of styles. Continuing in this tradition of compatibility are the guitarists' trade-off solos in "Screaming For Vengeance," which climax with an intense double-guitar harmony.

Over the last ten years Glenn Tipton and K.K. Downing have pushed and inspired each other to try new things. In doing so, they have had a similar positive influence on guitar players all over the globe who support and admire them.

the dialog

With such a proliferation of heavy metal bands these days, it must be hard to maintain your individuality.

Downing: We pride ourselves on one thing: We don't sound like anybody else. A lot of bands copy. That's something we wouldn't want to do.

What was the best compliment about your playing you have ever received?

Tipton: We get a lot of compliments, particularly about our sound. We have struggled and put a lot of effort into our onstage sound. We find that the slightly different sounds we've got really do complement each other.

Downing: Of course, we've both had different people come up to us and ask us to join other pretty famous bands. That's pretty complimentary.

Do you inspire each other to become more proficient on your guitars?

Tipton: Definitely yes. There are a lot of times when we are dishing out a quarter of the lead break each, and Ken will come up with something that's far faster than I thought he was going to do, so I have to push myself. It's a natural, healthy competition.

Downing: You can learn a lot of things over the years. We have picked up things separately and shown them to each other. It's like two people researching the guitar industry instead of one: You come up with new ideas and all sorts of things.

There aren't that many bands that have two equally competent guitarists.

Tipton: It hasn't always been easy. Obviously, there have been points in time when we didn't quite agree on certain things, but that's going to happen with anybody in the world under the same circumstances. We've overcome it, and it's paid off.

It seems as if Judas Priest's guitar work has progressed a lot since Rocka Rolla *and* Sad Wings Of Destiny. *Has there been anything that's inspired you?*

Tipton: Just the fact that it's been eight years. They were our first albums, and obviously we've improved. We would give up if we didn't. We put a lot of work and effort in.

Downing: A lot of it stems from natural songwriting. In the earlier days, we would tend to play a two-minute lead break over a straight *Em*. It's pretty difficult to incorporate a lot of interesting things in that. Now we have different sorts of key changes over solos, which help to create more interest. We can do more things around them. You remember when Cream used to go off on ten-minute solos just over a straight minor?

So the music itself tends to inspire a good solo?

Downing: It can very well, if it's more than ten seconds long.

How do you find the time to practice and compose with your busy touring and recording schedule?

Tipton: We don't practice very much anymore. I do practice, but usually on tour we get enough practice playing live.

How about as far as getting into new scales and things like that are concerned?

Tipton: Usually just prior to an album I try getting into a lot of new guitar themes. When you're writing songs for an album, you'll learn new things. You tend to just fall into little bits of lead and incorporate them all. I also listen to many bands for a few months prior to the start of writing an album. We do very little writing on the road because our schedules are so heavy. And a lot of the times when you get back to the rooms you just want to collapse.

So you don't do that much when you go back to your hotel — you don't get inspired to turn out tunes.

Tipton: No. We don't coast — we give our all. There are times when I do mess around with guitars on tour, but usually not. I don't think I've ever written a song on tour. I may have lots of little ideas.

Downing: On tour I'm always trying to improve what I'm doing right now with regards to sound onstage, little bits of solos. This is very important because on a tour you can forget what you started out playing. If you're not careful you can sort of deviate from night to night, and

NEIL ZLOZOWER

NEIL ZLOZOWER

eventually you play something completely different and forget what you wanted to do originally. It's important to keep reverting back and reminding yourself. But I think we are constantly trying to improve our sound and everything into something that's consistent.

Tipton: It's easy to fall into the trap of becoming a little bit mundane on a tour. You're very sharp when you start. As time goes on, if you're not careful — if you don't keep revising — your sound might deteriorate, or even little bits of lead playing might not be as sharp as they should be.

Why are Satan and devil themes predominant in your songs such as "Saints In Hell" and "Devil's Child"?

Downing: They are more interesting topics than singing about things a lot of bands do. Like "Electric Eye": It's science fiction. It's more interesting to everybody in the band than singing about a forest a thousand miles away or something.

Tipton: Over the riffs we've written, you couldn't sing about flowers and blue skies. It doesn't go together. We have made an attempt to update ourselves to an '80s feel. I mean, our lyrics aren't dungeon anymore: Ken mentioned "Electric Eye." I know there's "Devil's Child," but we've tried to update it. Rob was singing those lyrics in '74.

Is anyone in your band a satanist?

Tipton: Oh, no. Not at all.

Downing: It's just a heavy duty background. None of us were born rich. It's just basically what you were in school, really, and what you've grown up to be mentally. Obviously there're elements of science fiction, devil things, and sex in there. Nice things, you know, in the Hendrix style — "Purple Haze." The Beatles were doing strange stuff, too.

But Jimi Hendrix and the Beatles sang about drugs because they were into them.

Downing: It was a world trend at the time, if you remember. The world trend now is for movies like *E.T.*, *The Exorcist*, and things like that. It's all leather and chains.

Tipton: We try to push our lyrics more away from the medieval and into a more modern aspect, but still in keeping with what we do.

Does the guy who brings the song idea to the group usually end up playing the solo?

Tipton: It doesn't always follow. If you have an idea while writing a song, then you probably will write the lead break section. Say, for instance, "Electric Eye": I wrote the lead break section. But there's other stuff I write where Kenneth plays lead, and vice versa. We are really quite free. We usually write all the songs and then unless somebody's got something formulated that they really want to play, we just take a long time thinking which would actually suit us most.

How do you approach writing joint compositions?

Tipton: Somebody will have an idea. There are occasions when we'll both put the music for a song together, but then other times someone will come up with an idea and somebody else will pick up off it and improve it. We just kick everything around.

Downing: There's no real formula that we could tell potential songwriters. It's just do it the best way you can, whatever sounds good to you.

Tipton: The most difficult songs to write in the world are heavy metal. We really do base a lot of importance in our songs. We take a lot of time and put a lot of effort in. Far more energy goes into our songwriting than touring. We discarded four or five songs off the last album, and they were good songs. It just happened that we wrote five better ones. We had a bit more time on the last album than we've had previously. It's good when you've got time.

Downing: He's right. Heavy metal is the most difficult music to write in the world. If somebody said to us, "Write a pop song," there's a possibility it could get in the Top 10. But we've never tried. It seems that there are so many bands now and riffs that have been around for years, it's very hard to write heavy metal songs.

Do either of you sing well enough to sing lead?

Downing: No.

Tipton: I used to do lead vocals in a band, but I'm quite happy to just sing backup.

Are the majority of your solos on record worked out in advance?

Downing: They tend to be more worked out now than before, but we do leave some things open.

Tipton: There are certain more melodic things where I get a general feel for a lead break and then just touch it up in places. If you're working on scales or little licks, then you might throw those in instead of something that's a bit bland.

Downing: You don't sit down and start to work and build things. You get the tape of the backing track, listen through it once, and play exactly what you feel. Then you don't just work on that. You play a lot of different things and see which direction you want to go with it. If it's basically an ad-lib thing when it's actually composed, then I go with that.

After you record a solo, do you try to learn to play it the same way live?

Tipton: We stick basically to our recorded versions; they are going to sound almost the same. I've seen bands where the guitarist can't play the same solo he did on the album, and the song's lost something. It's not what I'm waiting for. It doesn't come in right, and it doesn't finish right.

So you try to stick to the same solo concept.

Tipton: I try to stick around the same framework, although I do allow myself places where I can ad-lib, because I need that. If you stick too rigidly, you'll drive yourself crazy playing it every night. There are some bits in songs that aren't too important where I might just deviate occasionally and have a bit of freedom.

Downing: I feel basically the same. Although I've got two or three ad-lib solos at the moment, I find I'd rather play set things onstage for the simple reason that every night my sound is different. If you've got a really good sound, you'll cook. But if the sound isn't good, it won't be any good. It probably sounds great out front, but I've got to have the sound together onstage for me to really get off on my own ad-libbing. And there's no such thing as the *perfect* sound.

What do you think a soloist should do?

Tipton: He should always have something to say. No matter how many notes are in there or if it's a fast lead break or slow, a solo should have feel. In the time allotted to you, it should definitely say something; otherwise, don't put it in.

Downing: I suppose that says it all.

Have you ever written chord progressions and thought of solos over them before you had a song to use them in?

Tipton: Oh, yeah. You work on different aspects. When you work on a song, you probably work on some lead bits. Sometimes it's good to put a chord sequence down to see what sort of note patterns you can play.

Have you ever written songs around a lead break?

Tipton: There's more than one that springs to mind. The title track on *Screaming For Vengeance* has a lead break that was built around a chord pattern which was there before the song was.

If a reader wanted to hear your essential work with Judas Priest, what cuts would you tell him to listen to?

Downing: I think basically anything that I've played. Maybe the live album, because it can show people that we can do what was originally on the studio version. If you want to, you can be just as good onstage. It's important to play a song as good as you originally did. For solos, I think *Unleashed In The East* is a good overall picture of Judas Priest.

Tipton: I think it's very important to get an interesting sound, so I would choose "Beyond The Realms Of Death." I'm not particularly impressed by that solo, but a lot of people seem to be, so it must have some of my characteristics in it. I prefer a lot faster solos; that's the one thing I've had the most compliments about. I prefer to play fast, but I don't think you should *just* play fast. Like I said before, it shouldn't be just a flurry of meaningless notes. It should be tasteful. It should say something.

Have you produced any unique tones on your records?

Downing: I'm sure if I were to listen to all the albums back again, I would definitely pick some songs and say, "That was a good sound. I'm really pleased with that." But I think we've always had a really good selection of different sounds with regard to lead. Most players will keep one sound throughout the whole album, but we've got a good mixture.

Tipton: We were recently going through our back albums for lead credits and discovered that sounds we used to think were great at the time sound a little bit timid now. Like the intro to "Invader," where I do some stuff with Echoplexes: At the time that was good, but now it's a little bit embarrassing. We've progressed. We've always chased new improvements. I think that's a healthy attitude to have.

Can you reproduce live any track you put down in the studio?

Tipton: Yes.

Downing: The hardest thing to do is copy your own solos; it's much easier to learn other people's. I often have to relearn parts of studio solos. I've thought, "Yeah, it sounds good. I'll put that in."

Tipton: The only time I have problems is when I have monitor difficulties. If I've got my sound okay and nothing's broke down, no problem.

Can you easily transpose notes you hear in your head to guitar?

Downing: Yeah. I would say so, after all these years.

Tipton: Yeah, it's easy. That becomes easier and easier, the more experience you get. When I first started, I tried to copy other lead breaks; I think every guitarist does. And it's not until you develop your own style that you realize how important it is to have your own characteristics. Sometimes I'd play my wits against a magical guitarist for hours, and never end up with what they were playing. You learn that's not important in the end. You just pick certain things from people and adapt them to your own style. That's far more satisfying.

Downing: Something I never did was copy other people's solos. Actually, I remember playing a couple of Hendrix things onstage once, but nothing apart from that. I mean, I couldn't play "Born To Be Wild" if you asked me. I suppose I could just hold it in my head and then play from the guitar, but I've never learned what other guitar players did.

What musical scales do you use?

Tipton: I've never been a big fan of scales, like diminished sevenths and things like that. I like freedom. I like feel.

Downing: I use major, minor, and chromatic.

Do you know the names of all the modes and scales?

Downing: Somebody invented some new ones [*laughs*]? Yeah. The names never really stick with me, although I did learn them all. I've found, however, that they don't sound like what I should be playing—suspended major minor, you know.

Tipton: I used to change just between major and minor, but now my runs aren't really made up from the scales.

Do you use all of your left-hand fingers?

Downing: I use them all. You mean somebody's made some money without using all four of them?

Tipton: We use everything—fingers, teeth [*laughs*].

Do either of you play slide?

Tipton: I do. I used to play a lot of it. I don't bother so

Judas Priest flank a Harley-Davidson motorcycle.

much with it now, because I think it's very dated.

Downing: A thing of the past, isn't it?

What goes through your mind when you're playing onstage?

Tipton: Lots of things, worldly problems. To be honest, when you do lengthy tours it becomes very easy to go onstage every night and play. You practice so often that you have time in the set for your mind to wander. I don't mean to say that it detracts from the energy we put out, but there are times when your mind wanders.

Downing: It becomes easy, and your mind does wander wherever it might go, such as to what you might want to do after you get offstage. That's when it can become dangerous.

What are the most difficult songs in your set?

Tipton: Actually, the first two songs—"Electric Eye" and "Riding On The Wind." The lead breaks are fairly fast in there, and there's no chance to warm up because we don't sound check. The crew does it for us.

Do you have to be in a special state of consciousness to play at your peak?

Downing: Yeah. When you're not quite so stiff and you can move your arms freely, when you've gotten plenty of sleep the night before and haven't got a hangover. If I have to play gigs in the morning, I don't think I do very good.

Tipton: You definitely have highs and lows on tour. If you have a bad cold, for instance, which doesn't show up as it would when you are at home, there's a general lack of energy. You just can't find everything in yourself like you could when you feel 100%. We're on tour seven or eight months a year, so we're going to feel good and bad during that time.

Do you prefer arenas to small clubs?

Downing: I think you've got to like to play in front of as many as possible.

Tipton: I can get off on either equally well. We did a gig in Chicago recently where people were packed almost back-to-back in a club with a very low ceiling. It reminded me of the old days. I really enjoyed it. The draw of the crowd at arenas is good, but I used to enjoy the clubs as well.

Do you do the same set night after night?

Downing: Yes.

Do you do any finger exercises to warm up before going on?

Downing: Oh no, those were the days.

Tipton: I warm up a little bit.

Do you play in any styles that you don't communicate on Judas Priest albums, such as classical, jazz, or flamenco?

Downing: Basically just bits of those three. I like to play the acoustic guitar. It's a very compact thing. You don't need amps and all that stuff, so it's easy to mess about with.

When you first started out, did you show promise in those styles?

Downing: Yeah, definitely. I could have been pretty good at classical, all of them.

Tipton: I like very melodic stuff. I'm interested in blues, anything with a lot of feel. You know, jack-of-all-trades, master of none. We have to channel all our efforts into what we are actually doing. You can't cover too many aspects of it and be very successful.

Downing: I was always very good at chords. I was one of those who never had a problem holding a barre chord down. It was pretty easy from the word go, especially with classical and jazz styles. Even if you have small hands, you should be able to stretch five frets.

Were either of you raised in a particularly musical household?

Downing: None whatsoever.

Tipton: Well, my mother taught piano. I didn't start getting into music, though, until fairly late. I wasn't any 11-year-old starter. I was in my late teens when I got fairly serious. My interest started out with the blues and then progressive rock and so forth. I used to be very interested in jazz when I first started, although I can't say it helped me at all.

Downing: I must have been 16 when I started playing acoustic guitar. I was trying to play Hendrix-type solos on an acoustic guitar with metal strings [*laughs*].

When you first started playing guitar, how many hours a day did you practice?

Tipton: I used to spend a lot of hours practicing. I never put the guitar down at one point; it was constant. I'd just put it down at night to have a rest, and then pick it up again. At that point I'd have so much work to do to match up to everybody else who was around that there was no time for rest, really. When I got fed up I would put it down, but it wouldn't be for long.

What did you think was most important to learn?

Tipton: Lead. Chords were easy for me. I know some people struggle with them, but I enjoy experimenting with chords, unless it's a demented 6*A♭* [*laughs*]. I can play any chord in the book, really. That's a very inventive aspect of guitar; there is so much you can do there, so many ways to be original.

Downing: To me the most important thing was finding out what notes you could and couldn't play. There are so many different ways of doing it. When you get to rock, you just have to give it all or nothing. That's my advice. I think it's important to learn the notes and the fretboard first and foremost, and then some scales. When you play a chord, you've got to know where it is. But apart from that, that's as far as you need to go if you want to become a rock star.

Did you ever formally study music?

Downing: Yes, for a time, but I was basically self-taught from books. I used to buy Beatles and Led Zeppelin books with chords written out. Sometimes they'd be written out wrong. I got pretty close to sight-reading at one time, but what can you sight-read that you'd want to play? I had a few piano lessons and some classical guitar, but there wasn't time. There is little time, anyway, and I have to concentrate on writing songs and playing lead breaks to those songs.

Tipton: I studied piano and can read music, and I learned guitar chords from books. I can learn from music, but I think there is a danger in reading too much because it tends to stunt inventiveness. You tend to rely more and more on what somebody else wrote. You also tend to eventually need that piece of paper in front of you to actually play songs, even if it's just to play chord sequences. If you learn something mentally, you don't forget it. If you learn it from a piece of paper, you keep

ROSS MARINO

NEIL ZLOZOWER

needing to refer back to that paper, and that tends to stunt you. I'm not saying that this is the wrong thing for guitarists to do, though. It just depends on what you want to get into.

Can you transpose piano parts to guitar?

Downing and Tipton: Oh, yeah.

Then why don't you have keyboards in the band?

Tipton: We've done keyboards on albums. We don't now because we don't think it's quite right; we wouldn't do it onstage. But in the early days we were experimenting.

What about synthesizer solos?

Downing: I don't like any of that shit.

Did any specific artists or solos influence you?

Tipton: I've always loved melody, and I try to incorporate it in heavy metal as much as possible without being too sweet. Here, I've got to refer to the Beatles, who I have always been a fan of. I can listen to them for hours on end. Jimi Hendrix was always a big influence. When I first started out, I listened to him inside out. Rory Gallagher and Peter Green were also influential. Rory Gallagher is the first person I saw who really exploited the harmonic thing. I couldn't understand how he did it when I used to watch him. I used to play a lot of early blues — Robert Johnson and stuff like that. But since that time I've tried to be into original solos. One of the keys to success is the ability to realize that there's a certain point where you drop influences and channel everything into your own style. So I can only point to earlier influences.

Downing: I was into virtually everything, and everything had to be an influence. I used to put records on and play along to them. I can remember when I only owned two or three LPs and wore them out; Deep Purple and Cream were pretty good. As soon as the song started, I'd play lead to it in whatever key it was in, put licks in that should have been there in the first place. Virtually all of Hendrix' music was an influence, and Free, too — there was so much feeling in *Tons Of Sobs*. Rory Gallagher was also important, plus some John Mayall Bluesbreakers stuff I used to love. Budgie was also one of my favorite bands; the original band was good live.

Have you ever heard anybody such as Edward Van Halen or Michael Schenker and said, "Wow! I think I'm going to try this"?

Tipton: I've got a great deal of respect for Van Halen and Michael Schenker, but I think there's a danger in copying people.

Downing: Van Halen used to play a couple of our songs in bars, and Eddie once told me that he was influenced by one of our solo changes with the tremolo. Rather then being influenced by people like Van Halen or Schenker, I think we're more influenced by good songs.

Tipton: There are a lot of guitar players around who are excellent. I've seen guitarists in bars who are unbelievable! I respect a lot of people, and they all have their own styles, which I respect as well. We are both lead guitarists so we take a big interest in it, but that's not all I can see. If somebody has talent in another area, I'm likely to appreciate them even more so. When I'm dishing out compliments, I lean towards people like Peter Green, who is one of my all-time favorites. He is not a brilliant guitarist, but he writes such good songs and has got such an emotional feel. Guitarists don't have to play a million notes a second.

Downing: Paul Kossoff is another one of those guys. In his heyday, we used to see him play small colleges and schools around where we came from. He really got that sort of thing together: He could have a lot of feel with just a couple of notes.

Before Judas Priest, were either of you ever in a band whose members went on to become famous?

Downing: No.

Tipton: I was in a group called the Flying Hat Band which supported Deep Purple in Europe. We used to play rock and roll. We were well before our time. That was my best claim to fame [*laughs*].

Was there ever any jealousy when you guys first started playing together?

Tipton: We got together when we were very young — about 21 — and there was healthy competition.

Did it get a little weird at times?

Tipton: Yeah, we've been through that. We've been together eight years.

Could you point to any big breaks in your career?

Tipton: I don't think we've had any big breaks. We've worked very hard for what we've attained.

Downing: I think *Sad Wings Of Destiny* really did a lot for the band. The live album was probably the next big break we had.

Tipton: Definitely *Sad Wings Of Destiny* was the first foothold we got in the States. It did a lot for us over here. We had a chance at the commercial aspect of it. "Diamonds And Rust" was one of the first things that got a lot of airplay over here.

Have you been equal writers throughout the band's career?

Tipton: Yes.

Downing: We still consider that we've got a long way to go with regards to writing.

Did either of you make any recordings prior to Judas Priest?

Downing: No.

Tipton: Just those amusing demos.

Have you ever been offered guest session work?

Downing: In the early days a couple of real big groups at the time asked us to play on a couple of their tracks. We didn't do it.

What were your early guitars?

Tipton: I started out with a semi-acoustic Hofner, and then my first all-electric was a short-scale Rickenbacker. It didn't sound right, but it was a great guitar. Then I changed to a Stratocaster; that got stolen, so I got another one. Eventually I got some money back on the guitar that was stolen, which gave me a chance to buy another guitar. I thought, "Well, the alternative is a Gibson," so I bought an SG, and that's the sound I've adapted ever since. My first amplifier was an AC-30 Vox. K.K. had a mongrel guitar.

Downing: Actually, my first guitar looks exactly the same as the one Eddie Van Halen plays now — guts hanging out. I put it together myself. The body was shaped like a Watkins Rapier, which was a cheap guitar. It should have had three pickups, but it had all the guts hanging out and just one pickup on it.

What's your main guitar today?

Downing: I've got a '64 Gibson Flying V that I'm in love with. There was a vibrato bar on it when I bought it. I took that off, and the guitar has been refinished. The pickups are Gibson P.A.F.s, I believe. That guitar has a very smooth, big sound. It's good for rhythm. Michael Schenker went to buy this guitar for himself the day after I had bought it from a little shop in Birmingham.

Tipton: I would have to say I have two main guitars, because I use a Gibson SG and a new Fender Strat. The Fender, which I sort of put together myself, has got two DiMarzio Super Distortion humbuckers and a tremolo arm on it. I usually use that for the wilder stuff. My classic SG is a cross between an SG Standard and an SG Special. It's got stock pickups and the innards from a Standard and a smaller neck from a Special, which I like. It's great, very easy to play. There is no vibrato on it. Those guitars are all I need; they give me everything I could ask for.

Do you own other guitars?

Downing: I've got five now — three V's and two Strats. My other Flying V is a 1970. It's got a Gibson Maestro vibrato bar that is pretty bad. I use my '70 or '71 sunburst Strat quite a bit. It's got a DiMarzio Fat Strat, which is a real good pickup. I've had my white Strat for years; that's the one on the back of *Sad Wings Of Destiny*. It has a '60 body, a new neck, and a Seymour Duncan pickup. Hamer also just built a Flying V guitar for me with a Floyd Rose vibrato unit on it. We've never used Floyd Rose units before. Standard units still work pretty good if you've got the guitar set up properly.

Tipton: I've got my old '61 Strat at home. It's completely original, except that it was a sunburst and has been refinished black. I use it in the studio sometimes for nice clean chords where we don't want any distortion whatsoever. I used that on "Beyond The Realms Of Death" — the little quiet electrical passage where there's no distortion.

Who does most of the vibrato work?

Tipton: We don't each concentrate on any particular aspect. Wild and tame, we both do it.

Could you give a couple of examples of the difference between solos cut with the Gibsons and the Strats?

Downing: On the new record I just use the V's for things I don't use tremolo on. If there's a tremolo part in it, I'll use the Strat.

Tipton: I used the SG in "Electric Eye," "Take These Chains," "Another Thing Coming," and "Screaming For Vengeance." I used the Stratocaster for "Riding On The Wind," although live I do those lead parts on my SG because we've got no time for guitar changes. Instead of using my tremolo arm, I go a half-tone flat and bend it down.

How do you set your action?

Downing: It's medium — not low, not high. If you want to push a lot of strings and it's too low, you can't get enough grip. I prefer to use Gibson jumbo frets, but they're not too good for tuning when you play chords down at the bottom.

Tipton: I was lucky when I got the SG. The fret wear was very even, and now it's just adjusted to the way I play. So it's gone down, but it's gone down according to the way I play.

How about out-of-phase wiring on your guitars?

Downing: No, not interested.

Tipton: Not interested, either.

What type of fingerboards do you prefer?

Tipton: I've got a maple neck on my Strat. I prefer the rosewood, though.

Downing: It doesn't bother me what they are made of. Mine are all different.

How do you set the controls on your guitar? Do you roll back the treble?

Downing: Everything's full up.

Tipton: I've got the tone controls on my guitar disengaged. I never use them. I play it in the treble position all the time. If I need any extra bass, I can get it from the pickups or from my board.

Downing: Tone controls are not good things. They aren't actually tone controls; they're just rubbish.

Do you take good care of your instruments?

Tipton: I regard them as tools. They've got to be very sturdy, and they've got to do a job.

Downing: I've got five or six chips on a new guitar, and I haven't played it yet. But it has to get through a hell of a lot more.

Tipton: They get a good pounding on the road, our guitars do. We have a road crew of about 35 people, and each of us has his own guitar guy.

What effects do you use?

Downing: The main effect I use is a custom-made treble boost. I use that on everything in the studio, my lead and rhythm tone.

Tipton: Same thing. It's always been part of my original sound. Its circuit is based on the original Range

NEIL ZLOZOWER

Master treble boosts, which aren't made anymore. The first person I saw use one was Rory Gallagher.

What other effects do you have?

Downing: Virtually everything is in our pedalboards, which were custom-made by Pete Cornish in England. Mine includes a Cry Baby wah-wah, a Roland Space Echo, and an MXR Phase 100 and distortion unit. It also has some things made by Pete Cornish — a fuzz box which we seldom use, a 10 dB gain boost that can beef up the solos, and an overdrive unit. There are line boosters between every effect.

Tipton: The actual power that comes in is the actual power that goes out. We've worked at making sure that we can switch any series of effects in. There's a combination switch so you can pre-program three or four effects and then keep them ready to go. But even if we've got three or four in, it won't change the basic sound. I always use my treble boost first. I can alternate from that to an MXR distortion unit, but one or the other is always switched in. I've also got an overdrive unit, a flanger, and some MXR effects — a Phase 100, a digital delay, and a 12-band graphic equalizer which I find very useful. LED lights let me know what's on. I have a send and return on my stock Maestro Echoplex, which I use quite a bit. There are various sends and returns in there, so if we wanted to send the signal to a rack mount we can. But at this point in time I don't use anything else. Apart from that, the board has been built from a lot of our experiences. It's a very reliable, sturdy board. It travels well and eliminates all sorts of noise.

Was it expensive to get someone to design your board?

Downing: Yes, it was, wasn't it? $2,000 is pretty expensive.

Tipton: I don't classify it as expensive. It's worth the money to me. It doesn't actually change our sound; it just makes it a lot more roadable.

Do you sometimes leave your wah-wah set in a halfway-down position?

Downing: Occasionally, yeah.

What kind of amps do you use?

Tipton: 50-watt and 100-watt Marshalls. If we're recording, we use just one 50-watt. We'll mike up four new ones live for the basic sound, but there's a stage full of them. These amps don't have the master volume on them.

Have these been custom-wired?

Tipton: No, but because we use treble boosts, we go into the bass channel and not the treble.

Do you strap channels together?

Tipton: No. We've got four separate outputs on the pedalboards. Those four lines go to four separate amps, so that each one is driven equally. You don't get any gain loss between one or the other, and you don't have to compensate on the volume. This allows you to set each amp up individually. So onstage we each drive two 100-watt Marshall heads to two sets of two cabinets with standard speakers. We also have a Yamaha practice amp in our dressing room, but it's very seldom we use it.

Do you ever blow speakers out?

Downing: We used to, for some reason, but I think they are making better speakers these days. We certainly are not playing any quieter.

Tipton: Our equipment is more sophisticated. Everything's smoother and more reliable.

Do your personal monitors just have guitar or the whole group?

Tipton: Whatever you want. I have guitar and drums in mine. By varying my position onstage, I can hear as much or as little of K.K. as I want. Ian is right behind me, so I can feel and hear him. The rest of it is basically finding the right positions onstage for certain songs.

Do you have your own sound system when you're headlining?

Tipton: It's all Tascho, the best rock and roll system in the world.

How many watts are you guys packing?

Downing: I don't know. It's like saying you've got a 100-watt amp, you know. What's 100 watts? Every amp that comes out of the Marshall factory differs. People go, "Wow, they're a big band with a 1000-watt PA!" How do you measure that type of thing?

Do you use a strobe tuner?

Downing: We just use a Korg tuner.

Tipton: I've always found that a strobe is a lot more trouble than it's worth. I can get my guitar perfectly well in tune with the Korg.

What gauge picks do you use?

Downing: Very light.

Tipton: It's best to use a light gauge because if you want any more strength in the pick you can always bend it. The pick definitely affects the tone.

Downing: I think that whether it is made of plastic or nylon affects the tone more than the actual thickness of it.

What are your strings?

Downing: Guild, gauged .007, .009, .012, .018, .028, and .036, high to low.

Tipton: I use two .009s, .014, .022, .034, and .038.

Do either of you employ a wireless transmitter?

Downing: I do. I have a Schaffer-Vega and a Nady.

Tipton: I've tried them, and they just don't agree with me. I think the key to a really good guitar sound is not in the special effects or anything like that. It's ten years of experience. It's eliminating all the little things that go wrong — little transistors that don't work right. It's consistency, reliability, and good tools around you. A good sound comes from the half-hours you spend on winter days in somebody's little workshop with sawdust on the floor, and then trying the setup in church halls or little youth clubs in England and eliminating everything that goes wrong. These are all little things that you can't put your finger on; it's a lot of experience that's rolled up and compact. Our boards and setups are very, very good because we've put a lot of time and effort in to eliminate all the bad parts of them.

If you could materialize a new guitar device just by fantasizing about it, what would it be?

Downing: Well, you've got the new Floyd Rose and these guitars that don't go out of tune, but you still have to compete with different things like temperature changes. These tuning devices are not actually 100%. I've always thought of having something that would fix to the guitar and automatically adjust the string if it goes out or stretches a bit. I'm sure somebody is going to do one. It would have to be electronic, obviously, maybe

NEIL ZLOZOWER

something you could press between songs that would bring the strings back to their original tension.

Tipton: Maybe I would like a guitar that wrote its own songs [*laughs*].

Do you have any endorsements?

Tipton: Only Guild strings. They give us lots of free strings, which are pretty good. Actually, we've got some acoustic guitars, too, but I don't know if that's an actual endorsement. It's great. We actually fell into a trap at one point when we had been inundated with people who gave us free products. It's really not worth it, though, because there are only certain guitars worth using, as far as I'm concerned. Electrically, there's only Fender and Gibson. Yamaha makes great acoustic guitars.

Have you started recording your next album yet?

Tipton: We haven't even started to write it yet. It will probably come together in the summer. We have three more albums to do for CBS.

How many tracks do you use for guitars?

Tipton: It depends. For basic rhythm sounds, we just take one track each.

Downing: We have obviously double-tracked on many occasions, but you'll usually find that if you've got a pretty good sound and a pretty good producer, you can cut just one track.

Tipton: You start to overkill if you put too much in there. You don't get that crispness. We have over-tracked.

What's your recording process? What do you record first?

Tipton: Nowadays we try to get a live backing track — drums, bass, and two guitars. In the early days it was just drums first and then they put the bass over it. We do a lot of ambient recording for the actual backing track. We put ambience mikes up so that the tracks have more life in them. We don't always manage to achieve this, but that's what we hope for. At least one track is always ambient. [*Ed. Note: Ambience means the characteristics of the room's acoustics imparted to a sound.*]

How prepared are you when you begin recording?

Tipton: We have things worked out pretty well. Last time, we took off a week in between putting the backing tracks down and the solos, and it helped a lot.

How much money do you spend on an album?

Tipton: We spent a lot on the last album because we did half of it in Spain and then mixed it in Florida. We dropped a lot of the tracks because we had a Christmas period and a tour, which gave us a chance to breathe and write more stuff. I don't know what we spent on it, but that was one of our more expensive albums. Normally we don't spend a great deal. We find that if you sit down and rehearse adequately, there's no reason to go in the studio and waste time.

Downing: I would say we spend 150 grand, maybe.

Have you had any platinum records?

Tipton: No. Very soon. We've crossed gold [500,000 units sold] fairly easily on three or four albums, but we've never quite made platinum [1,000,000 units].

What was your biggest album to date?

Downing: Probably *Screaming For Vengeance*. Even as successful as we are — you know, Madison Square Garden, two nights at Long Beach Arena — all the bands you've got over here are not in the same vein as us. The Foreigners, the Journeys, and all the pop bands will sell four or five million in the first two weeks. That's pretty hard to compete with.

Tipton: We're still chasing.

Do you think that the new wave of British heavy metal is dying?

Downing: The same thing will happen to that as it did to punk and new wave: The good will stay and the bad will just fade.

Tipton: It's a shame that England is over-influenced by the press. It's not the kids' fault. In the States, kids tend to make up their own minds about what's good and bad. I think the press will build up the new wave heavy metal thing and then destroy it, just like they did with actual new wave.

Downing: So much of those new wave or heavy metal bands sound like something we did seven or eight years ago. The only good thing about it is that the bands in Britain are given a chance at least to be heard. That's great, because we've always flown the flag for Britain, so to speak.

If your band was to lose its market, would you keep on with what you're doing now, or try to match the musical trend?

Downing: I don't think there's any danger of losing our market.

Tipton: We've stuck to our guns for the last eight years — weathered the storms, swam against the tide, suffered abusive bombardments from the press — and it's paid off for us. We enjoy playing Judas Priest music. We love it.

Downing: The writers and the press haven't picked on all these new wave heavy metal bands, have they? Judas Priest looked and sounded like that five, six years ago. I suppose we can take it as a compliment, but when we were struggling to come through, we used to get knocked so much: "Judas Priest sounds like so and so." The press was always on our tail, trying to put us down.

Tipton: The funny thing was that when they used to accuse us of sounding like people, it was completely absurd. We got accused of sounding like acts we sounded absolutely nothing like, such as Joan Armatrading and the Rolling Stones.

Downing: One guy knocked us in every way possible. At the end of one interview, he said, "After all, what hope is there for a band that sounds like Deep Purple, Black Sabbath, and Led Zeppelin all rolled into one?" Any band that sounds like those three all rolled into one can't be all bad.

What advice would you give guitarists concerning avoiding stagnant periods?

Downing: They should learn a few Priest solos [*laughs*]. I don't know. Is there such a thing as a rut anymore?

Tipton: You should just give yourself inspiration. If I get bogged down while writing songs or leads, I always go out and buy some new albums that I've never heard before to find new trails to follow. Go out and buy half a dozen new albums that you know you're going to get some sort of inspiration from. It's great in the States because you hear so much on the radio that it just lends itself to fresh, brand-new ideas.

What advice would you give a young guitarist want-

ing to get started in the business?

Downing: Everybody plays guitar these days.

Tipton: I really don't envy kids starting out today because the competition is so rough, particularly in the States. There's not any advice you can offer them other than they're going to have to put a lot of work in.

Downing: I can't say, "Be good," because obviously you have to be pretty good. Get a band that's together to where you all *look* good. Think of an image, get a good name together, and stick with it. You've got to stick with it. Don't you just hate bands that keep changing like the scenery?

Tipton: If you get a good band together — especially when there is any money starting to fly around — it's very important to maintain a level of friendship and overcome any grievances. You've got to sustain. Like K.K. says, stick at it. You have to operate as a unit, not five separate entities, so that you can beat everybody else — not just musicians, but financial problems as well.

Downing: Don't be impatient — that's the other thing. They're all impatient these days. I suppose we were in the beginning, too. We considered ourselves stars eight years ago. Why we weren't internationally famous and rich, we couldn't understand.

Do you think being a star begins in your own mind?

Tipton: Of course it does. You've got to take what K.K. says with a pinch of salt. The word "star" in itself is a joke, you know.

Downing: If you come from L.A. and you look good onstage and you can pack them in all the time at local clubs, that's the very start. You can't get a big head and say, "We should be up there with Van Halen, Sabbath, and Priest." This is a big country; we've been around it a few times ourselves.

Any chance for a solo album from either of you in the future?

Tipton: There's a possibility. I think everybody has got that thought tucked away. When the momentum eventually drops with the band, I'll probably fall into it. I've got quite a few ideas, but at the moment everything is J.P.

Downing: People do solo albums when they've become really big. They've reached their goal in what they are doing, or they fail and split up and do a solo album. We haven't reached either one of those, so everything is where it is.

Tipton: There are a lot of personal projects that people want to get out of the way. I think there isn't a musician in the world who hasn't got that idea tucked away. If you just wrote for Judas Priest and stopped there, you're not really pushing hard.

Downing: Judas Priest is the ideal act for me to be a part of, to write for and play with. If I did a solo album, it would probably sound exactly the same because that's what I want to do.

— Mike Varney

JUDAS PRIEST: A SELECTED DISCOGRAPHY

Rocka Rolla, Gull [dist. by JEM], IMP 7001; *Sad Wings Of Destiny,* Janus, 7019; *Sin After Sin,* Columbia, PC 34787; *Stained Class,* Columbia, JC 35296; *Hell Bent For Leather,* Columbia, JC 35706; *Unleashed In The East,* Columbia, JC 36179; *British Steel,* Columbia, JC 36443; *Point Of Entry,* Columbia, FC 37052; *Screaming For Vengeance,* Columbia, FC 38160.

BILL O'LEARY

Eddie Van Halen's Debut

NEIL ZLOZOWER

The release of *Van Halen* in February 1978 changed the direction of American rock guitar. An incredibly gifted player, Eddie Van Halen dialed amazing tones from a home-made guitar and introduced new fingering techniques to metal. He was interviewed for this November '78 *Guitar Player* feature during Van Halen's first U.S. tour.

* * * *

Edward Van Halen's clean, powerful lead playing was first recorded eariler this year on his band's predominately heavy-metal debut album, *Van Halen;* at the time he was 21. Eddie immigrated to the U.S. from the Netherlands during the rock and roll heyday of the late '60s and soon abandoned his piano for drums and electric guitar. He spent years playing small clubs, beer bars, backyard parties, and dance contests, collecting the band's current lineup along the way.

Van Halen's discovery in March 1977 — described by Eddie as "something right out of the movies" — came one night when Mo Ostin, then president and chairman of the board of Warner Brothers, and producer Ted Templeman saw their act at the Starwood club in Los Angeles and signed them. With Eddie's brother Alex on drums, Michael Anthony on bass, and lead singer Dave Lee Roth, the band recorded 40 songs in three weeks, including "Runnin' With The Devil," a searing guitar solo titled "Eruption," and a remake of the Kinks' classic "You Really Got Me." Eddie joined the legion of musicians on the road when Van Halen embarked on a nine-month tour in February.

Eddie was born in Holland on January 26, 1957. His father, a professional saxophonist and clarinetist who played live radio shows, got Eddie and Alex interested in music at an early age. "We both started playing piano at age six or seven," Eddie recalls, "and we played for a long time. That's where I learned most of my theory. We had an old Russian teacher who was a very fine concert pianist; in fact, our parents wanted us to be concert pianists."

In 1967 the Van Halens moved to the U.S., and Eddie got his first taste of rock and roll. "I wasn't into rock in Holland at all," he says, "because there really wasn't much of a scene going on there. When we came to the U.S. I heard Jimi Hendrix and Cream, and I said, 'Forget the piano, I don't want to sit down — I want to stand up and be crazy.' I got a paper route and bought myself a drum set. My brother started taking flamenco guitar lessons, and while I was out doing my paper route, so I could keep up on the drum payments, Alex would play my drums. Eventually he got better than me — he could play 'Wipe Out' and I couldn't. So I said, 'You keep the drums and I'll play guitar.' From then on we have always played together."

Eddie bought himself a Teisco Del Rey electric guitar — "a $70 model with four pickups" — and began to copy licks off of records. "My main influence was Eric Clapton," Eddie says. "I realize I don't sound like him, but I know every solo he's ever played, note-for-note, still to this day. My favorites were the Cream live versions of 'Spoonful' [*Wheels Of Fire*] and 'I'm So Glad' [*Goodbye*]. I liked Jimi Hendrix, too. But now no one in Van Halen really has one main thing that he likes. Dave, our singer, doesn't even have a stereo; he listens to the radio, which gives him a good variety. That's why we have things on the *Van Halen* album that are a change from the slam-bang loud stuff — like John Brim's 'Ice Cream Man.' We are into melodies and melodic songs. You can sing along with most of our tunes, even though many of them do have the peculiar guitar and the end-of-the-world drums."

Eddie and Alex Van Halen formed their first bands while attending high school in the suburbs of Los Angeles. During the early '70s they teamed with a bass player to form Mammoth, the last band they played in before Van Halen. "I used to sing and play lead in Mammoth," Eddie explains, "and I couldn't stand it — I'd rather just play. Dave Lee Roth was in another local band, and he used to rent us his PA system. I figured it would be much cheaper if we just got him in the band, so he joined. Then we played a gig with a group called Snake, which Mike Anthony fronted, and we invited him to join the band. So we all just got together and formed Van Halen.

"By the time we graduated from high school, everyone else was going on to study to become a lawyer or whatever, and so we stuck together and started playing around cities in California — Pasadena, LA, Arcadia. We played everywhere and anywhere, from backyard parties to places the size of your bathroom. And we did it all without a manager, agent, or record company. We used to print up flyers announcing where we were going to play and stuff them into high school lockers. The first time we played we drew maybe 900 people, and the last time we played without a manager we drew 3,300 people."

The band worked on their own material and got gigs playing Southern California clubs and auditoriums, including the Santa Monica Civic, the Long Beach Arena, and the Pasadena Civic Auditorium. Soon they were working as the opening act for performers including Santana, UFO, Nils Lofgren, and Sparks. Their appearance at the Golden West Ballroom in Norwalk, California, brought them to the attention of Los Angeles promoter Rodney Bingenheimer, who booked them into the Starwood. They played the club for four months, and there met Gene Simmons, Kiss' bass player, who financed their original demo tape sessions. "We made the tape," Eddie says, "but nothing really came of it because we didn't know where to take it. We didn't want to go around knocking on people's doors, saying, 'Sign us, sign us,' so we ended up with just a decent-sounding tape."

While playing the Starwood, the band also came to the attention of Marshall Berle, who would eventually become their manager. It was through Berle, Eddie explains, that the band had its fortuitous meeting with Ted Templeman and Mo Ostin: "We were playing the club one rainy Monday night in May 1977, and Berle told us that there were some people coming to see us, so play good. It ended up that we played a good set in front of an empty house, and all of a sudden Berle walks in with Ted and Mo Ostin. Templeman said, 'It's great,' and within a week we were signed up. It was right out of the movies."

Van Halen entered the studio soon afterwards and

emerged in three weeks with enough material for at least two albums. "For the first record," Eddie recalls, "we went into the studio one day and played live and laid down 40 songs. Out of these 40 we picked nine and wrote one in the studio — 'Jamie's Cryin'.' The album is very live — there are few overdubs, which is the magic of Ted Templeman. I would say that out of the ten songs on the record, I overdubbed the solo on only 'Runnin' With The Devil,' 'Ice Cream Man,' and 'Jamie's Cryin'' — the rest are live. I used the same equipment that I use onstage, and the only other things that were overdubbed were the backing vocals, only because you can't sing in a room with an amp going without having a bleed on the mikes. Because we were jumping around, drinking beer, and getting crazy, I think there's a vibe in the record. A lot of bands keep hacking it out and doing so many overdubs and double-tracking that their music doesn't sound real. And there are also a lot of bands that can't pull it off live because they have overdubbed so much stuff in the studio that it either doesn't sound the same, or they just stand there pushing buttons on their tape machines. We kept it really live, and the next time we record it will be very much the same.

"The music on *Van Halen* took a week, I would say, including 'Jamie's Cryin'' — I already had the basic riff for that song. My guitar solo, 'Eruption,' wasn't planned for the record. Al and I were dinging around rehearsing for a show, and I was warming up with this solo. Ted came in and said, 'It's great; put it on the record!' The singing on the album took about two weeks."

Eddie's strategy with the band, he says, is "I do whatever I want. I don't really think about it too much—and that's the beauty of being in this band. Everyone pretty much does what they want, and we all throw out ideas, so whatever happens, happens. Everything is pretty spontaneous. We used to have a keyboard player, and I hated it because I had to play everything exactly the same with him. I couldn't noodle in between the vocal lines, because he was doing something to fill it up. I don't like someone else filling where I want to fill, and that's why I've always wanted to play in three-piece bands."

Eddie assembled his main guitar with parts he bought from Charvel. "It is a copy of a Fender Stratocaster," he says. "I bought the body for $50 and the neck for $80, and put in an old Gibson patent-applied-for pickup that was rewound to my specifications. I like the one-pickup sound, and I've experimented with it a lot. If you put the pickup really close to the bridge, it sounds trebly. If you put it too far forward, you get a sound that isn't good for rhythm. I like it towards the back — it gives the sound a little sharper edge and bite. I also put my own frets in, using large Gibsons. There is only one volume knob — that's all there is to it. I don't use any fancy tone knobs. I see so many people who have these space-age guitars with a lot of switches and equalizers and treble boosters — give me one knob, that's it. It's simple and it sounds cool. I also painted this guitar with stripes. It has almost the same weight as a Les Paul."

Eddie's other guitars include an Ibanez copy of a Gibson Explorer, which, he says, "I slightly rearranged. I cut a piece out of it with a chainsaw so that it's now a cross between a V [Gibson Flying V] and an Explorer, and I put in different electronics and gave it a paint job. I've also recently bought a Charvel Explorer-shaped body and put a Danelectro neck on it and an old Gibson patent-applied-for pickup. And I also found a 1952 gold-top Les Paul. It's not completely original — it's got a regular stud tailpiece in it, and a tune-o-matic bridge. I have rewound Gibson patent-applied-for pickups in it, too. I use a Les Paul for the end of the set because my Charvel is usually out of tune, and the Les Paul's sound is a little fatter.

"Nobody taught me how to do guitar work; I learned by trial and error. I have messed up a lot of good guitars that way, but now I know what I'm doing, and I can do whatever I want to get them the way I want them. I hate store-bought, off-the-rack guitars. They don't do what I want them to do, which is kick ass and scream. Take the vibrato setup, for example. You have to know how to set it up so it won't go out of tune, which took me a long time to get down. It has a lot to do with the way you play it—you can't bring it down and not bring it up. Some people just hit the bar and let go — you have to bring it back right. Sometimes you'll stretch a note too far with your fingering hand, and it'll go flat. Here you have to pull the bar up to get it back to normal. I've also found that a gauged set of strings will work better than one you make up. Like, I used to use heavier bottom strings with light top strings, and it didn't work very well. I also buy a different spring from Fender for my vibrato — one that's a little looser — and this makes a big difference. You also have to watch out for the little string retainers Fender uses, because sometimes the strings can get caught in them and go out of tune."

Onstage Eddie uses a Univox echo unit that is concealed in a World War II practice bomb. "I had a different motor put in it," he says, "so it would delay much slower and go really low. I use this for 'Eruption.' I also use two Echoplexes and a flanger for subtle touches. And I use an MXR Phase 90 phase shifter that gives me a treble boost for solos, too."

On a recent return flight from Japan, Eddie's original 100-watt Marshall amps were lost in air freight, and he's replaced them with Music Mans, Laneys, and new Marshalls. "I like three 100-watt amps for the main setup," he says. "After I do my guitar solo I change guitars and amps to the second setup. The third setup, also three amps, is for back-up. I have each guitar plugged into a different setup so that if anything goes wrong, all I have to do is grab another guitar. This saves my worrying about trying to fix the amp. I use voltage generators, which can crank my amps up to 130 or 140 volts. Amps sound like nothing else to me when they are cranked so high, but you have got to keep a fan on them because they blow so often. You have to retube them every day, and they usually don't work for more than ten hours of playing."

Eddie seldom formally practices with his guitar, preferring instead to "play when I feel like it. But I am always thinking music. Sometimes people think I'm spacing off, but really I'm not. I am always thinking of riffs and melodies. Lately I've thought up acoustic-type riffs."

Eddie's first U.S. tour hasn't altered his feelings about rock and roll. "I have never given up on rock," he says. "There are people out there who used to say that rock is dead and gone — bullshit. It has always been there, and

ROSS MARINO

it is still the main stadium sellout thing. If you want to be a rock guitarist, you have to enjoy what you are doing. You can't pick up a guitar and say, 'I want to be a rock star' just because you want to be one. You have to enjoy playing guitar. If you don't enjoy it, then it's useless. I know a lot of people who really want to be famous or whatever, but they don't really practice the guitar. They think all you do is grow your hair long and look freaky and jump around, and they neglect the musical end. It is tough to learn music; it's like having to go to school to be a lawyer. But you have to enjoy it. If you don't enjoy it, forget it."

Asked his plans for the future, Eddie Van Halen answers, "Man, just to keep rocking out and playing good guitar!"

— Jas Obrecht

Van Halen Comes of Age

By the end of the '70s, Van Halen had sold over 7,000,000 albums and toured the world twice. As America's premier metal guitarist, Eddie was imitated by players who borrowed everything from his fingering patterns to his instrument designs. Eddie explained some of his techniques for the first time in this extensive April '80 cover story.

an introduction

Very few guitarists have had as intense an impact in as short a time as Eddie Van Halen. The sparkplug of the band that bears his family name, he exploded into ears around the world in February 1978 with the release of *Van Halen*. On this debut album Eddie wrestled devastating feedback, kamikaze vibrato moans, sustained harmonics, white-hot leads, and liquid screams out of a cranked-to-the-max homemade guitar that combined a Fender Strat-style body with the electronics of a Gibson Les Paul. Even on this first effort, underneath the raw intensity of Eddie's solos — many of which were spontaneous first takes — lies a strong melodic and rhythmic sensitivity.

The immediate success of *Van Halen* catapulted the band on a 10-month world tour, during which Eddie stunned audiences with his seemingly off-hand ability to instantaneously convey to his fingers what he heard in his head. He toted a suitcase full of guitar parts with him, building and fixing instruments in his spare time. In November 1978 Eddie was presented in the pages of *Guitar Player* for the first time. By the end of the year, companies had cloned his trademark guitar, players had begun borrowing his licks, and Eddie had walked away with *Guitar Player*'s Best New Talent poll award.

For *Van Halen II*, released early in 1979, Eddie slapped together another Strat-style guitar and took up where the first LP left off. Besides pulling off several imaginative, fat-toned solos with the dizzying skill of a stunt pilot on a grand finale spin, he furthered his exploration of new and unusual guitar sounds. In the opening of "Women in Love," for instance, he achieves a chimelike effect by fingering notes with his left hand while simultaneously tapping each note's harmonic counterpart on the fingerboard above — a technique he also uses in "Spanish Fly," a fast flamenco-style nylon-string piece.

Van Halen set off on another world tour in March 1979, spending eight months playing the U.S., France, Belgium, Holland, England, Japan, and Canada. *Van Halen II* went gold in two weeks after 500,000 copies were sold; seven weeks later the record was declared platinum when sales climbed over 1,000,000 units. (Since the release of *Van Halen*, the group's name has never been off the charts.) In December 1979 — just one year after he won Best New Talent — Eddie edged out veteran guitarists Jimmy Page, Carlos Santana, and Steve Howe to win Best Rock Guitarist in the *Guitar Player* Readers Poll. He also topped readership polls in Japan.

Accolades were not limited to record buyers and poll balloteers here and abroad, though; players, too, began acclaiming his guitar wizardry. In the August '79 *Guitar Player*, Ted Nugent proclaimed him "a fantastic guitarist." Three months later Cheap Trick's Rick Nielsen discussed Van Halen's deft use of the vibrato bar. Then, in the first cover story of the '80s, Pat Travers declared Van Halen the state-of-the-art rock guitarist, adding, "I don't think there's anybody better for saying more, getting a better sound, or just taking advantage of the straight Stratocaster-style sound."

Van Halen came off the road in December 1979 and almost immediately went into the studio to record their third LP, *Women And Children First*, in only eight days. Once again, Eddie proved that his playing is not limited to rock styles. On "Could This Be Magic" he performed an impromptu Hawaiian-sounding acoustic slide part, and also played the steel-string on "Take Your Whiskey Home." And with the enthusiasm of a mad scientist ready to pull the switch, he continued his quest for weird sounds, using his guitar to duplicate a prop plane revving up, shaking his bass *E* string against the pickup to heighten the intensity of a passage, and banging away on an electric piano hooked up to his pedalboard and Marshall stacks. The electric solos continue in the fiery tradition of the first two albums.

The interview below was conducted while *Women And Children First* was in its final mixing stage. During the seven-hour conversation, Eddie unhesitatingly discussed his guitars, techniques, and views on the art, revealing some information for the first time. He celebrated his birthday a week later on January 26. And now, at age 23, he's the youngest cover story artist in *Guitar Player*'s history.

the interview

When you started playing guitar, how much time did you spend with it?

All day, every day. I used to cut school to come

ROSS MARINO

JON SIEVERT

home and play, I was so into it.

Were you self-taught?

Definitely for guitar. I never had a lesson in my life, except when a friend of mine a long time ago showed me how to do barre chords. I just learned from there.

How did you teach yourself?

[*Duplicates Eric Clapton's solo in "Crossroads" from Cream's* Wheels Of Fire *on his electric guitar.*] I know that song note-for-note, and also "I'm So Glad" [*Fresh Cream*] and the live version of "Sitting On Top Of The World" [Cream, *Goodbye*]. I used to know all that stuff.

Did your brother Alex jam along on drums while you were learning?

Actually, I started playing drums first. I bought the Surfaris' "Wipe Out." I loved that song and said, "I'm going to go out and buy myself a $125 St. George drum set." So I got a paper route to pay for it. I'm out throwing the paper — five in the morning, in the rain, with a bicycle with a flat tire — and my brother is practicing on my drums. He got better, so I said, "You take my drums."

Is this when you got your first guitar?

Yeah. It was a $70 Teisco Del Ray electric with four pickups. I used to think, man, the more pickups, the better. And look at what I've got now! One pickup and one knob.

How did you develop your speed?

Well, I'll tell you. They used to lock me in a little room and go, "Play fast!" [*laughs*]. I was actually trained to be a classical pianist. I had this Russian teacher who couldn't speak a word of English, and he would just sit there with a ruler ready to slap my face if I made a mistake. This started in Holland, and both my brother and I took lessons. Then when we got to the U.S. my dad found another good teacher. Basically, that's where I got my ear developed, learned my theory, and got my fingers moving. Then when the Dave Clark Five and those bands came out, I wanted to go [*plays the riff from "You Really Got Me"*]. I didn't want to go clink, clink, clink. I still play piano, and I also play violin.

Did your piano study influence your guitar playing?

Things like this are classical [*plays the continuous left-hand tremolo passage from "Spanish Fly"*]. I know that had something to do with piano. I'm sure some things psychologically come out, but I don't actually sit down at a piano and try to apply it to guitar.

Were your parents supportive of your move to the guitar and rock and roll?

My father yes, but my mother no. My mom wanted us in the U.S. and out of Holland. She was afraid we'd get into music like my father. She still doesn't think it will last, but she's proud. My dad was one of the baddest clarinet players of his time. He was so hot — unbelievably. And he had *tone*. My dad is the person who would cut school and smoke cigarettes, and my mom would be the cheerleader. Complete opposites — the conservative and the screw-up. If you sat there and talked to my dad, he'd make you roll over and laugh. He's just like me and Al — 16 years old. His whole life has been music; that's all he knows.

Do they ever go to your concerts?

Yeah. My dad cries when he sees us play because he

loves it. You know, he's so happy. It really is like his dream come true: The family music tradition is continuing, and it's also his name. Like when I was in school, everybody said, "Forget my parents. They're assholes." Not me. I was always the weirdo. I'd say, "Hey, I love my parents. I'll do anything for them. They've always busted their ass for me." On my dad's birthday last year we retired him and bought him a boat. I want to make my people happy.

What made you decide to build your own guitars?

A Les Paul to me was just the cliched guitar, the rock and roll guitar. I liked the sound, but it didn't fit my body. I'd have to wear it too high to be able to stretch as I do, and it looks funky. So I wanted to get that type of sound, but with a tremolo. And Bigsbys have got to be the worst. So I bought a '58 Strat years ago when we played high school dances, and Dave and Al just turned and started throwing sticks at me! They said, "Don't use that guitar. It sounds too thin!" You know, single-coil pickups. They had a real buzzy, thin sound unless I used a fuzz box, and that's even worse. So I sold that and then two years later I bought a router and dumped a Gibson PAF pickup into a '61 Strat. It got very close. All of a sudden the band said, "That's okay. It doesn't sound like a Strat anymore." Then I heard that a company called Charvel made exact duplicates of Fender guitars, but out of nicer wood.

Is this where you got the wood for your first homemade guitar?

Yeah. The very first one was the black-and-white striped one on the first album. I went to Charvel and had them rout a body out for just one pickup and one volume knob. I had to cut my own pickguard to cover everything up because it was originally a three-pickup Strat body. I used the vibrato tailpiece from a '58 Strat for that guitar. I also had Charvel make me a really wide neck. I hate skinny necks. I like them to be almost as wide as a classical guitar across the fingerboard, but thin in depth. I left it bare wood because I hate to slip and slide when I start stretching strings. Now at the same time, I built what I call my shark guitar, which is actually one of the first Ibanez Destroyers [shaped like a Gibson Explorer] made out of Korina wood. I made the mistake of taking a chainsaw to it and putting a bunch of weird stuff on it.

Did it lose some tone?

It lost the tonality I want. Now, kids can't tell. They can buy a DiMarzio pickup and stick it in anything and go, "Yeah, it's rock and roll!" But it was that distinct little tone that I look for that was cut out of the guitar. Then I went to Charvel and bought the parts for a Destroyer with a vibrato. I got tired of playing it, and so I had a friend of mine carve a dragon biting a snake out of the Destroyer's body.

How long did it take you to build the black-and-white Strat?

Not really too long, but it took me a while to build up to doing that. I used to have an old Gibson ES-335 that was my main experimental guitar. That was the one I refretted and painted and totally screwed up! I mean, I did everything you can imagine to that guitar to ruin it. But I learned from it. It's too bad, because that guitar would have been worth some bucks today. But I learned what I know of building guitars, so I guess it's worth it.

Have you since modified the black-and-white Strat?

Yeah. A company started copying it, and I said, "Man, I better change it." So I really went to town painting it all freaked out, and I put three pickups back in, but they don't all work — only the rear one works. I just did it to be different, so every kid who bought one like that model would go, "Oh, man, he's got something different again." I always like to turn the corner on people when they start latching on to what I'm doing. Here I am just a punk kid trying to get a sound out of a guitar that I couldn't buy off the rack, so I built one myself and now everybody else wants one.

Did you make another guitar for your second album?

I made the yellow-and-black Strat. It has an ash body by Charvel. It was my idea to have it rear-loaded so I wouldn't have to have a pickguard, and Charvel routed it for me. The pickup that's on the photo is not really what I use. I had just finished slapping it together and painting it when they shot the album cover, and just stuck some garbage pickup in it to look like a complete guitar. Then I took the pickup out of my first guitar and stuck it in there, but it didn't sound too good. I hate the fuzz box, real raspy sound. So I put a PAF magnet in a DiMarzio pickup and rewound it by hand, which took a long time. I actually ruined about three pickups, and by the fourth time it worked. I didn't count the windings; I just did it by sight.

Was that the guitar you took on your second tour?

I used that one plus the original one from the first album for the first half of the tour, and then I ran into Floyd Rose and he showed me his special bridge and nut for keeping a Strat in tune. I said, "What the hell, I'll give it a try." I'm up for anything. So I had Boogie Bodies make me a mahogany body that's fit to my size, and I put the Rose device on it. The body is a Strat-style, but it's 2½" thick, which is thicker than a Les Paul. The Rose tailpiece gets a thin sound, and I thought a chunky piece of wood could make up for the tinkiness. It works a little bit. That guitar has a Gibson PAF and just one volume knob. It's real simple.

What is your overall opinion of Floyd's vibrato device?

I like it and I don't. For one, on my guitar it sounds real brittle-bright, and I have to do some heavy equalization to get my tone. That's why I don't like to use it in the studio. We just go in there and play live, and I depend on making my guitar sound good out of the amp instead of fixing it in the mix. Number two, if you pop a string, you can't even one-note your way through because the whole guitar goes out of tune. Sometimes I'll hit a chord and tune really quickly. With this device you can't — you have to unclamp it. On top of that, sometimes when I jump off the drum riser the neck shifts just a hair, and then I can't tune it. But it has advantages: When you're using the bar, it *will not* go out of tune.

What are the most difficult aspects of building your own guitar?

Making the neck fit the body. Another problem is that the strings on a Stratocaster are spaced differently than a Gibson's. If you use a humbucking pickup, the strings don't line up with the pickup poles. So I've tried slanting the pickup so the high *E* string will be picked up by a front pole and the low *E* will be picked up by a rear pole. For the sound I like, it is also important to get the space between the bridge and pickup right. I do it almost like a Les Paul. If I put it too far towards the neck I get the Grand Funk and Johnny Winter tone, and if I put it too close to the bridge I get a real trebly Strat sound. So I move it up towards the neck a little bit from the Strat sound to get a beefier tone.

Do you carry any special tools or extra parts with you when you're on the road?

I bring along at least five extra necks, three different bodies, ten different pickups, some machine heads, and a couple of different tremolo pieces in case one breaks — you know, just spare parts mainly. See, like if we're six months through the tour and the frets are starting to go bad on one neck, I'll slap another neck on instead of refretting it, because I don't have time to refret while I'm traveling. In tools I carry screwdrivers, chisels, chainsaws — very simple stuff [*laughs*].

Have you any special methods of refretting necks?

Yeah. I hate the way people refret necks. I do it real simple: I sand them down with some 400 wet-or-dry sandpaper and then use some steel wool. I hate flat frets because the more space you have for the string to rest on, the more room you have for the intonation to be off. I like big frets height-wise, but I make them come to a peak. From a side view, one of my frets would look like the tip of a pick. It doesn't come to a complete point, but it would be rounded as opposed to flat. Another thing is that you have to put them in right. Fender has a machine that puts them in from the side rather than from above, and a lot of people take them straight out and rip the wood. I toured the factory and saw how they did it and said, "No wonder I ruined so many Fenders by pulling them straight out!"

Do you do anything special to your pickups?

I usually use old Gibson PAFs, and I always pot them. I submerge the whole thing in paraffin wax, and this cuts out the high obnoxious feedback. It's kind of a tricky thing because if you leave it in there too long, the pickup melts. I take a coffee can and melt down some wax — the same kind that you use for surfboards — and put the pickup in it. See, one of the reasons a pickup feeds back is that the coil windings vibrate, and when the wax soaks in there, it keeps them from vibrating so much. It will still feed back, but it's controllable. After I dip the pickup in paraffin, I put copper tape around it. You have to be really careful if you do this to a pickup like a DiMarzio. You can throw an old PAF in there and let it soak it up; it doesn't melt. But with DiMarzio's, if you blink, all of a sudden your pickup's ruined.

Do you own any stock factory-made guitars?

Yeah, I have a new Gibson ES-335, and two '58 Les Paul Jrs. — a single-cutaway and a double-cutaway. I've got a whole load of Japanese Strat copies. I also just purchased two vintage Les Pauls, a '59 flame top and a '58 gold top. These are pretty much in immaculate condition. I bought them as an investment; I don't play them. My main stage guitars are the ones I build myself for under $200. I have an acoustic, too; the one I used on "Spanish Fly." It's an Ovation nylon-string, not the real expensive model. I've never owned a steel-string.

Are there any guitars that you'd like to build in the future?

I'll have the next one built, and it will probably be difficult and cost a lot of money. What I'd really like now is like a three-quarter size 335. I was playing a 335 for a while before we got signed, and it sounded fine. But the other guys would go, "Come on — you look like Roy Orbison" [*laughs*]. Really, here's this skinny punk kid playing a Ted Nugent axe, you know. They said, "You're rock and roll; you ain't Roy Orbison. Either get some dark glasses or get rid of the guitar." So I dumped that and started playing the Les Paul again. So what I would like is a 335 to fit my body, and maybe not quite as hollow as some 335s. I'd like a solid beam all the way to the back of the guitar and maybe a little extra wood in there. The one I have now lacks a little bit of tone. It's too acoustically toned, too hollow.

Would you put a vibrato bar in the 335?

Yeah. I love 335s. I can haul ass on those things. When I pick up a stock 335, you probably wouldn't even recognize my playing. It's more jazzy, more fluid and fast — kind of like Allan Holdsworth. One of the reasons I started using a vibrato was that my playing got so fast it was just too much. So now I break it up a little bit. It's like a race car racing down the road and crashing every now and then.

What are your views on using a vibrato bar?

It's more of a feeling as opposed to an effect. I don't really use it for freak-out effects; I use it to enhance a little more feeling. I really don't have any special chops with it. I just grab it when I feel like it. It calls for a totally different technique. I have special tricks for keeping it in tune, but it still goes out. You have to play with it. Like if you bring the bar down, the *G* and *B* strings always go sharp when you let it back, so before you hit a barre chord you have to stretch those strings back with a real quick little jerk. The vibrato is actually like another instrument. You can't just grab it and jerk the thing and expect it to stay in tune.

What's the advantage of playing with your hand on the bridge?

I like getting a muffled effect with the side of my hand. It gets more tone. It's a definite texture you can use in combination with straight picking.

How do you hold your pick?

Between my thumb and middle finger. Sometimes when I play fast, I'll put the tip of my index finger on the corner of the pick.

Do you ever use your other fingers to pick?

No. I can't fingerpick for anything. I've never had the time.

Did you use a pick for "Spanish Fly"?

Yeah, except for the part near the end that sounds like Montoya or something.

Do you ever use the side of your pick to get high-pitched harmonics?

Sometimes. I do in "I'm The One" [*Van Halen*]. I also get harmonics by hitting a note with my left-hand finger while I tap my right index finger on the fingerboard exactly one octave up. When it's an exact octave, you

Van Halen, 1980: Dave Lee Roth, Alex Van Halen, Eddie Van Halen, Michael Anthony.

NEIL ZLOZOWER

bring out the harmonic plus the lower note.

Do you tap on top of the fret wire or behind it?

On the fret, I guess. Like in "Spanish Fly," I start out by tapping harmonics and then do hammer-ons and pull-offs with my left hand while I tap above with my right-hand index fingertip. Now this is my latest: I hammer-on and pull-off with my left hand and reach behind my left hand with my right and use my right index finger below my left hand, so that it acts as a sixth finger. In other words, my right-hand finger changes the lowest note. See, the way I play is in my fingers. I could play a Strat or a Les Paul, and it's going to sound like me. People say, "Oh, how do you get that sound?" They could play my guitar, and it wouldn't sound the same. I have a style of playing where no matter what amp or guitar I use, it sounds like me.

How far can you reach on the fingerboard?

On the high *E* string I can reach from the 5th fret to the 12th. From the 12th fret I can hit any note on the fingerboard above. That's how I get weird noises.

Are you learning new things on the guitar all the time?

Yeah. Like if I sit down and play by myself, I play completely different than I would with the band. I just really go for feeling in my playing. All our albums have mistakes — big deal, we're human. But they reek of feeling, and that, to me, is what music is all about. It's not like Fleetwood Mac. You know, they spend so much time and money on their albums. I think that if something is too perfect, it won't faze you. It'll go in one ear and out the other because it's so perfect. Like our stuff, to me, keeps you on the edge of your seat. It builds tension whether you like it or not. It slaps you in the face.

Like in "Ice Cream Man" [Van Halen] *when the band comes in?*

Exactly. It's almost like you're just waiting for us to blow it — waiting for something to go wrong, but it doesn't. That's what creates the feel, the tension: just like winding something up and waiting to see when it's going to break. It's just inner feelings coming out; it's not conscious. The way I play is the way I am.

When you're playing onstage, what do you think about?

Nothing. It's like having sex, actually. I swear to God. It's definitely my first love. Got in a fight with my girlfriend before. I used to go over to her house and play my guitar in her bedroom, and she'd go, "You love your guitar more than you do me!" And I'd go, "You're right!" Hey, I'm sorry — it's part of me.

How many times a day do you pick up a guitar?

All the time. Sometimes I play it for a minute, sometimes half an hour, and sometimes all day. There's no schedule; I don't run by schedules at all. Usually I play before I go to sleep, when I wake up, when I come home, when I'm bored.

Do you usually use an amp?

When I'm at home I use a little old white Fender Bandmaster. I plug into the extension speaker so I can crank it all the way up and it fuzzes out. It's actually like at full volume. You get tube distortion and it sounds real good. Like a Marshall has two outputs, and you can use either one and get a full output. With the Fender, you have a main speaker jack and if you want the extension one to work, the first one has to be plugged in. If you bypass the first one and just plug into the extension speaker, you get a real low signal, but you get the same sound as if you plugged into the main one. You blow a transformer every eight months, but it's worth it. It sounds great. That's what I use at home.

What do you look for in a solo?

Feeling. I don't care if it's melodic or spontaneous. If it's melodic and has no feeling, it's screwed.

What should a good rock and roll song do?

Move you in any way. Depress you, make you happy, make you horny, make you rowdy. Anything. If it doesn't, it's like Fleetwood Mac! Excuse me, I should point out that I love *Rumours* — that's a hot album.

When your band is putting together new material, do you work on both words and music?

No. Dave writes the majority of the lyrics and I write the music. I don't consider myself a songwriter to begin with. I've written songs on the piano, but they're not Van Halen. It's very easy to write a song on the piano. You just pick some chords and squeeze a melody out of it; I learned that in school. So when I write on guitar I always come up with a theme riff — you know, some powerful opener — and then a verse, a chorus, a bridge, a solo, back to the bridge, chorus, and then the end.

How do you decide what to do with the solo?

Sometimes it's spontaneous, sometimes it's set. Like the solo in "Runnin' With The Devil" [*Van Halen*] was set. And the same with "Ain't Talkin' 'Bout Love" [*Van Halen*]. By "set" I mean that I figured out something melodic instead of just going for it. When I wrote "Ain't Talkin' 'Bout Love" I thought it was about the lamest song I ever wrote in my life. It took me six months before I even worked up the nerve to show the guys, but kids go nuts for it! I love the beginning — *Am* and *G*.

What were some of your spontaneous solos?

"Ice Cream Man" was one — that was a first take. The solo In "You Really Got Me" was totally spontaneous. Next time you listen to it, turn the balance to one side, because the way Ted [Templeman] produces, my guitar is always on one side. Listen to it — there's only one guitar, no overdubs. But it sounds full.

Do you repeat solos from night to night, or do you change them around?

I rarely repeat. Sometimes I remember the way I did it on the record and kind of follow it, unless they are melodic solos like in "Runnin' With The Devil" and "Ain't Talkin' 'Bout Love." You know, if I start noodling around, kids go, "Hey, that ain't the same song!"

Are there some songs you stretch out on in concert?

"Feel Your Love Tonight" [*Van Halen*]. My guitar solo without the band, definitely. "You Really Got Me" ends with a long jam.

It sounds like a lot of your solos are built off of lines rather than chords.

Well, the thing is, in rock and roll you only have so many chords. If you start hitting chords like this [*plays 7ths and 9ths*] in rock and roll, forget it! They have emotion, but they don't fit power rock. They're so dissonant that the vibrations of the overtones with that much distortion sound like shit. That's why most rock and roll songs are simple — straight major or minor chords. You start dickin' with chords like the 7ths and 9ths through a blazing Marshall, and it will sound like crap. It's very tough to come up with an interesting solo when you're just in one key. But see, there are ways to get around it — you can be playing in *E* and you can solo in *D*. There are certain chords that are relative to the key you're playing in, like in the key of *A* you can play around an *F#m.*

You seem to end a lot of phrasings with a blues feeling.

Yeah, well, I started out playing blues — the *Blues Breakers* album where Eric Clapton's on the front reading the Beano comic book. I can play real good blues — that's the feeling I was after. But actually I've turned it into a much more aggressive thing. Blues is a real tasty, feel type of thing; so I copped that in the beginning. But then when I started to use a wang bar [vibrato], I still used that feeling, but rowdier, more aggressive, more attack. But still, I end a lot of phrasing with a bluesy feeling. I like phrasing; that's why I always liked Clapton. He would just play it with feeling. It's like someone talking, a question-and-answer trip.

On your records, Michael Anthony's bass parts are subdued compared to what you do. Is this intentional?

Yeah. He's a damned good bass player. He plays *bass.* He's not a Jack Bruce; he doesn't play guitar on bass. When Al and Mike are playing, it's an open world for me. I can do whatever I want. They're right there backing me up, feeding me. Whereas if he was a Jack Bruce, I'd be in competition with him. Everyone is hot, but in their own pocket. A lot of it has to do with the mix on records, whereas live it comes off much better, much more powerful. I kind of like it because most bands sound like hell live and great on records. I think we sound good on record but better live. I'm totally happy with our records, but live it comes out better.

How do you warm up before going onstage?

Just scales. Fast or slow, depending on how cold my fingers are.

Do you put new strings on every night?

Yeah, Fender 150XLs. I stretch them to death. With that new Rose thing, I boil the strings so they stretch, because if you just put them on and clamp it down, the strings stretch out on the guitar. I just take a pack and let it boil for 20 minutes in the hot water. And then I dry them in the sun, because otherwise they rust. But I only use them one night anyway, so who cares if they rust?

Does anyone take care of your guitars besides you?

Rudy Leiren — he's my roadie.

How do you tune up before a show?

I tune all my guitars myself. We tune a quarter-step down, so it's like right between *E* and *Eb*; this is for vocal reasons. I used to tune down to *D,* but Mike couldn't get his bass tone. He'd get too much slap. When we go in the studio, man, I don't strobe tune or anything. I just pick the guitar up and if it's in tune, I say, "Mike, tune to me," and we play. Why does it have to be the same? Who says it has to be tuned to *E*? Why the rules? Fuck the rules! I mean the main reason I get all the weird stuff I do on guitar is because I don't do it by the rules.

Do you experiment with open tunings?

No, because that's kind of a rule too that's been done. I don't care that much about things that have been done, where most players have only done what's been done. They look at the guitar as if that's all it's for. They don't even go beyond to think. Like they don't know how I get some of the weird noises I make, but it's just the guitar. Just do anything to it! I could drop a guitar and get a noise out of it. The guitar is not designed for one purpose. You can do anything with it. I'll do my damnedest to squeeze every noise out of this thing I can.

What is your philosophy on using effects?

What I'm really into doing is squeezing anything out of the cheapest possible thing. Like whenever I get something made or built or designed I always say, "Make it as cheap as possible." I'll walk into this music store where I buy all my stuff, a place in Pasadena called Dr. Music, and they laugh at me. Because I ask them what they have, and they go, "Oh, got this new this, got the new digital delay or something or other," and I go, "Got anything cheaper?" Because I can get wierder noises out of them than the expensive state-of-the-art shit.

Do you feel the state-of-the-art ones have too much control in them?

They don't have enough. You pay so much, and they're so precious. You can't take them around, you can't kick them, you can't drop them. If you ever saw my pedalboard!

What's in it?

It's a piece of plywood with two controls for my Echoplex on it, an MXR Phase 90 that I've had for years, and an MXR flanger. They're all taped to a piece of board with black duct tape. And like a lot of big-name players laugh themselves silly when they see it, but after they hear me, then they go, "Can I plug in?" Some of these guys have got four out-of-phase switches, and a this and a that, and a biamp crossover, and blah, blah, blah. And I just go, "Is it on? Is it working? What's it for? What's it do?" I can't tell! At least when I use an effect, you know I'm using it. My main tricks are in my amps.

What kind of amps are you now using?

Well, in the studio I use my old Marshall, my precious baby. It gets a slightly different sound. Live I use new Marshalls. I made the mistake of taking my main one out on the road last year and I lost it on the way back from Japan. It was flying around India somewhere and six months later, thank God, I got it back. This is the one I bought when I was a kid. I didn't even know what I had until now. It's very old; it has a Plexiglas front. It used to be the house amp at the Pasadena Rose Palace; whoever played there has played through it. It's a real good amp — unbelievable balls!

How do you modify your amps?

Okay, I use a combination of two different kinds of amps. They're both Marshalls, but one kind actually has less power than the other, which is boosted. I use them together. The ones that have less power have a giant capacitor in conjunction with the fuse; if anything happens, the fuse blows first. The capacitor has something to do with the computerized ignition system of a car. I can't give you the exact specs, but it looks like a stick of dynamite, only fatter. What it does is suck juice. I hook it up to the fuse holder and the mains, and it lowers the voltage about ten volts so the amp lasts a little bit longer. It doesn't really change the sound, but whatever I use, I use to the max. I just turn it all the way up. So this capacitor lowers the voltage and the amp lasts a little longer. I still have to retube them once a week. [*Ed. Note: This is not a recommended procedure for modifying amps and should not be attempted by anyone inexperienced in the field of electronics and amp modification.*]

What is done to the other kind of amps?

I use a Variac, which is like a dimmer on a lighting system. It's an autotransformer which goes all the way from 0 volts to 160. In the studio I crank it up to 140 and watch the tubes melt! [*Ed. Note: Again, this is not a recommended procedure for modifying amps, as Paul Rivera of Rivera Research and Development points out: "You can cause severe damage to the amp besides melting tubes. Since a Variac is an exposed transformer, by hooking it up incorrectly you could get the hot of the AC line on the chassis of the amp and electrocute yourself. Anyone wishing to attempt this sort of modification should go to a knowledgeable repairman."*]

Do you lose many amps during your shows?

Yeah, but I have so many of them. I have like 12 to 15 100-watt Marshalls onstage in pairs of four, hooked up together. Then I have three switches where if the first stack blows, I can switch in the next one. That's about it for live. I have such a big setup: 80 12" speakers for my last setup, which was the equal of 20 Marshall cabinets. The next one will be World War III. But it's not for overblitzed noise.

Is it to refine the sound?

It's to make a good tone even louder. Some people get a sound like an amplified AM radio. I like it to be like a nice home stereo amplified — you know, the difference between tone and no tone. I have some other tricky stuff in my amps which I don't even want to talk about because if someone reads it in the magazine they are going to hit up Jose, an old guy from Argentina who knows a lot of tricks and does stuff for me. He doesn't want people to know who he is because he's getting mobbed. He also puts little things inside my MXR stuff, like permanent gain controls that boost when I kick them on. I don't even know what they're called. They reduce noise and boost the signals.

Do you have the sound you want?

Sometimes. It depends on the arena, depends on my mood. It's dependent on a lot of things. I'll tell you, the best sound I ever get is sitting home alone playing through that little Bandmaster cranked on 10.

What do you use as an onstage monitor?

We use two giant Showco M-4s [four-way cabinets], which are actually like a complete system in themselves. They have the highs and lows and everything. The only thing I add to the mix is a teeny bit of my voice, so I can hear if I'm in tune with my guitar and my brother.

Do you ever have trouble hearing yourself?

Never. Dave and Mike won't even come to my side because I'm so loud. But there is a difference between being just loud and having what I call a warm, brown sound — which is a rich, toney sound. I guess a lot of people are tone deaf and can't figure it out because they just crank it up with a lot of treble just for the sake of being loud. Anyone can do that. I can actually play so loud onstage that you won't hear anything else, but I don't really like to do that. I like to get a balanced sound.

How loud do you play in the studio?

Very loud. I use four 100-watt Marshalls, which are cranked up to close to 600 watts with the Variac. I like to

BILL O'LEARY

feel it, you know, make my arm hairs move. If you stand in front of a big PA you vibrate. It's the way I get off. I don't wear ear plugs, either, so I'm surprised I'm not deaf yet. We used to get kicked out of clubs because I refused to turn down. It's the only way I could get a sound — crank it all the way up.

Do you use wireless transmitters?

Yeah, I always do because I bounce around a lot. My first one was a Schaffer-Vega. It took me a long time to get it working right with my system because at the time my amps were so powerful that the thing was overdriven and wouldn't work. It was too much power. Then when I got weaker amps I could use it. If you use it with too high of an amp it will just freak out; you get the weirdest feedback noises you ever heard in your life. And then I got a Nasty Cordless. Now the Schaffer-Vega is tuned to a fixed frequency, and one of the advantages of the Nasty is that you can dial in the frequency, just like a radio. The Schaffer-Vega has a built-in compressor in the transmitter, which is kind of cool, depending on what amp you use it with. I think that the Nasty is weaker. Like with the Schaffer-Vega I'm always reaching at my knob, trying to get 11 out of it instead of 10. And with the Nasty, I'm reaching for 14, so I use an equalizer to boost it. But it is actually a cleaner sounding system. When we played the Budokan in Japan I couldn't use either one because there were heavy radio signals everywhere.

When you go into the studio to record, how ready are you?

We're ready with the structure of the song — that's about it. We jam on tunes a few times in the basement. When I get to the studio, I tell Ted, "Just put a mike to my amp; let's get going." You know, they are always dicking around with the mikes, the speaker mix, Al's snare tone, and this and that. I really get sick of that because I'm just sitting there ready to go: "Come on, let's go while I feel like playing." You know, after four cups of coffee and a bottle of wine, I don't feel like playing. And then they yell, "Let's go! We're ready."

Do you have a good idea of what you're going to play?

Solo-wise, no.

Have you ever tried recording direct-to-disc?

I wouldn't mind. We record very live. The only thing that I think wouldn't work on direct-to-disc would be vocals. See, I stand right next to my brother when I play. I don't use headphones; neither does he. If I was playing direct-to-disc, how could I sing, playing at that volume, unless I played in a booth, separated. Then I just wouldn't get the vibes of playing with Alex.

Let's discuss some of your parts on the Van Halen *album. How did you do the descending growl at the end of "Eruption"?*

That's a $50 Univox EC-80 echo box, a real cheap thing that works off a cartridge. It's like a miniaturized 8-track cartridge. One day some kid turned me onto it and all of a sudden I hit a note, turned it all the way up, and got that growl. I go, "Whoa!" So I mounted it in an old World War II practice bomb that I picked up in a junkyard. I've read reviews in papers that have said, "Eddie Van Halen with a synthesizer solo." Actually all it is is a $50 piece of junk.

Did you plan the solo in "I'm On Fire?"

No. It's so funny — I wanted to do a melodic solo and the guys go, "Pretend you're John McLaughlin!" So then that solo came out. I don't even know what key I'm playing in! I just started playing and it fit perfect. That's how a lot of it works — totally spontaneous. It's not like I decided, "I'm going to start here and end up there."

How did you get that scratchy sound in "Atomic Punk"?

A phase shifter was on, and I rubbed the strings by the bridge with the heel of my hand — I've got calluses on it. I do the same thing on "Everybody Wants Some" [*Women And Children First*]. I just love doing weird things.

What's the sound at the opening of "Runnin' With The Devil"?

Car horns. We took the horns out of all our cars — my brother's Opel, my old Volvo, ripped a couple out of a Mercedes and a Volkswagen — and mounted them in a box and hooked two car batteries to it and added a footswitch. We just used them as noisemakers before we got signed. Ted put it on tape, slowed it down, and then we came in with the bass. It sounds like a jet landing.

How many tracks did you use for "Ain't Talkin' 'Bout Love"?

Two. I soloed on the basic track, and if you listen *real* closely on one channel, I overdubbed the solo with an electric sitar.

In the solo section of "You Really Got Me" there's a staccato part that sounds like a car lurching. It's right before Dave starts in with the "ooohs" and "ahhhs."

Yeah. I hit the *G* string at the 7th fret and bent it up to [the note] *G* and flicked my toggle switch back and forth.

Was there much of a difference in how the first and second albums were recorded?

I don't think we spent as much time on *Van Halen II*. We toured from the second week in February until December 5th, 1978, and then on December 10th we went into the studio. We didn't spend as much time getting the sound. I like the guitar, but I'm not particularly pleased with the drum sound. I like the drum sound on the first album much better.

On the songs "Somebody Get Me A Doctor" and "You're No Good" you have an effect that sounds like a volume pedal.

That's just the knob of the guitar.

Did you double-track the harmonic intro to "Women In Love"?

Yeah, I played it twice. It sounds like a Harmonizer, and live I get the same effect using the Harmonizer. I like that chime, clock-like sound.

How long did it take you to cut Women And Children First?

We finished the music in six days, and the whole album took eight. I don't understand how people can take any longer. I'd say we did it for between $30,000 and $40,000.

What is the strange effect at the beginning of "And The Cradle Will Rock"? It resembles the sound of a prop plane starting up.

I pinged my strings above the nut and asked Ted to play it backwards so the attack comes at the end of the note. In conjunction with this, I scraped the springs in the back of my guitar. I also took my vibrato bar all the way down so that the strings were limp and then with my left thumb I flapped the low *E* string around the 3rd fret. Sounds great; I love it.

Is there a piano later on in that song?

Yeah, it's a Wurlitzer electric piano that I ran through my MXR flanger and my Marshalls. I just banged on the keys — broke two of them doing it. Who would ever think of doing anything that lame? But it sounds good. You could never tell I had classical training on piano. I bought that piano in Detroit and started pounding on it one night in the bus and wrote "And The Cradle Will Rock."

How did you do the clicking sound in the middle of "Romeo's Delight"?

I shook my low *E* string against the pickup.

What kind of a 12-string did you overdub in "Simple Rhyme"?

It's a Rickenbacker electric. At first it didn't sound right through my amp, and I asked Ted, "Can you doctor it up later in the mix?" Then I told him to forget it. I wanted to make it good out of the amp before it's recorded. My theory is if it doesn't sound good coming out of the speaker box, it ain't going to happen on tape.

How did you come to play acoustic slide on "Could This Be Magic"?

They just handed me a guitar and a slide and said, "Come on, you can do it." I said, "Okay, I'll do my best." And I never in my life ever even played slide before! I'm going, "No, let me practice," and the guys said, "Come on, man, just play." I pulled it off decent. I think I used an old Gibson acoustic, and it was in standard tuning.

Your part almost sounds Hawaiian.

Yeah, it does. It almost sounds like Andy Griffith on the front porch. We wanted to get a horse in there at the end, or a cow going, "Moooo." That song is funny as hell! That's one thing — slide never interested me, because you're going like that [*moves little finger up and down fingerboard*]. Why? I like to use all my fingers.

You don't have an instrumental on Women And Children First.

No. What for? Maybe later on I'll do one if I figure out some finger thing that's just totally different. "Eruption" was the first one, and then the second one I did was in a flamenco style ["Spanish Fly"], but it was still the same type of thing. And what could I do this time? I didn't want to do one just for the sake of doing another solo, so I'm going to wait until I have something really good. Something that sounds classical — electric or acoustic — like some Bach stuff. I've been listening to a lot of classical music, especially Debussy. Goddamn, that mother wrote some hot shit!

Have you ever thought of doing a solo album?

I never will until maybe years from now. All of my energy goes into Van Halen; it's my family. I'm not going to leave my family until one of the members passes on. But still, I have a whole backlog of tunes that we've never done. So if I ever do a solo album, which I don't see in the near future, I'd have plenty of ideas.

Has seeing other guitarists ever inspired a change in your playing?

Allan Holdsworth — that guy is bad! He's fantastic; I love him. He's got a rock *sound*. I love his solo in "In The Dead Of The Night" on the *U.K.* album. I love the solo in

GLEN LA FERMAN

"Hell's Bells" on *One Of A Kind*. [Drummer] Bill Bruford plays hot on that album. Holdsworth is the best in my book. I can kind of play like him, but it doesn't fit our style of music. He's a real artist. He plays a guitar like mine, too. He wears it up high, like a jazz guitar. I could play all that stuff, too, if I played with my guitar up that high, but how would a rock and roll kid look with a guitar up like that? I do have to sacrifice the amount of movement I do onstage for the way I play. I like playing much better on a stool. I don't do it, though, not even in the studio, because then it would sound like I'm sitting on a stool.

So the movement of your body is really tied in with the way you play?

Definitely. 100%. I never do anything the same. I have no choreographed steps where I have to be in any part of a song. I'm wherever I want and do whatever I want whenever I feel it.

Are there other players you like to listen to?

Randy Hansen is hot. I know him real well; he's a good friend. Now he's coming out with his own stuff, and I hope to God he succeeds. Rick Nielsen is very funny; I love the guy. He's [Bowery Boy actor] Huntz Hall. They [Cheap Trick] are the comedians of rock and roll, whereas Kiss are the circus of rock and roll. The reason I think we're happening is because we are one of the only *real* bands out there. We're not punk; we don't dress weird. We play good music — or at least *I* think so. Half of the critics think it's thud rock bullshit. They label us heavy metal old hat. Name me a heavy metal band that's done what we've done. I sound like I'm bragging, but I don't mean it that way. I'm not saying that all the things I come up with are genius-brand riffs, but neither is punk. Punk's like what I used to do in the garage.

What do you think when you hear other players using your licks?

I guess they always say that imitation is the highest form of flattery. I think this is a crock of shit. I don't like people doing things exactly like me. Some of the things I do I know no one has done, like the harmonic runs and the clock chime-like sound. The "Eruption" solo: I never heard anything done like that before, but I know someone must have figured some of it out. What I don't like is when someone takes what I've done, and instead of innovating on what I came up with, they do my trip! They do my melody. Like I learned from Clapton, Page, Hendrix, Beck — but I don't play like them. I innovated; I learned from them and did my own thing out of it. Some of those guys out there are doing my thing, which I think is a lot different.

Do you feel that your playing is constantly progressing?

I don't think it's ever progressed — just gets weirder all the time. How much can you progress? I'm as fast as I can possibly get. I can't picture myself being too much faster. I mean, you can only hear so much. What I'm trying to do is be weirder and different.

Do you get in slumps?

Yes and no. You always reach a plateau, and then moving up from there is a bit tough. But for me it's not that hard.

How do you do it?

Just continue to play and play and try different chops. It's especially hard for me after touring for ten months and playing the same songs. Now, depending on the beat of the song, I play differently. I'm a very rhythmically oriented guitarist. I really work off of rhythm, so if the song's fast, I play a certain way. If it's blues, I play completely different. So if I do the same set for almost a whole year, I get into a rut of that style, and it takes me a month or two to change and come up with new things. That's my rut.

How do you prepare for a tour?

What we do is go into a small room or a basement for two weeks and do physical training. It's like getting ready for a boxing match — real heavy duty jumping around, going through the set. We play without a PA, just instruments. Then we rent a big place and do the full show. I'll tell you, I'd sell my guitars to go on tour. It's a world vacation, a way of life.

What's it like?

It's living out of a suitcase, being in a different town every night, getting a squeeze here and there, seeing the world, experiencing different cultures — Japan, France, Germany. It's traveling. I've always wanted to travel and make music.

Do you find that you get enough time alone?

We have that sometimes. See, like if we play Paris and we party out too late that night, I'll sleep and pass on the sightseeing. But sometimes I'll pass on the party and take a day and go out and trip around. So it's whatever you want to do.

Do you make money on tours?

We break even because we put all our money into sound and lighting. We tour to sell records; the only thing that sells us is our live show. Everything we do is a complete reverse of other people. All we ever knew was our live show. Like when we went in to record the first album, I said, "Hey Ted, I've never done overdubs." Just the thought of playing to a machine, to me, would lose feeling. So I said, "Can I just play live?" You know, go for what you know. So I did and Ted freaked out. He said, "Whoa! It doesn't even *need* another guitar." What we did was apply our live show to plastic, whereas people like Boston and Foreigner do it the opposite way: They work it out in the studio and then have to rehearse before they go on tour. Live shows are the bottom line for us. On this next tour, we're going to be taking out the largest lighting system ever taken on the road.

What's it worth?

Money-wise, I don't even know. I know it's taking all of our money, though. We're betting the whole wad that we will sell. And if not, then we won't. But we always bet our all — give it all or nothing. We are not about to go, "We can save a little money here if we don't do that." We design what we want, have it built, and then say, "How much money have we got?" If we don't have enough, we say, "We've got to get it."

So you look at money mainly as a tool to advance your art?

I don't even look at money. So far the only thing I've done with money is retire the old man and stuff like that. I haven't bought anything for myself except for my guitars and my Jeep. You know, I've got everything I want, which is music, a squeeze now and then, and a car you can mess around in. It's mainly music: That's all I really care about. [*Sings "It's my life and I'll do what I want."*]

Has the attainment of success — stardom, some would say — matched what you imagined it would be?

To tell you the truth, I'm not into the star bullshit at all. A lot of people get off on it — let their hair grow long, buy a Les Paul and a Marshall, and be a rock and roll star. I don't even consider myself a rock star. I enjoy playing guitar. Period. I had an English class where I had to do an essay on what my future plans were — what I wanted to do in life. I said I wanted to be a professional rock guitarist — not a rock star. What is a rock star? It's a mystical image kids have. I'm considered a rock star because kids label me as one. That's kind of why I hate going out partying and playing the part of a rock star, because I don't know how a rock star is supposed to act. If I act too normal, they'll go, "Oh, that's him? That's all he is?" And if I act too much like, "Hey, I'm a bitchin' rock star," they go, "Hey, this guy's egoed out." So I don't show my face too much. I'm pretty much a loner. I just can't get along with people; they don't understand me. So I spend a lot of time alone, playing my guitar. It's just more satisfying. I don't like to waste my time acting, because I'm no good at it.

What are the major disadvantages of the rock life?

The disadvantages of being a rock star is your private life is gone, but your sex life increases. And you have to do interviews. I hate doing interviews.

Why?

Because they always fuck me over. I don't feel like I have anything to say, because if I really say what I feel, they'll twist and bend it and make me seem like I'm egoed out and that I'm God, you know. But I'm not at all; that's one thing I just never expected. I did an interview once and said that my main influences were Clapton and the usuals. And they said, "Not Jimi Hendrix?" I go, "No, actually I didn't like Hendrix at all. He was too much flash for me. I got off on the bluesy feeling that Eric Clapton projected, although I don't play like Clapton or sound at all like him," which doesn't sound egoed out. I don't sound like him. But when I read it back they made it seem like, "I don't play like Clapton. I'm better than all of them." I called the guy up and said, "Hey, man, that's the last time I'm doing an interview with you," which I guess was bad to do, too. The thing is that kids only know me through what they read. I feel like going door-to-door, saying, "Hey, this is bullshit. Don't believe it." But the kids do.

How can you keep journalists from exploiting you?

Don't talk to them. But then again, then they *really* think I'm egoed out. But they don't understand; it's just that I ain't got nothing to say. Like playing the guitar is part of me. I just feel like saying, "Everything I've got to say is in notes." It really is. I project more feeling out of playing than I can with my mouth. I'm no extrovert. I'm a quiet person. That's probably why I do all those weird things on guitar. The only thing I like talking about is the guitar, which is why I wanted to do this interview.

How do you view your career with the band?

We're looking at it as a lifetime thing, like the Stones. We're not out there for the quick buck. A lot of acts burn themselves out by playing all those stadium shows; they overexpose themselves. They just grab the bucks and go for it. I don't care about money. We need it to survive, but I can survive with whatever — musician soup, if I have to. We put our all into the music and the production. Look at the greats: Elvis, the Who, the Stones — they have no gimmicks. They're personalities. And that's what we are, too; or that's what we need to keep striving for. It was kind of scary when all these bands were doing a glitter trip a few years ago. We had to gamble: Should we go that way or just bet on ourselves? It's a lot easier to have a gimmick. But if you lay your personality on the line and they don't like you, you're gone. So far we've gone the personality way, and it's worked. And that's how a band lasts — being real. We're not bullshitting the people; we're not a circus.

That spirit comes through on your records.

Well, it's our whole attitude; it's the way we feel. We're there to party with the people. We're not there to show off. We're not out to prove anything, although we do have an aggressive attitude towards everything we do.

What do you picture yourself doing in 30 years?

Same thing we're doing now. That's what I want. I don't know what's gonna happen in the future — maybe somebody else in the band will get egoed out and quit or something — but I'd love Van Halen to be forever. And if not, I know I can always make it playing guitar somewhere, because I'm getting hit up left and right now: "Will you play on my record, will you do this, will you do that?" And I go, "No, Van Halen is my family. I'm not gonna wash your dishes. I'll wash dishes for Van Halen alone."

— Jas Obrecht

A SELECTED EDDIE VAN HALEN DISCOGRAPHY

With Van Halen (all on Warner Bros.): *Van Halen,* BSK 3075; *Van Halen II,* HS 3312; *Women And Children First,* HS 3415; *Fair Warning,* HS 3540; *Diver Down,* BSk-3677. **With others:** Nicolette Larson, *Nicolette,* Warner Bros., K-3243; Michael Jackson, *Thriller,* Epic, QE 38112, Brian May & Friends, *Star Fleet Project* (mini LP), Capitol, MLP15014.

ROSS MARINO

Van Halen's Michael Anthony

Although his role on record is largely supportive, Van Halen's founding bassist aggressively steps out onstage to showcase metallic slices of his considerable skill. He was questioned during the band's *Fair Warning* tour for this October '81 feature.

an introduction

Since 1974 Michael Anthony has played bass in one of the world's leading heavy metal acts, Van Halen. This year the group's stage shows include an extended bass solo in which Anthony simulates the sound of an airplane flying around, and then leaps upon his instrument. Theatrical stuff. Otherwise, Mike's main role on vinyl and stage is providing support for Eddie Van Halen, who claims, "Anthony is a damned good bass player. When my brother Al and Mike are playing, it's an open world for me. I can do whatever I want. They're right there backing me up, feeding me."

Anthony was born in Chicago on June 20, 1955. His father played trumpet in big bands, and at seven Michael began a serious study of the instrument. After deciding to play bass in a junior high rock band, he paid $15 at a pawnshop for a Victoria electric guitar and took off the highest two strings. At 14 Mike moved with his family to L.A. and played trumpet in his high school marching band and concert orchestra. In the early '70s he enrolled at Pasadena City College to study brass instruments and piano. In hours off, he gigged on bass with a local lineup called Snake.

Michael met drummer Alex Van Halen in a jazz improvisation class in 1974, and soon afterwards Eddie invited him over to jam with their already-established band. Anthony remembers, "I went and played with Alex and Ed for like three hours in a little garage they were rehearsing in. I swear, they tried to put me through every beat change and off-beat thing they could think of, and I caught them all! Right after we were through playing, they just said, 'You want to join the band?' I said, 'Sure!'" Anthony has since toured the world with Van Halen and appeared on all four of their albums.

the interview

Has your formal education in music helped your bass playing?

Yeah, I think in some ways it does. The jumping around and all that, you just get from watching what everyone else does. But the background that I got from playing bass in jazz improvisational stuff helped me a lot, even though playing behind Ed I'm kind of restricted. I've got to keep pretty much straight because he gets off real wild at times. There's still a lot from my education that I can apply to what we're doing, like the harmony classes are helpful when we're figuring out different harmonies and stuff like that. But basically it was the jazz that helped me get the most out of bass.

What do you think are the most important things for a beginning bassist to learn?

I'd say take up the piano [*laughs*]. To me, that's the universal instrument. Once I started playing it, I really began to appreciate music a lot more. It broadens everything out. From there I started dinking around with different instruments, and I play a little bit of guitar, trumpet, some trombone, and a lot of other brass instruments.

Do you play any bass styles that aren't represented on your albums?

Yeah, because the style that I play live is almost completely different than what I play on albums. On albums you need that real solid rhythm, especially when Ed does a solo. Basically everything that we do in the studio is live, and so you don't want it to sound like three different people playing three different songs when you go off on a solo. Alex and I work out a real solid rhythm thing, so that when Ed does go into a solo and that rhythm guitar drops out, there's still a solid foundation pumpin' away. Live, I can get away with going off and doing a little more of a lead-type of playing, which I can't do on the albums.

Would you say your playing is constantly expanding? Are you learning new things all the time?

Yeah, I am now. Sometimes maybe for a month or two I'll get into a rut, like when we're gigging really heavily and I don't get out and listen to any new kind of stuff. I'm always hunting for new and different kinds of basses. I'm not like Ed — I'm not to the point where I build my own guitar from scratch. I'll buy something that's already in the store, *then* I'll rip it apart and put my own kind of pickups in it and stuff like that. And it seems like every time I pick up a different bass — depending on its feel — it kind of alters my style. So if I start to feel stifled for a while — let's say playing a Fender Precision — then even if I pick up a Jazz Bass or something like that, where the neck is radically different, I find myself playing a lot of different licks. So I'll change by playing that for a while, even if I don't use it onstage.

What is the extent of your bass collection?

I've got about 14 basses right now. I just bought an old '63 Fender Jazz Bass that I really like. I don't have it out on the road. A long time ago B.C. Rich built me a bass that was everything that I wanted, including having a thin neck. On most of my basses, I have the neck shaved until it's right in between a Precision and a Jazz width. I like them very rounded, almost like a half-circle.

What other kinds of modifications do you usually have done?

Right now I'm using Schecter pickups. I use the one split P-Bass style, and I have that rewound so it's a little more powerful. Live, it gets a nice round, full tone. And you know the body's bottom horn when you get up around the 24th fret? I always cut that back. I don't understand why companies build 24-fret basses and the bodies always start right around the 20th, 21st fret! I like to use every fret and always have a problem playing the high notes, so the first thing I do is cut that horn so I can play all the way up the neck.

Do you leave the switching stock?

When I first buy a bass I will. I used to use a lot of double-pickup things because I'd use the front pickup if I was playing with my fingers, and then switch over to the front and back when I was playing with a pick. But now, with the way I'm winding them, I just use one pickup, which is a lot simpler. I've tried a lot of different basses with all the preamps and stuff like that, and that's nice for somebody who is playing in a little club. You can hear it really nice coming out of the amp, and you're not playing loud. But for what we're doing onstage, just one pickup that's got the sound is all you really need.

What kind of compensations do you have to make when playing at such high volumes?

Right off the bat, you can't play fast. You lose it. A lot of times I'll try to do a fast lick, and right away things will start getting muddy, especially if I'm doing something that's down low. So I find myself playing a lot more slower stuff live.

Do you use a wireless transmitter?

Yeah, I use the Schaffer-Vega because I move around so much. In fact, if that breaks down and I have to use a cord, I feel like I'm in a cage.

What kind of strings do you use?

I like Rotosound round-wounds.

Do you favor using your fingers or a pick?

I use a pick and my fingers about 50% each. I use a pick to get more of an attack and if I'm doing a lot of chords. Actually, I started playing bass with my fingers, so that's where I can get all my speed from. So if I'm doing quicker things, then I play with my fingers.

Do you use any unusual techniques?

Not really. Just the basic two-finger plunk. I was getting into a little bit of funk-type playing for a while, so sometimes I'll slap it a few times with my thumb. The first time I got turned on to this was through Mother's Finest. I met their bassist, the Wizard, and immediately went out and bought all their albums. I haven't got a real vibrating fast thumb, but I have a good time and apply a lot of that slapping to what we're playing. I'll slap with my thumb and then use my third finger to pluck from under the string.

What does your amp and effects setup consist of?

Right now I'm using six Ampeg SVT heads, which are all modified — they're like 400 watts RMS. My rack has a Roland DC-30 Chorus Echo, an MCR flanger, an ADA flanger, an Electro-Harmonix Micro-Bass synthesizer, an MXR envelope filter, and sometimes a DBX Disco Boom Box, which was originally developed to put on your stereo when you're playing disco. It adds a lower harmonic and can be synthesized. I use that if I have to do something fast, like a one-note thing.

During your solo onstage, you create the effect of an airplane flying around.

Right. That's a combination of the echo, the MXR flanger, and the Micro-Bass synthesizer. I use the synthesizer because it's got a sub-harmonic on it that sounds really good, and it's really clean. It's also got a changeable square wave that can warp the high-end. The echo just keeps it going, and I use the flanger to actually make the effect of the plane-type thing flying by. Don't ask me how I came up with it, because one night I was just sitting around playing with them all together, and it just came out.

Do you have to be at high volume to make it come out that way?

Not really. But what I'm really trying to create is a lot of low end pumping off the stage.

Do you change your solo around night-to-night?

Besides the basic things that we all do together, I never play the same thing twice. My solos are always changing, especially when we are finishing up our third night somewhere and a lot of people I see in the front row are probably who I've seen the last two nights.

In your bass solo you're kind of aggressive towards your instrument.

Yeah.

Do you ever wreck anything?

Yeah, all the time. Every time I smack it on the ground. I've got a million holes in it. I'm always replacing strap locks. All my keys are bent. The only kind of bass I can jump on is one with a neck that goes all the way through the body. If I used a bolt-on neck, it would snap right in half.

What is the best brand of bass to jump on?

[*Laughs*] Right now I'm using a Yamaha Broad Bass 2000 that I received in Japan as a present when Yamaha came and followed Ed and me around in '79. Out of all the stock basses I was trying, I thought that was the best that had come out at that time. One thing led to another, and I started jumping on it! It's really weird because in the world of heavy metal or whatever you want to call it, there's the guitar hero, and that's basically it. A drummer can do a long solo, but even that starts to get boring. That's why Alex does some really nice, compact things. And the bass player is always the one who stands next to the drummer and does nothing. Only somebody who has actually played music can appreciate . . . well, that's where all your Jack Bruces and Tim Bogerts and all the other good rock bassists come in. They are only known by other musicians.

The most accomplished musicians aren't necessarily the most famous.

During our second year out, I was doing a thing with a fuzz — all sorts of weird stuff — and the New Barbarians had just finished playing before we did. Some chick came running up to me and said, "Yeah, yeah, Stanley Clarke did like this ten-minute bass solo, but jeez, when you got up there, you made them sound like shit! You sounded like World War III!" And I said to myself, "Hey, this is one of the typical kids." I'd love to get out there and show all my chops, but I think, "This is what we're playing to, and this is what they appreciate." And since I've been jumping on my bass this year, I swear I cannot believe the compliments that I get from people. It kind of throws me for a loop, too. It's fun; I'm having a good time doing it. I'm not out to jump after any kind of #1 in a bass player poll. I can sit at home and play what I like to play — just jam with some friends.

Do the limitations of rock bother you?

Sometimes they do. I know I'm helping Ed sound good. There's a lot of times when I'll get frustrated because I can't play what I want to play. The other guys'll say, "Why don't you just sit back and play this," and I'll kind of grit my teeth and go, "Well, okay." But for the most part it's really good. It's a little restricting playing behind a guitarist like Ed, but it feels good because of who he is.

How does the band arrange material before recording?

Ed usually starts out with a basic lick. We rehearse in the basement of our singer Dave's father's house in Pasadena. We'll get like a case of beer and a tape recorder, and just start playing. We'll play a riff over and over again and it develops out of that. Ted [Templeman], who produces our albums, has gotten so close to us that he's almost like a fifth member of the band. He'll come down and listen to us play and put his suggestions in. We'll throw in different pieces from old material that we haven't used. We've still got tons of unused material that we did on our first work tape.

Has your method of recording changed over the different albums?

No, not at all, except that the new album [*Fair Warning*] took a little longer to record — five weeks. We always write our stuff to be played live because when we're onstage, there's no rhythm guitar. Even though we've got all the wonders of the studio that we could use, that's the way we do it. And if we don't get it on the first two or three takes, we see no point in it. We don't want it coming out sounding perfectly in-tune after playing it so many times. We don't want to burn out, so we stop right there and go on to something else or take a break and drink a beer.

What are your favorite recordings with Van Halen?

Let's see. From the new album, I like "Mean Street" for a straight-ahead rocker. And I really liked doing "Push Comes To Shove," because Ed turned me on to Percy Jones, the bassist in Brand X. I really got into his style of playing, so at the very beginning of the song I cop a little of his stuff. Playing that was really fun, real different from anything we've ever done before. But it's still got the Van Halen flavor. When we first heard it back, we'd just go, "Wow!"

Are there any other bass players that you admire or have been influenced by?

Shoot, I grew up listening to everybody. When I first started playing, I listened to a lot of blues and session people, like Harvey Brooks with Electric Flag. From there I just listened to everybody. I played in a band for a while that did a lot of Blue Cheer, so I listened to their bass player, Dick Peterson. Then I got into Cream. Between them, Jack Bruce and Tim Bogert influenced me the most for my rock style. I'm starting to really get into fretless stuff now. There's so many different harmonic sounds that you can get with one. I always listen to Jaco Pastorius.

What are the pressures of becoming so famous so fast?

I don't even really think about stuff like that. I thank God that we didn't happen real quick, like a Boston, where all of a sudden you just zoom right there. With us it was more of a steady thing, not really fast. I think that was great for us because it didn't really affect anybody in the band.

Is success what you expected?

Yeah, and more! It's everything I'd always dreamed of wanting to do, and now we're there.

Most young players have ideas of the good side of the rock lifestyle. What are its disadvantages?

Not getting enough sleep [*laughs*]. I can't even think of any negative things, really. It's all in everybody's head. It's how you pace yourself. As far as the playing goes, I'm having the time of my life. As long as I can keep doing it, it's just great for me.

Do you play outside of the band?

No. Sometimes when we're off the road I'll jam for a set with friends that might be playing in a little club or bar. I like to get a different input from playing with other people. But I've never actually wanted to go out and play with anybody else. I'd just like to keep doing what we're doing now.

Do you have any advice you'd pass along to young bassists?

Yeah, just stick with it, no matter how hard it gets. We've hit some really bottom times, times when we thought that we'd always be playing in a club and have to always play other people's material. We just decided to make the break and play original stuff. A lot of bands do it and lose a lot of money, so they go right back to playing clubs because they think that's where the money's at. I painted house numbers on curbs and stuff. The main thing is just to stay with it.

— Jas Obrecht

MICHAEL ANTHONY: A SELECTED DISCOGRAPHY

With Van Halen: (All on Warner Bros.): *Van Halen,* BSK 3075; *Van Halen II,* HS 3312; *Women And Children First,* HS 3415 ; *Fair Warning,* HS 3540; *Diver Down,* BSK 3677.

THE NEW WAVE OF METAL

JON SIEVERT

JON SIEVERT

Randy Rhoads

Randy Rhoads was the first American metal hero of the '80s. The soft-spoken veteran of LA's Quiet Riot joined the Ozzy Osbourne band in the fall of '80. During the next year, Randy appeared on Ozzy's *Blizzard Of Ozz* and *Diary Of A Madman* albums, laying down some very sophisticated — and influential — metal guitar. Months after Randy was killed in a plane crash, *Guitar Player* interviewed his family, friends, and fellow musicians for this November 1982 *Guitar Player* cover story.

an introduction

Randy Rhoads had become one of rock's most acclaimed guitarists at the time of his death earlier this year. A magnificent performer, he rose to fame quickly and became a hero to legions of young players. He left us a legacy of only a few albums, the best known being two records with Ozzy Osbourne. By all accounts, though, Randy's considerable talents extended far beyond the realms of heavy metal. He lived for music, and was well loved and respected by those with whom he grew up, studied, or played. They tell his story best.

a biography

Delores Rhoads

My son Randy was born on December 6, 1956, in St. John's Hospital in Santa Monica, California. He has one brother whose real name is Doug, but who goes by the name of Kelle Rhoads when he sings. His sister is Kathy. Randy was the youngest. His father, who has always been a music teacher in public schools, left when Randy was 17 months old, and I raised the three children by myself. In 1949 we started building a music school and store in North Hollywood called Musonia, which I still own. We couldn't afford a TV or stereo until quite a bit later than most people, so there was not a lot of music to listen to at home. Randy just had to develop things on his own. Of course, I was always on the classical side. I played professionally for a short while, and also taught music — especially trumpet — in the public schools.

Kelle Rhoads

All Randy ever wanted to do was play the guitar. I don't remember him ever saying he wanted to do anything else. I can remember really well the time *before* he played guitar. He was a very intelligent kid who got good grades in school, and he didn't even have to try. And the thing that should underscore anyone's understanding of Randy is that he was so kind. Man, he was probably the kindest human being I ever met. I don't think he could have offended anybody, and I never saw him get mad. And he was like that as a child.

Delores Rhoads

Randy started taking lessons in my school when he was about six-and-a-half. We had an old Gibson acoustic that belonged to my father. Randy picked that up and just loved it from the very first — as soon as he was large enough to hold it and do something. I had a guitar teacher in the school at that time who was a pretty good rock player — I guess rock was just beginning to come up. So Randy studied with him. It was not too long until the teacher came up to me and said, "He knows everything I know! I can't teach him anything more. He's gone beyond me already." Randy just loved it so much. He played all the time; he never put it down. He was so dedicated. In all the years I had been teaching — and that's a good many years — I've never seen a student who just *loved* it so much. In his early teen years, when Randy talked on the phone he would hold the receiver with his shoulder and practice at the same time.

I still have the first electric guitar Randy played on —an old, large, semi-acoustic Harmony with f-holes. He started playing that when he was about eight years old. The guitar was really Randy's only instrument, although I did teach him some piano and a bit of reading music after he was pretty good on the guitar. He knew enough piano to work out harmonies and chords to use when writing songs. He could read all the scales and chords. I had a straight little group for the students to participate in — it was like a school orchestra — and Randy played in that when the guitar was almost larger than him. But he loved it, just because it was playing.

Randy Rhoads

I tried lessons on and off when I was young, but I couldn't stick with it. I didn't have the patience. When I went back to lessons in my teens, I took classical guitar. It did wonders for me. When I was 12 or 13, I started jamming, and that's when I said I wanted to do this for real. When I first got up and played for people, it was a fluke. These guys used to jam on a mountain in Burbank, and I thought I wanted to get up and play. When I first did it, people started clapping. A friend had shown me the beginning blues scale. That sort of showed me how to connect the barre chords to a little scale. From then on, it was just add-ons. [*The Randy Rhoads quotes appearing in this article are from previously unpublished interviews conducted by John Stix in 1981 and 1982.*]

Delores Rhoads

When Randy was a teenager and even before, we used to ride on the trains to Chicago, New York, the Southwest, and on down to New Orleans. Randy would always take a guitar with him, and he would never leave it anyplace! It was in a big case, and we had to carry it on the train and wherever we walked. I remember we once had a little bit of a layover in Chicago, and we walked towards a drugstore. Some really creepy looking characters started to follow us, and I thought they were going to try to steal the guitar. We ran to get back into the station just to protect that guitar! When we'd travel on the train, he'd say, "You know, Mom, I imagine what it will be like if I ever get to tour. It's going to be exciting to go different places."

Kelle Rhoads

The first band that I was in was the first band Randy was in. We got the group together when Randy was about 14 and named it Violet Fox after my mother's middle name, Violet. I played drums. Randy played rhythm guitar on a big, red Ovation; at that time, he didn't think he'd ever be a lead player. This band was together for four or five months, and we played some parties and some little shows at my mom's school.

Delores Rhoads

We have always lived in the same house in Burbank. In fact, Randy was still living at home even with Ozzy, although he was on the road a lot and stayed with Ozzy in England. Randy was raised in a religious environment. He went to First Lutheran Day School through sixth grade, and then he had to go to John Muir Junior High. By the time he was 13 or 14, his little group was playing for parties and picnics, in the park, and down on the Burbank Mall. He was playing a lot by then. I used to go with him and load up the equipment. Alice Cooper became the big thing with my sons. Then their tastes changed as they grew.

Kelle Rhoads

I took Randy to his first rock concert, and he was *amazed*. It was Alice Cooper in 1971. He never saw anything like it, and he couldn't talk for four hours. I think that kind of showed him what he could do with his talent, and that's partly what made him decide to play rock. Before that, he played rock guitar and I played drums, but we never really thought about it.

Delores Rhoads

When Randy went to Burbank High, he decided that school was not that necessary. The only thing he wanted to do was play all day. I said, "You have to finish your education." About halfway through, I went to the board of education and asked special permission for him to go to adult school at hours that were convenient for him and wouldn't interfere with his playing. That was the way he finished school. He was mainly in little neighborhood groups until Quiet Riot.

Quiet Riot was really a popular local band in the LA area. They made a couple of Japanese albums. They were supposed to tour, but that never materialized. I guess the management was not as good as it should have been. Nevertheless, they played a great deal. They performed four or five nights a week, every week. Randy wrote most of their music, and the singer, Kevin Dubrow, wrote a lot of the lyrics.

Rudy Sarzo

I met Randy in late 1977, when I started playing bass with Quiet Riot. They already had a couple of albums out on CBS Sony in Japan and had management, but they were just playing locally. Although my picture is on the *Quiet Riot II* album, Kelly Garni played bass on both albums.

I thought Randy was a totally excellent guitar player. It didn't hit me how good he was until I had played with him for a while. People would tell him do this or do that, and he would say, "Okay, sure, no problem," and then he would go on and do whatever he felt like doing. He never really compromised that much, but the material that had to be played was compromising for him. He had to play along with the songs, but if we did something with a pop flavor, he would come on and just do a blow-your-head-off type of a lead on top of that. Quiet Riot didn't do much traveling — we went from Oxnard down to Riverside. We mainly were an LA club band, doing weekends at the Starwood or Golden West Ballroom. We didn't get an American record deal, which is one of the reasons why Quiet Riot broke up.

Randy Rhoads

Rudy and I used to gig a lot in LA. It was something to do, and I guess I thought Quiet Riot would make it. But now that I'm away from it, I know that it wouldn't. I hate to say that. It was kind of like I was growing up at the time and didn't know it. There is a lot more room for a guitar in Ozzy's band than there was in Quiet Riot.

Delores Rhoads

Randy never had any real great guitars until he was playing with Quiet Riot. The owner of one of the rehearsal studios they played in bought Randy that white Gibson Les Paul that he played all those years. That was the first really good guitar that Randy ever had. He loved it.

Karl Sandoval

Four or five months before he parted from Quiet Riot to join Ozzy, Randy came to my shop and asked me to

JON SIEVERT

COURTESY DELORES RHOADS

make him a guitar. He had gotten referrals from other people I had made custom guitars for. We had several meetings to discuss the details of what he wanted on the guitar before it was even written up. He had pictures drawn: He wanted a Flying V shape, tremolo unit, double humbucking pickups, and one volume and one tone control per pickup. The guitar has an old '60s non-adjustable Danelectro neck that has been shaved and modified to look somewhat like an arrowhead. It has a rosewood fingerboard and a wide, flat feel. The action is very comfortable. The tuners are standard Schallers.

The thing that was different about it was the Strat-style side-mount jack underneath the V section, which was one of his ideas. He also wanted the toggle switches at the end of the wing. Polka dots were used because they were like his trademark, and the inlay on the fingerboard is supposed to resemble bow ties. Both of these were his ideas, too.

Rudy Sarzo

The most unusual thing about Randy was the fact that he didn't have to play copy material to survive. So he didn't have the same background as a lot of players who have to go out and do disco, blues, or Steely Dan music. Randy didn't need that because he had been teaching for about ten years. Instead of going out to play clubs, he would teach and make excellent money. So his playing influences are very unusual — mainly classical music and late '60s, early '70s English rock guitar players. Later on he came to really admire Gary Moore and Eddie Van Halen. Those were his two top guys. By the time he got to England, he was not like a typical American guitarist who has influences of R&B, country, and things like that, because he never played that.

Randy Rhoads

I have a lot of influences from everywhere. I like a lot of classical music and blues rock. As far as the classical, I just like it. I think it's a real technical thing. I wouldn't call myself an accomplished classical player at all, though. Again, I never had the patience to go through it. I wish I could be good at it.

There are many great players. Eddie Van Halen is great — I don't want to get near competing with people like him. I love Allan Holdsworth's playing. He's got a lot of great jazz scales. Andy Summers of the Police is definitely unique. Pat Metheny does some great acoustic stuff. John McLaughlin is technically great, but his is not one of my favorite styles. Leslie West was very important to me. He has a great feel. He is powerful and moody. I like Earl Klugh. Jeff Beck can do anything — he can play one note and it's great. Ritchie Blackmore was great; I loved his expression. I love B.B. King. I like Michael Schenker's and Steve Lukather's playing a lot. I also like Ronnie Montrose, especially with Edgar Winter. I like the way he bends; I could never bend like that. I liked all the English players in the '70s who used a lot of vibrato.

But I don't own any rock guitar albums. I listen to a lot of background music that I don't have to think about. I don't listen to music to achieve anything from it. I just listen to relax and be social. Mostly I like mellow jazz and classical. If I'm out in public, I like to hear blaring loud rock, but never in my own house. I can't listen to my own records at home.

Delores Rhoads

With Quiet Riot, Randy would teach during the day up to the time when he had to go play, which was around 7:00 at the latest. On days that he didn't play, he would teach a heavy schedule. In fact, Randy taught in my school for many years. He always said that was one thing that built him up strongly, because he played with the students, which encouraged them so much. He was a very successful teacher who built up a large group of students because he could relate well with them. He had his own way of presenting material, even in the rock field. His playing inspired the students a great deal. You know, there are *so many* good guitar players because it's such a popular instrument. The minute I heard Randy playing anyplace, though, I knew it was him because he played with such feeling and had such a live, brilliant sound. His technique was so fast — he could make his guitar playing sound like the music of a great concert violinist. That always amazed me. I'm not saying that because he's my son, but because I analyze it as a musician who has heard many players. Later on, when time allowed it, Randy would give seminars in some of the large music stores.

Keith Baim

I am a former student of Randy's. I took lessons from him for about six months when he was teaching at his mother's school. I was extremely fond of Randy and had a great deal of respect for him as did his other students, who numbered in the forties or more. Randy had much more than talent: He had charisma. He was friendly, and, above all, enjoyed teaching and helping others become better players. He was more than kind, and almost always placed my name, as well as the names of many other students, on the guest list just about any time he played in Hollywood. Quiet Riot was LA's favorite local band, and Randy was LA's favorite local guitarist.

I always looked forward to my lessons. He'd almost always run late, and we would spend about half an hour a week laughing, talking, and learning. He would say, "Keith, make your guitar a part of you. Use it to express how you feel!" He emphasized that phrasing is the most important aspect of one's playing: "People don't talk in a monotone, and you shouldn't play guitar that way. *Accent* your playing." He worked very hard with me to help me develop my own style. Needless to say, he was a huge influence and was more inspiration than is imaginable.

Randy Rhoads

The way I started to get a style was by teaching. People wanted to learn everybody's licks, and at first this was okay. Then I thought, "Wait a minute—you've got to get your own style." So I started combining what they wanted to learn with a bit of technique. Every day with every student I'd learn something. When I started to get a lot of students, I thought, "Enough with the licks. I'm going to have to get them to learn to find themselves." When you teach something to a student, it clicks in your head. You may find the answer to another problem you may have been trying to figure out.

I taught eight hours a day, six days a week, every half hour a different student. I had little kids, teenagers, and even some older people. When you sit there and play all day long, you're going to develop a lot of speed. I learned to read, too, but I have to look at it, think about it, and then play it. About the third time I do a piece, I can read it.

I think half of your sound comes in the way you play. A lot of it is in your hands. If you practice with a lot of muting and then go out and do it louder onstage, you've still got the same sort of sound. You can't be lazy. You have to want to play. You have to love the guitar. I did. As a matter of fact, I was afraid of competition because I thought that everybody was better than I was. It was so close to me, I thought everybody was great. Therefore I couldn't copy licks; I just learned on my own.

Rudy Sarzo

Quiet Riot ultimately had an outrageous following. It was great! Randy was the focal point of the band, the guy the kids would come to see. If you went out in the audience, you'd see a bunch of little kids with his haircut, wearing little polka dot bow ties and vests, trying to be like him. And then there were a lot of clone Randy Rhoads guitar players in bands.

Delores Rhoads

How Randy got into Ozzy's band is kind of a funny little story. I used to ask Randy, "What if someone did come along who was really big and asked you to go with him?" He said, "Well, of course, I would have to take that opportunity." Ozzy was looking for a lead guitar player. He had been in New York and LA for weeks and weeks, and couldn't find anyone. He was just ready to go back to England and say, "Forget it. I can't find who I want." A bassist who knew Randy suggested that Ozzy listen to him. They called Randy, who was teaching that day in my school until about 10:30 P.M. He said, "Oh, it won't amount to anything, Mom. I won't even bother to go down." I said, "Randy, even if it doesn't materialize, it's good for you to meet people who have been in the business for years." He was reluctant, but he took his little practice amp and went down. When he came back, he said, "Golly! I only played about two minutes, and Ozzy said, 'You've got the job!' I don't know what I got, but I got something!"

Randy Rhoads

Apparently Ozzy went through every player in L A after he quit Black Sabbath, and I never knew about it. I never looked for outside things; I was stuck in a rut. To be honest, I wasn't a big Black Sabbath fan. They were great for what they did, and obviously they did it well and made it huge. I respect that. I don't want to get into it too much, but I wasn't a fan. I'm not sure why I got in Ozzy's band. Possibly he knew a certain sound he was looking for, and all of these other players tried to show off too much. I just started making a few harmonics. Perhaps it was my personality, because I was real quiet. I still don't know. I was 22 when I joined his band.

Delores Rhoads

Two weeks later Ozzy called and said, "Well, we're getting things together, Randy. Are you ready to come to England?" Randy was flabbergasted! He said, "Oh, oh, I can't go now! I've got a cold, and I can't leave until I feel a little better." Randy always had respiratory problems and was susceptible to colds. Many times he played with a fever of 104°. If he was supposed to play, he would play.

Randy and Ozzy finally got it together. It all happened so fast, Randy couldn't get his thoughts together. It was like a whirlwind. He went to Ozzy's house in England in October or November of 1980; this was his first time out of the country. They started getting into it really strong with just the two of them. Then they auditioned people for the rest of the band and recorded the first album in March or April.

Ozzy Osbourne

I fell in love with Randy as a player and as a person the instant I saw him. He had the best smile in the world. Randy was the best guy in the world to work with. There is no comparison between him and [Black Sabbath guitarist] Tony Iommi, and I can only compare the two because those were the only guitar players I had ever worked with. I was attracted to Randy's angelic attitude towards the whole business. I didn't have to teach him anything; all that he was lacking was guidance. He listened to every word I spoke to him, and we had a great rapport together.

When we were working on the albums, I would give him a melody and he would work a riff around it. Every hook he ever came up with, I loved. He was original. We discovered that most heavy metal bands stick to one key—I don't know about keys or read music or really understand notes because I just get up there and scream and jump around. But Randy said to me that most guitar players in modern bands fluctuate between *A* or *E* or whatever. So we made a rule that almost every number that we recorded on an album was never played in the same key.

COURTESY DELORES RHOADS

A teenage Randy practicing at home on a Gibson SG.

Randy Rhoads

Ozzy's music is both of ours. A lot of times he'll have a melody, and I'll have a riff that fits in. He hums something and I go, "Hey, I have a chord progression that will go with that!" "Goodbye To Romance" and "Mr. Crowley" were done that way. A lot of other times I'll be sitting practicing, and he'll say, "I like that — remember it." Naturally, I never can. So we'll do it right there and build a song.

Max Norman

I met Randy at a place in London where the band was rehearsing. This was about two weeks before I engineered *Blizzard Of Ozz*. The recording of that album, which took just over a month, was done at Ridge Farm. Usually all four people would be there playing in the same room for the basic tracks. We would lay down the vocals, drums, bass, and rhythm guitar simultaneously. As long as we got a good bass and drum track, we would take it from there. Then the guitars were overdubbed.

Randy was always very nervous in the studio. He was extremely careful about what he played. If there was one thing out, he would go back and do that again. That's a pretty good policy, because a lot of those tracks — especially the lead guitar tracks — were triple-tracked.

He was the best guy at overdubbing solos and tracking them that I've ever seen. I mean, he would blow me away. He would actually play the whole solo three times. "Crazy Train" is an example of that. If you listen to it really close, you'll hear there's one main guitar around the center and two other guitars playing exactly the same thing, panned pretty much to the left and right, but back somewhat. You just hear them as one guitar. In fact, when you hear solos of his that really come out, a lot of times that's because there's three parts there, which means you get a very stable image.

Randy did quite a bit of overdubbing during the *Blizzard Of Ozz* sessions, and we would spend considerable time in the control room going through the songs one by one. He had a lot of ideas and arrangements. We would take half an hour just to get a sound, and then it would take a long time for us to get some of these things down simply because he wanted to get just one little twiddle right. The great thing about it was that he had the parts so together that it didn't sound like there were that many there. Everything kind of jigsaws into each other.

Randy would usually rip one solo down, and if there were a couple of little mistakes, instead of going back and patching those, he would go back and do the whole thing again. He was extraordinary because he would know exactly what he played — a very astute player. A lot of Randy's outro solos — solos on long fades at the end of the tracks — were first takes. A lot of the other ones were quite well written in his head beforehand; he would work on them for a long time to get them right. Some of his solos were perfected over a few days. He'd fire a few, listen to them, and then he'd say, "Oh, yeah, okay. I see what's going on." Then I'd make a tape loop up for him, and he'd sit down and run the loop around maybe 20 times. He would forget about it for a day, and then come back and try another one. By the time we got close to recording the solos, he would play the whole thing straight through.

Randy did a great deal on all of the tunes. He was instrumental in writing a lot of the actual key rhythms, and he was almost totally responsible for the overdub sections. For instance, most of the musical backing on "Revelation (Mother Earth)" is Randy's. It's his chord pattern, pretty much most of his ideas filling up the overdubs. There are six guitar parts on "Goodbye To Romance."

Pretty much all the guitar tracks were done with Randy's polka-dot Flying V-type guitar, which had an extraordinary top-end. He also had a creamy white Les Paul that we used; that was pretty good, chunky. He ran his guitar into his onstage effects board and then into his 100-watt Marshall stack pretty much all the time. That amp had a real nice straight sound, actually, with both cabinets plugged in and stacked up. It was one of the older models without the master volume.

We originally put Randy's amp in a fairly live room downstairs underneath the control room and shut the doors. I used a close mike and a distance mike down there, and all of the original rhythm tracks were done like that. A lot of them, though, were replaced later on because we opened those sliding doors and cranked the Marshall up and turned it out towards the studio and used even more mikes. This gave it a much bigger sound. The room had concrete walls and the amp was placed about three feet from the back wall, so the sound would funnel out from the concrete chamber into the rest of the studio, which is an old barn. I'd have a Shure SM-58 close mike on the Marshall in the concrete room, an AKG 451 mike just outside of the room on the steps, and a couple of Neumann U-87s out in the middle of the studio. The controls on the Marshall were pretty much flat-out.

The effect that I used a great deal on that album was an AMS 1518, which is a very clean British digital delay with a VCO [voltage-controlled oscillator] on it. You can slightly flange with it and do some strange grindy things if you get it at the right setting. Plus you can use it to get a hollow, tubey effect. If you listen to the rhythms on "Crazy Train," you'll hear there's a real grind to them. That particular sound comes from the AMS. "Suicide Solution" has four rhythm guitar tracks with a bit of AMS, which contributed a lot to its fullness. At the very end of that song he used feedback and his vibrato bar.

Randy wanted to do an acoustic guitar instrumental called "Dee" on *Blizzard Of Ozz*. That was written for his mother. I miked that the same way I did all of the other acoustic guitar parts; I had him sitting out in the middle of the floor of the studio at night when everything was real quiet, and I miked him with an AKG 451 at a distance of about three or four feet. I believe he did "Dee" with two guitars, a steel-string and a gut-string. It is very difficult to tell because the guy was a master at syncing up.

Randy Rhoads

"Revelation" and "Mr. Crowley" are my favorite cuts on the first LP because both of them have a heavy classical influence. I think the relationship between heavy metal and classical music is great. It has been going on like that for a long time. Look at Deep Purple: It's heavy, but it's a way to bring a melody in there, too. Leslie West was one of my all-time favorite guitar players. I love his feel. He used a lot of classical lines, but he was really into it when he did it.

Delores Rhoads

Randy went on the road after recording *Blizzard Of Ozz*, first touring the United Kingdom. Later the band zigzagged across the U.S. Randy loved playing L A , because it was his local scene. The first time he appeared there with Ozzy was at the Long Beach Arena in June 1981. He was really looking forward to that. He had so much trouble with his custom pedalboard, he was just beside himself. No one could figure out how to repair it. I said, "Look, Randy, you played many, many years without that pedalboard. You just give it all you've got." So he played the concert without it, but he was upset because he felt that it added a great deal. Randy was always a bit of a worrywart — he wanted everything to be so perfect!

Randy Rhoads

My weakness is my insecurity. I don't go up there every night with a lot of confidence. If the sound is not right, I'll get paranoid. My strength is my determination — I just want to keep getting better. I want people to know me as a guitar player, the way I knew other people. I don't want to be satisfied with myself. My other weakness is my girlfriend, who distracts me. She is the one person who can take me away from my instrument, which is something that never happened in the past. She is also my strength at the same time.

Pat Thrall

I saw Randy play in Santa Monica on the *Blizzard Of Ozz* tour, and man, the guy blew me away so bad! He actually gave me a bit of a scare. It was the first or second time he'd played L A , so he was really showing off. He was so on, it was ridiculous. I went backstage, and the first thing I said to the guy was, "Well, I guess I better get my paper route back [*laughs*]." He really got a kick out of that.

The stuff that he would do live and what he'd do on albums was very different. He had a lot of musical knowledge, and some of the scales that he employed onstage were a little more out there. As far as serious rock and roll guitar goes — somebody who's got the sound and uses the [vibrato] bar — I had never really heard anyone apply diminished scales and all that the way he would.

Max Norman

I was amazed when I saw Randy play live because he managed to make it sound like there were at least two guys there. Onstage, Randy was more dynamic than in the studio insofar as he was leaping between three different parts and trying to cover them all. He was basically playing in a three-piece band onstage, although there was a keyboard player who was very much kept in the background. He had to work real hard on the rhythm in this context, and I think Randy was very good at that. He would pull the lead solos one note short in order to get back into the next section for the rhythm.

Randy Rhoads

I've gained a lot of experience since the *Blizzard Of Ozz* tour, which comes out in my playing. A year ago I was probably more in practice from all the teaching gigs. I had more time to practice, but my styles have changed now. I've learned more about live playing. I don't feel I have to overplay because I'm basically in a trio, although we do have keyboards on the side that fill in a little bit. In

fact, I think I could do more. I'm still learning my way around the big stage. I like the sound of two guitarists in other bands, but I couldn't play with another guitarist. It's just too confining. I like to have the freedom.

I've still got a long way to go. Ozzy is so big and such a humble guy. He helps me a lot. He always says something will happen, and it does. He educates me about record companies and the kids in the audience. He's just predicted everything along the way. My old band was really into trying to get to the top. The only way we knew how to do it was by going over the top. I learned from Ozzy that you don't need to do that if you're good. Now I move when I want to move, not because I think I have to. I learned that from his personality. I don't want to be a ham and throw in the kitchen sink, but I still want to get my mark in. You're only as good as you are.

ROCK CONCERT

Van Halen

AND

Quiet Riot

Saturday

April 23

Glendale College Aud.

1500 N. VERDUGO RD.

8:00 pm

$3.75

A PING PRESENTATION

The early days: A poster for a college concert where Randy's group shared the stage with Van Halen.

Kelle Rhoads

Randy wanted to be a rock star up until the time he got it. After that he just wanted to be a fabulous musician. He was a musician first. Being with Ozzy sure gave him a chance to see the world. Going from a local boy to doing that — what an incredible leap! It really made him a lot more worldly wise, and yet it made him more humble. It gave him more respect for his talent. People always told him he would make it.

Delores Rhoads

After the first tour they started the second album. It was very cold over there, and Randy was so miserable with a cold. He said, "We can't get out; we have to just stay in. All I do is write music all day. Then we go in and rehearse and record it, to see what we want to change. It's like being in prison!" It was a hard album for him because Ozzy wanted certain things, and he was not the easiest person to work with. Randy worked hard and he wrote a majority of the music.

Max Norman

My role on *Diary Of A Madman* was pretty much the same as on the first album. I had a little more influence, I guess, on the second one, which I co-produced. The first one kind of fell together; the second was a lot more organized. My recording strategy changed a little, too. The placement of the drums changed. Randy's playing was better because there was a tour between the two albums. He was just getting better all the time. He was getting really hot on the second album; the improvements are really noticeable. Stuff that used to take a long time to do didn't take so long anymore. Plus he had a lot more ideas about what arrangements he wanted.

All of the backing tracks were recorded the same way and the basic miking and speaker setup was the same, but we got into very curious extremes when recording some of the guitars. We did a lot of stuff in the control room to change the tonality of the sound around, such as running him through a little compressor on the board before going into the amp. I would help his guitar EQ by putting it through the board first.

The solo in "Flying High Again" was triple tracked, with Randy playing the same part each time. I used the AMS on that. We had a little bit of trouble getting "Little Dolls" to work very well. We may have only put one solo track on that, instead of three, which is why the guitar sounds a little in the back.

He did the swells in "Tonight" with his volume knob. Near the end of that tune he flicked his pickup selector switch back and forth. The jam concluding that song went on quite a long time after the fade, about another two minutes. It was amazing, but some of the tracks are pretty long, and we had to do some early fades. There is some tantalizing stuff, and I wish it didn't go out quite there. But both of the albums were long.

"You Can't Kill Rock And Roll," which has kind of a slow tempo, has quite a few rhythm tracks: a couple of heavy-duty power-chord tracks, one steel-string acoustic track, and probably two or three other guitar parts. At the end there, Randy said, "Just roll it round to me, and

NEIL ZLOZOWER

Randy's mom, Delores Rhoads: "The white Les Paul Custom was the first really good guitar that Randy ever had. He loved it."

COURTESY DELORES RHOADS

Randy onstage with Quiet Riot. The popular Los Angeles-based band recorded two albums for CBS Sony in Japan before Randy joined Ozzy Osbourne.

I'll wax some stuff on the end." The main lead guitar going out of there was pretty much one-take.

"Believer" begins with some unusual guitar work. Randy was just messing around before the track comes in, and we just left it on there because we liked it. There are a few little bits and bobs like that; those little accidents that happen, and you think, "God, that sounds great. We'll leave that on there."

"Diary Of A Madman" is another one where we did one steel-string acoustic and a nylon-string acoustic. There are a lot of guitars there. We did work a lot on those textures, which was one of the areas where he was a real master. I learned a lot about getting those textures and rhythmic magic from Randy.

All of the studio tracks we recorded were released on *Blizzard Of Ozz* and *Diary Of A Madman*. The only other material that's available is from some live shows from last year, which I have been doing a little bit of work on.

Randy Rhoads

We played the songs on the first album a lot before we recorded. I had time to sit back and say, "I don't like this lead," or, "That's not what I'm looking for." For the second album I sort of had to put the leads together in the studio, that's it. Be happy with it or else. I didn't have time to search for what I wanted to play. Possibly if we had more time to write it, it would have been different. We could have played the songs more. We sort of got a basic form for the songs and went right into the studio. I was wrapped up in the middle of everything to the point where I couldn't get a hold on it. Considering how it was done, I'm happy with it.

Epic Records Press Release

November 30, 1981: On December 29, Ozzy Osbourne will embark on a four-month U.S. tour in support of *Diary Of A Madman*, his second Jet/CBS LP. A road crew of 25 Broadway and Las Vegas technicians will travel with him to stage this living horror flick. In addition to the trap doors and hidden passageways onstage, a giant motorized hand has been constructed to dramatize Ozzy's stage entrance and exit. The concert's only restriction is clearly printed on the ticket: "No normal people admitted." Sales of *Blizzard Of Ozz* currently top 6,000 records each week.

Rudy Sarzo

Randy was 99% responsible for getting me into Ozzy's band for the *Diary Of A Madman* tour. I came in after that album, although my picture is on that one, too. By the time that album was finished, the old bass player, Bob Daisley, was kicked out.

The difference between Randy's playing with Quiet Riot and Ozzy was day and night. When Quiet Riot was working very hard in L A to get a record deal, we had to be ourselves, but also try to please the record labels. So we were more pop-oriented, and Randy's playing was a little more restrained. Ozzy told him to just go all the way and be totally himself, be totally *out* in his playing: "Be the best Randy Rhoads you can be."

Randy was a progressive guitarist. By that I don't mean a style, but that every day he would progress on a song, play it different. It would still be the same song, but he would elaborate on it. Randy didn't like to jam, though, in the sense of getting together with a bunch of people and playing in one key. The jams we had would actually be writing; they'd turn into songs.

Tommy Aldridge

Randy was in London when I first met him. I was playing drums with Gary Moore for a live EP, and he came by to hear us. I started with Ozzy in April of last year, when both of the albums were already recorded. One of the reasons I took the gig was that I got off so much on playing with Randy.

I've performed with a lot of guitarists, including Gary Moore, Pat Travers, and Pat Thrall, and there is no comparing them to Randy at all. In every respect, Randy was by far the best musician I ever worked with and probably ever will. The small amount of actual recorded music he left behind is infinitesimal compared to what he was capable of. And he was such a giving, loving kind of guy.

Randy Rhoads

In every show there is a five-minute piece where Tommy Aldridge and I each get to do a bit of a solo. Five minutes between two people is not very much time, and the kids we play for aren't interested in musical expertise. If I sat down and played some classical music, most of the kids — besides those who were interested in the classical side — wouldn't be impressed. They're headbangers. Ozzy has an incredible following, and most of his kids are non-stop. I've experimented with a few things and tried to get some classical things in, but I really couldn't work them into this set. The time calls for flash. It's very heavy and everything is very powerful. The solo features are only there to show off Tommy and me. At the same time, they're not supposed to represent anything like, "This is what we can do." It's just a quick flash pot going off.

Don Airey

Before I became the keyboardist for Ozzy's band, Gary Moore, Tommy Aldridge, and I made an album together. I knew Ozzy quite well before then because I had worked on a Black Sabbath album when he was with them, and he had tried to get me to join Sabbath. So I finally ended up joining him the day after Christmas 1981 for the *Diary Of A Madman* tour.

I didn't get a rehearsal with the band. They've got this massive set and massive production, so more or less my first run-through was my first show! I wasn't actually on the stage, I was off on the battlements of a castle; "Keyboard Corner" is what it was called. It was absolute chaos for the first two weeks, and I wasn't sure what to play because nobody told me. But then I got together with Randy and saw how he wanted it. It was more keyboards being used for effects rather than an integral part of the band — a bit of drama and a few surprises here and there.

It was a hard band to join because they had been playing for a year on the road, and they were *tight*. To come into that band was really quite a challenge. I was frightened to death when I heard them. I'd never heard anything as heavy, and Randy was phenomenal. After a month or two I got the hang of it, and it really started to sound very good. It was the best band I'd ever played with. Tommy Aldridge is a great drummer, and Randy was certainly the most exceptional person and musician I've ever met.

Randy was an all-encompassing player. His guitar sound was so huge. Sometimes he'd more or less be playing three parts at once. I'd just say, "What do I do? What do you add to that?" I really had to come up with a few things. Randy would hear the tapes afterward and go, "Wow!" Randy could get some very unusual tones, including one that was like very clean and had fierce distortion — I don't quite know how to put it. I hadn't heard anybody use that kind of sound before. It almost sounded as if he had a ring modulator on the guitar, which he didn't. It was just him. The three months I had on the road with him were very exciting. It was quite a strange tour, actually, with snow all the time. It was freezing! Quite a grueling experience, but very exciting for me musically.

Kelle Rhoads

When Randy was on the road, instead of like partying out after he played, he would go to a Top-40 club and say, "Hi, I'm with the Ozzy Osbourne group. Can I jam with this band?" And he'd get up there with them just so he could play. He really was a musician's musician.

Near the end of his career, Randy also used to go to a lot of pawnshops to look for guitars. In the last four

JON SIEVERT

months of his life he bought a couple of really rare Les Pauls. One was a black '57 that was virtually untouched.

Grover Jackson

I made a couple of the guitars that Randy played up until his death: the white offset-V kind of instrument, and the black one. These have "Jackson" on the peghead. Randy contributed quite a bit to their design. He came in Christmas of '80 with a crude line drawing of a guitar, and said, "Can you make this?" I said, "Well, let's change this and that." I added the head design to it, and he and I worked together and made the white one. He contributed 50% or better of its design.

The instruments have long, fairly small bodies that are easy to get around. They have a neck-through-the-body solid maple construction, 22 frets, a 25½" scale, and Seymour Duncan pickups: a Jazz model in the neck position and a Distortion. They have binding on the neck and around the head, and a special pearl inlay that Randy came up with. The white one has one of Charvel's standard tremolo units on it.

One of the main differences between the white one and the black one is that the black one has a pickguard and a lengthened, thinned-out rear wing. Randy complained that too many people thought the white one was a Flying V, and he wanted a more distinctively shark-finned design, more off-center. When we actually got the black one made as a wooden, unfinished guitar, Randy came in and said, "More." I literally took it to the bandsaw and cut a chunk out of it with him standing there. He said, "Yeah, yeah. That's it!" It was a pretty creative process.

I got the black one to him just before the tour, and then a few months later he was gone. I am going to market a version of the black one as the Randy Rhoads Model, although he wanted to call it the Randy Rhoads Concorde or just the Concorde. He really wanted to see that guitar happen.

Randy Rhoads

What do I look for in a guitar? Small frets. I can't play the big frets. Every time I get a guitar, I have really small frets put in it, almost like an acoustic guitar's. I like the sound of a double-coil pickup, but I also love the Strat sound. I'm looking for an old Strat, but not for live playing. For what I need to hear in a trio, it's not fat enough. As far as strings and picks, I use regular GHS strings, gauged beginning with a .010 or .011 for the high *E*. I like them because they have a real metallic sound. I also use a medium-gauge pick.

As for effects, I use an MXR Distortion Plus, an MXR equalizer, a Cry Baby wah-wah, an MXR chorus, an MXR flanger, and a Korg echo. I don't practice with the gadgets too much. I do use the Distortion Plus a lot, but that's it. I used to use them more because I had time to learn what I wanted to do with them, but I don't need them that much with this band.

Delores Rhoads

In the last few months, Randy was strongly into classical music. He was seriously studying harmony and advanced theory. He had written out all of the modes and recorded them. As a matter of fact, he was going into this field very, very heavily at the time of his accident. He would call me and ask questions. Being on the road was a problem for him. He didn't know what to do with his time, and he wanted to further his music. So he really had started on something that I think would have been extremely great. He would have combined something in the way of classical and rock that probably would have been unique.

Ozzy Osbourne

Randy's heart was in the classics, to be honest; he wanted to be a classical guitar player. In fact, with the first record royalties he received, he went out and bought himself a very, very expensive classical guitar. He sat there for days and nights working on his music theories. As a matter of fact, right before he died he had been up for four days and nights — plus gigging — working on his theory because he wanted to get into a university and get a degree in music. And every town he went to, he'd find a tutor. On days off I'd get in the bar. He wouldn't: He'd practice all day, every day. He didn't take drugs, and he didn't drink too much. Every day of his life he practiced.

Kelle Rhoads

In the last six months of his life, Randy was getting *extremely* involved with classical music. He was very interested in a couple of classical composers, and he would study their music. One was an obscure Baroque-period composer named Johann Pachelbel. He was very influenced by him. He also liked Vivaldi. He was really into Baroque music because of all the layers and modes. I have every reason to believe that he would only have played rock for another nine or ten months. He was planning to go back to school to study and really pursue a classical career. What he could do on clasical guitar was just sensational.

Guitar Player Magazine

December 1981: Randy Rhoads wins Best New Talent in the *Guitar Player* Readership Poll.

Rudy Sarzo

Last year Randy got voted Best New Talent in *Guitar Player*. When something like that happens to a young guitar player, he could do two things: He could say, "Hey, I've made it, and I don't need to get any better at this!" or he could do the opposite, which is what Randy did. He went totally into his playing. He stopped partying

JON SIEVERT

COURTESY DELORES RHOADS

Randy and luthier Karl Sandoval collaborated on the design of the polka-dot solidbody.

hard when he realized that people were paying attention to what he was doing. On the first tour he was a little crazy, but by the last tour he was totally serious — little or no drinking. He spent all of his time in his room, playing electric or classical guitar.

On days off, we would be in the middle of like Anytown, U.S.A. When we would get to the hotel in the morning after traveling all night, Randy would open up the telephone book and look up the music schools. He would go and take classical guitar lessons. He would come with his books and ask questions about reading, fingering positions, pieces, and stuff like that. He was coming along incredibly well.

Of course, in a lot of places he would go to the wrong school. He would have to face some young, 18-year-old girl teacher who would totally freak out when she found out who he was. Actually, many times he wound up giving them lessons, but he would pay for it [*laughs*].

The more recognition he got, the better he wanted to get. He was an incredibly humble guy. Every time anybody would ask him for an autograph or tell him a compliment, he would smile real shy. That was his nature.

Randy Rhoads

I'm in my second year with Ozzy now, and the question is: How do you stay on top of yourself? I've really got to start getting a hold on it now. It's no longer a case of just try your best. I've got to be great now, and I'm sort of bored with my own playing. I'll pick up the guitar and it seems like it's the same thing. I used to play constantly. In fact, I couldn't put it down. Now that I'm on the road, I practice less than I did because I don't have the time. I need total stimulation from somewhere.

The best way to keep improving is to have a guitar lesson every day. The cost of bringing a tutor on the road would be ridiculous, but I am wondering if someday it might be done. Sure, if you sit with the guitar long enough every day, you're going to improve and sometimes accidentally come up with things. But sometimes it's hard to put yourself in that frame of mind. If I had a tutor, it would be more of a responsibility: I'm paying this guy, and it's my commitment to keep at it. In fact, I wouldn't mind going to college, although it doesn't fit in with the idea of heavy metal.

Delores Rhoads

Being on the road was difficult for Randy. When he was traveling with Ozzy, his big hobby was those tiny, Z-scale model trains that they make in Europe. He had a lot of layouts and would make the little houses and all that. I think that relaxed him from playing and tension, and maybe it reminded him of riding on trains as a child. It was hard for him to be away from home and the family. He loved being on the road, and it was what he wanted to do, but he missed us a lot.

Kelle Rhoads

I could always tell when the road was really bad or when he really hated it, because when he got home, if he intensely got into those model trains, he was bummin'. I don't think he liked being on the road at all. See, people like my brother shouldn't get involved with rock and roll. They are higher people. I don't think he could understand a lot of it because he wasn't raised that way. A lot of times there were things that conflicted with the way he was brought up and his own morality. He saw a lot of things that really blew him away.

Those trains were important to him, but another thing that was real important to him was anything that had to do with family matters. The guy really was into family situations, like Christmas. What he could do to a Christmas tree! He never wanted to take them down, but he could decorate a house so fast, and it would all look incredible.

Tommy Aldridge

Toward the end there, Randy wasn't very happy. I don't know so much if it was the road he became disenchanted with, or if it was what he was doing. He was so young and he had so much ability. His vocabulary was so vast, and his potential was so much bigger than he even knew. He definitely wanted to be elsewhere, to move in a new direction. He wanted to go back and teach, to write some pieces out, and to take advantage of some of the classy session offers and flattering invitations that he was getting. With our schedule, he just didn't have the time. He was always asking me about lawsuits, how can I get out of this, how can I get out of that. I felt so much for what he was going through, but I honestly couldn't think of a way that he could get out of his situation, you know.

Randy Rhoads

Five years from now I would love to have people know me as a guitar hero. I'd love to do a solo album, but I haven't met the right people in the business yet. I'm not at the level where I meet people all the time. It has to be the right time for the right thing. I really haven't been able to think; I just go, go, go. Lately, I've just been trying to hang onto myself, to keep up with everything.

I'm locked into something right now, and it's not my own pace. Therefore it's kind of stifling sometimes. Playing sessions would be nice; I could do a different sort of playing and spread my name in different areas. Now it's very limited. Being with Ozzy is almost like being in Kiss. That's why I'm thinking of going back to taking lessons and teaching all day long. Now it's a combination of stopped ideas and constant touring. I've got to put it together.

Delores Rhoads

Randy left L.A. on a Monday in March. He had just had ten days at home and had all three of his wisdom teeth pulled. He was miserable. At the end of the week he caught another cold — typical Randy — and when he left that morning, he was so sick! I said, "Please call me when you get there, Randy." He did, and that was the last time I ever talked with him.

Associated Press

March 20, 1982, Leesburg, Fla. A small plane crashed into a mansion here and burst into flames yesterday, killing the lead guitarist of the Ozzy Osbourne rock group and two other people, police said.

The crash killed guitarist Randall Rhoads, 25; the pilot of the Beechcraft Bonanza — Andrew Aycock, 36; and Rachel Youngblood, 58, the group's makeup artist and hairdresser. The plane's pilot was also the group's bus driver.

Tommy Aldridge

It was 7:30, 8:00 in the morning, and I had just woke up. All of a sudden there was an airplane wing flying through the side of the bus. The guy who was flying the plane had no business being there because he had been driving all night. It was like being on a movie set. Don Airey and I were running around with a fire extinguisher, but it was useless. It was the heaviest thing I have ever gone through. Randy had so much that he wanted to do, and he was so prolific. I just want to say how lucky I feel to have been associated with the gentleman and to have heard him night after night.

Delores Rhoads

Ozzy and the rest of the band went to the funeral as well as all of the people from Jet Records. Members of Ozzy's band and Quiet Riot were pallbearers. My teacher Arlene Thomas, who was a close friend of Randy's, sang and played acoustic guitar. Randy is buried in San Bernardino, which is where I grew up and want to be buried. I had a small bronze guitar put in on one side of his name on the gravestone, and on the other side the RR signature that he used. I know he would have wanted that.

Don Airey

Randy's death was the hardest thing I've ever gone through. It's something that none of us will ever really understand. I know a lot of people say, "Oh, the band —partying and drugs." But it wasn't like that at all. Randy was so serious about what the band was doing. Randy and Ozzy wanted nothing less than the best, and I think it was headed that way. We're going to keep going as best we can.

NEIL ZLOZOWER

Rudy Sarzo

The other day I was driving to Jet Records and I turned on the radio. "Crazy Train" was on, and I listened to it. You know, Randy is the kind of player that every time you listen to a song, you hear new things, different things. There will be a live album out by Christmas as a tribute to Randy. There you will hear the difference between his live playing and the albums. It's like *more.* He does everything, like an attack. He blazes you with his guitar. Not to take credit away from Brad Gillis' guitar playing with us, but there was only one Randy.

Eddie Van Halen

Randy Rhoads was one guitarist who was honest and very good. I feel so sorry for him, but you never know —he might be up there right now, jammin' with John Bonham and everyone else.

Delores Rhoads

Randy was such a kind, warm person. I have tons of letters and cards, even from fans who never met Randy but just heard him play. They have written so much to me! I still get long-distance calls from people who just want a little connection with Randy, and I'm that one, I guess. They just want to know a little something about him personally. It's unbelievable. Neither he nor I realized at the time that he was making such a name for himself.

Kelle Rhoads

I can't think of anybody who deserves to be in heaven more. I think he will be remembered the way James Dean is: somebody who died real young and was able to make a few accomplishments. He was totally outstanding, but God took him back.

Ozzy Osbourne

Randy was so unique that I don't think people will ever fully realize what a talent that guy was — not only in rock and roll, but in every other field. He was phenomenal in the classics. We loved each other very dearly. I swear to God, the tragedy of my life is the day he died. I've been doing this for a long, long time now with my life, and if ever I could say that I met a natural born star, it was a guy called Randy Rhoads, God bless him. Long live Randy Rhoads! If I could only put it in one word and people would believe me, as crazy a reputation as I have, he was the most dedicated musician I ever met in my life. He was a master of his art.

— Jas Obrecht

RANDY RHOADS: A SELECTED DISCOGRAPHY

With Quiet Riot: *Quiet Riot I,* CBS Sony (Japan), 25AP 880 [produced by Derek Lawrence and Warren Entner; recorded at Wally Heider Studios, Hollywood, in late 1977]; *Quiet Riot II,* CBS Sony (Japan), 25AP 1192 [produced by Warren Entner and Lee de Carlo; recorded at The Record Plant, Los Angeles, June/September 1978]. **With Ozzy Osbourne:** *Blizzard Of Ozz,* Jet, JZ 36812; *Mr. Crowley,* Jet, 12003 [a 3-song English EP with live cuts of "Mr. Crowley," "You Said It All," and "Suicide Solution"; recorded in October 1980 during the first Blizzard Of Ozz tour of the United Kingdom]; *Diary Of A Madman,* Jet, EZ 37492.

Def Leppard

JON SIEVERT

Steve Clark

Hailed in their hometown press as leaders of "Heavy Metal's New Wave," Def Leppard emerged internationally in 1980. Interviewed in their native England for this March '82 feature, Def Leppard has since released *Pyromania* and toured the U.S. twice. Pete Willis left the band in 1982, with Phil Collen coming in on guitar.

the artists

Leading the "Rock Brigade" of what might best be called the new British invasion is Def Leppard, who in less than four years has gone from a group of teenage school friends jamming after classes to a highly polished heavy metal quintet with two popular Mercury albums, *On Through The Night* and *High 'N Dry*.

While Def Leppard's hard-driving musical attack owes a debt to Led Zeppelin, UFO, Rainbow, Thin Lizzy, AC/DC, and other institutions of metal madness, it also exhibits more subtle, refined melodic touches — phased single-string passages, 6- and 12-string acoustic phrasings, octave lines, and bluesy wah-wah leads. Primarily responsible for fusing flash with finesse are Leppard's two guitarists, Pete Willis and Steve Clark.

Both Pete and Steve were born in Sheffield, England, in 1960: Pete on February 16, and Steve on April 23. But that's where the childhood similarity ends, at least musically. Willis is a self-taught rocker who first became interested in guitar at age seven after hearing Jimi Hendrix's "Voodoo Chile" [*Electric Ladyland*] on the radio, while

Pete Willis

Clark studied classical music for two years before abandoning nylon strings for steel. Steve remembers: "I hadn't really played guitar until I was about 14, except for messing about with a few chords. When I wanted a decent instrument, my dad said, 'I'll buy you one if you learn to play properly.' So, I bargained with him: If I learned to play the guitar and took lessons, he'd buy me one. That did it.

"I drifted away from classical, eventually, when I started discovering Led Zeppelin and bands like that. But the lessons, including sight-reading, were really good training for what we do now. Pete didn't have any training at all, so he tends to play different styles than me — which makes for a good combination. I know the musical rules and he doesn't; you put it together, though, and it sounds good."

Def Leppard played its first gig as a group in July of 1978. Until then, both Willis and Clark were pursuing more typical careers. Pete went to school two days a week and worked the remainder of the time as a draftsman at the British Oxygen Company. "The firm sent me to college," he says. "I was studying for a degree in engineering, but I never stuck it out, because things became a bit impossible. By this time we were doing concerts at clubs, and I wasn't getting home until four in the morning. I'd get three hours sleep, then have to get up and go to work. I was falling asleep at my board and everything. So, when we finally got signed by the record company, I went in and told the boss where he could stuff his board — you see, he started getting real nasty with me after a while. That was a great feeling, actually."

Willis and Clark first met in a college class. According to Pete, "I used to see him reading a guitar book, so I thought he must play guitar. Next thing, I met him at a

Judas Priest gig, and invited him down to a rehearsal for a jam. When he came, he played the entire solo of 'Free Bird' perfectly, so we immediately asked him to join."

Steve Clark used an old Ibanez Les Paul-style electric for that audition. It wasn't until '79, when Def Leppard signed their recording contract, that he could afford another instrument. Clark quickly switched to Gibsons, purchasing three Les Pauls — a Standard, a Custom, and a Deluxe — which are stock except for Grover tuners and, on the Deluxe, Seymour Duncan '59 pickups. Pete Willis plays Hamer Standards exclusively. "I have three on tour with me," he says, "but I've modified them. I stuck an electrolytic capacitor between the middle volume and tone controls, which sort of compresses the sound. It's like using a wah-wah pedal, where you have the pedal set at a certain point in its range that creates a rich tone. I've also replaced the regular pickups with Seymour Duncan '59s, and put Grover tuners in."

Each guitarist uses GHS strings and plays through one 100-watt Marshall 800 Series tube amp, driving two cabinets with four 12" speakers. Clark's only outboard devices are a Morley Volume Booster (which, he says, he uses to add punch to leads) and a Cry Baby wah-wah; Willis plugs straight into the amp. "We try to get effects manually, if we can," Pete adds. "Take a song like 'Bringin' On The Heartbreak' [*High 'N Dry*]. There's a slow, sort of fingerpicked section that sounds slightly flanged, but it's not. I recorded my track, and Steve recorded his, and we put the guitars a bit out of tune with each other to create that effect."

Just about every new band has to contend with criticism that they sound too much like someone else. So it's been with Def Leppard. But Pete Willis, although only 22, speaks like a veteran rock warrior as he comments on Leppard's musical approach. "People have criticized us in the past," he comments, "saying that we just took all these different influences, mixed them up, and threw them onto albums. But that's what we like doing, you see. We don't want to play one type of music and that's it, because of the different influences each band member brings into it. Look at someone like AC/DC; you wouldn't get them to put a song like 'Bringin' On The Heartbreak' on an album. It's just not their style. We don't like to think that way, though. We enjoy playing slower or quieter or just different songs now and again."

This philosophy also carries over into Leppard's guitar approach. "I think a solo should go with the feel of a song, rather than just playing to sound flashy," Steve Clark says. "If it's a driving sort of beat, then just let it go, but don't do it all the time. I think it's just maturity that allows you to express yourself in ways other than speed." Willis, likewise, shares Clark's feelings about building solos: "Sometimes you'll get a person who thinks, 'This solo's great! Let me write a song around it.' I think people have finally gotten wise to that approach, though, and there are few who can really pull it off nowadays. They have to be very good, like Eddie Van Halen."

If you're a new band breaking into the world of concert rock and roll, you'll undoubtedly experience both the exhilaration and the frustration of playing before larger audiences — and headliners. "It's difficult in the support situation to put on your show when you're only allowed what the headline band will let you have," Clark says. Commenting further on the subject, Willis adds, "There's only a certain amount that you can do with, let's say, a 40-minute set, limited lights, limited stage room, limited this and that. We want to use our own monitor system, PA, and lighting rig, which are now in England. Def Leppard should be in the States again around May '82, and we're headlining. It should be a lot better, with a longer set and more involved stage show."

Def Leppard is still a young enough band to be very much aware of the many pitfalls facing musicians in today's profit-oriented rock music scene. Both Willis and Clark have paid their dues during the last four years, and offer sound advice about ways to avoid getting burned financially. "Just be careful of contracts," warns Pete. "Always get them checked over by a lawyer; that's the main thing. There are some contracts that you can't even begin to understand. If you sign them, that's it! Thank you, and good night.

"Management is crucial, too. One management company we had, all they were interested in was money. When we recorded our first single and got in the charts, they started seeing nothing but pound signs in their eyes. So, we have a score to settle with those people. We were thinking of delivering a half-ton of maggots to one of their houses [*laughs*]."

Financial hassles aren't the only potential problems a youthful group could face. There are concerns such as developing artistic integrity and proficiency, too, that are often overlooked by players in their quest for popular recognition. Pete shares one experience he had after a Def Leppard concert in Newcastle, England: "This guy came backstage and said he was in a local band. He asked, 'How come you're here after a year-and-a-half, when we've been at it for four years?' I said, 'I don't know, really. Do you practice a lot? Do you put a lot of time into your music?' And he answered, 'Oh, yeah! We practice every week — once a week.' When we were at work with our regular day jobs, we used to practice every night and all weekend. In fact, we actually wrote the first album nine months before ever playing a live concert. We wanted to do it right from the start and be polished."

Steve Clark adds to this by telling how Leppard's apparent "overnight" success was, in fact, far from it: "The thing that keeps you going at first is your belief that the band's getting bigger and better, but the only way to find that out is if the kids are coming to see you. We used to play our own songs in smaller clubs for £20, or something stupid like that, and then gig in workingman's clubs where you could earn £100 a night. A workingman's audience is anything from 20 to 70, and you just play chart hits. Most of the people who frequent them have been on the job all day and are just going there for a drink. They're not there to see you — they'd rather be playing bingo or something. It was a matter of survival; the money we made kept us going. Actually, you learn a lot by doing this. Being able to handle an audience that's 50 years old sort of teaches you how to handle younger audiences, too."

This year will be Def Leppard's time to headline. Whether or not they succeed in establishing themselves as a member of rock's upper echelon will depend a great deal on the continuing musical growth and dedication of guitarists Pete Willis and Steve Clark. Their chances look good, but what else would you expect from a band from Sheffield — the foremost producer of British steel.

— Jim Schwartz

A SELECTED PETE WILLIS/STEVE CLARK DISCOGRAPHY

With Def Leppard (on Mercury): *On Through The Night*, SRM-1-3828; *High 'N Dry*, SRM-1-4021; *Pyromania* (Phil Collins added on guitar), 810 308-1.

Watch for these forthcoming titles:

THE BIG BOOK OF BLUEGRASS
Edited by Marilyn Kochman
Foreword by Earl Scruggs

Interviews, playing hints, note-by-note solos for guitar, banjo, mandolin, fiddle, and dobro. Equipment maintenance, building, and repair. The history, the personalities, the greatest artists and their music, including Bill Monroe, Earl Scruggs, Lester Flatt, David Grisman, Ricky Skaggs, Sam Bush, and many more. From the pages of Frets Magazine.

hardcover/$24.95 (tentative) 0-688-02940-X
paperback/$12.95 (tentative) 0-688-02942-6

Available in Winter 1984:

ROCK KEYBOARD
Edited by Bob Doerschuk
Foreword by Keith Emerson

Fats Domino, Little Richard, Jerry Lee Lewis, Al Kooper, Leon Russell, Booker T. Jones, Elton John, Billy Joel, Michael McDonald, David Paich & Steve Porcaro, Brian Eno, Rick Wakeman, Thomas Dolby, and others—exclusive interviews, true history, astute analysis from the pages of Keyboard Magazine.

paperback/0-688-02961-2

GUITAR GEAR
Edited by John Brosh

A comprehensive, practical guide to buying, maintaining, repairing, customizing all guitar equipment, accessories, and effects. How gear works and how it's made. Amps, bass guitar, guitar synthesizers, latest developments, information, insight, and inspiration from the pages of Guitar Player Magazine.

paperback/0-688-03108-0

THE ART OF ELECTRONIC MUSIC
Edited by Greg Armbruster and Tom Darter
Foreword by Dr. Robert A. Moog

The first definitive book: the creative and technical development of an authentic musical revolution. From the Theremin Electrical Symphony to today's most advanced synthesizers. Scientific origins, the evolution of hardware, the greatest artists — in stories, interviews, illustrations, analysis, and practical musical technique. From the pages of Keyboard Magazine.

hardcover/0-688-03105-6
paperback/0-688-03106-4

From your bookstores or directly from the publisher.

Quill
A Division of William Morrow & Company
105 Madison Avenue
New York, NY 10016